Reading Scripture as a Political Act

Reading Scripture as a Political Act

Essays on the Theopolitical Interpretation of the Bible

Matthew A. Tapie and Daniel Wade McClain, editors

Fortress Press
Minneapolis

READING SCRIPTURE AS A POLITICAL ACT

Essays on the Theopolitical Interpretation of the Bible

Copyright © 2015 Fortress Press. All rights reserved. Except for brief quotations in critical articles or reviews, no part of this book may be reproduced in any manner without prior written permission from the publisher. Visit http://www.augsburgfortress.org/copyrights/ or write to Permissions, Augsburg Fortress, Box 1209, Minneapolis, MN 55440.

Scripture quotations are from the New Revised Standard Version Bible, copyright (c) 1989 by the Division of Christian Education of the National Council of the Churches of Christ in the USA. Used by permission. All rights reserved.

Cover image: The Temptation by J Kirk Richards

Cover design: Joe Reinke

Library of Congress Cataloging-in-Publication Data

Print ISBN: 978-1-4514-7963-8

eBook ISBN: 978-1-5064-0149-2

The paper used in this publication meets the minimum requirements of American National Standard for Information Sciences — Permanence of Paper for Printed Library Materials, ANSI Z329.48-1984.

Manufactured in the U.S.A.

This book was produced using Pressbooks.com, and PDF rendering was done by PrinceXML.

For Carolyn and Kate

Contents

	Contributors	xi
	Foreword **Stephen E. Fowl**	xv
	Introduction	1
1.	Empires and Enemies Re-Reading Lament as Politics **Rebekah Eklund**	19
2.	The Politics of Friendship in the Gospel of John **Peter Dula**	37
3.	"Before the Eyes of Their Own God" Susanna, rape law, and testimony in *City of God* 1.19 **Melanie Webb**	57
4.	The Politics of Fasting in Basil of Caesarea **Mark DelCogliano**	83
5.	Contemplating Genesis 1 as a Political Act in Late Antiquity **Daniel Wade McClain**	101

6. The Apocalyptic Figure of Francis's Stigmatized Body 127
   The Politics of Scripture in Bonaventure's Meditative Treatises
   Travis E. Ables

7. "For He is Our Peace" 149
   Thomas Aquinas on Christ as Cause of Peace in the City of Saints
   Matthew A. Tapie

8. War and the Ethics of Evangelization 169
   The Great Commission in Sixteenth-Century Spanish Political Thought
   David M. Lantigua

9. The Unexceptional King 195
   Political Theology in Shakespeare's *Richard II*
   Anthony D. Baker

10. *Ressourcement* and Resistance 219
    La nouvelle théologie, the Fathers, and the Bible, against Fascism
    Kevin L. Hughes

11. Inhabiting Scripture 239
    Wesley's Theopolitical Reading of the Bible
    D. Stephen Long

12. The Scriptural Logic of Barmen and the Jewish Question 259
    Susannah Ticciati

13. The End of Sacrifice 285
    John Howard Yoder's Critique of Capital Punishment
    John C. Nugent

14. A Broken Body Reads Mark   *303*
   Craig Hovey

Contributors

Travis E. Ables studies Christology and anthropology in the Augustinian tradition, and has a special interest in medieval Franciscanism and mystical traditions. He is the author of *Incarnational Realism: Trinity and the Spirit in Augustine and Barth* (Bloomsbury, 2013), and is writing *The Body of the Cross: A Theological History of the Atonement* (Fortress). He is currently an independent scholar living in Arvada, CO.

Anthony D. Baker is Associate Professor of Theology at Seminary of the Southwest in Austin, Texas. He is the author of *Diagonal Advance: Perfection in Christian Theology* (SCM, 2011), as well as various journal articles and book chapters. He is currently working on a book on Shakespeare and theology.

Mark DelCogliano is Assistant Professor of Theology at the University of St. Thomas in St. Paul, Minnesota. His research focuses on patristic doctrinal debates, theological developments, and scriptural exegesis in late antiquity. His books include the monograph *Basil of Caesarea's Anti-Eunomian Theory of Names: Christian Theology and Late-Antique Philosophy in the Fourth-Century Trinitarian Controversy* (Brill, 2010), as well as several volumes of translations of patristic texts, most recently *St. Basil the Great: On Fasting and Feasts* with Susan R. Holman (St. Vladimir's Seminary Press, 2013) and *St. Basil the Great: On Christian Doctrine and Practice* (St. Vladimir's Seminary Press, 2012).

Peter Dula is Associate Professor of Religion and Culture and Chair of the Department of Bible and Religion at Eastern Mennonite University in Harrisonburg, Virginia. He is the author of *Cavell, Companionship, and Christian Theology* (Oxford, 2011).

Rebekah Eklund is Assistant Professor of Theology at Loyola University Maryland, and is also an ordained minister in the Evangelical Covenant Church. She is the author of *Jesus Wept: The Significance of Jesus' Laments in the New Testament* (Library of New Testament Studies; T&T Clark, 2014), and co-editor with John E. Phelan Jr. of *Doing Theology for the Church: Essays in Honor of Klyne Snodgrass* (Covenant Press; Wipf & Stock, 2014).

Craig Hovey is Associate Professor of Religion at Ashland University in Ashland, Ohio and is executive director of the Ashland Center for Nonviolence. He is the author of numerous books including *Bearing True Witness: Truthfulness in Christian Practice* (Eerdmans, 2011), *Nietzsche and Theology* (T&T Clark, 2008), *To Share in the Body: A Theology of Martyrdom for Today's Church* (Brazos, 2008), *Speak Thus: Christian Language in Church and World* (Cascade, 2008), and co-editor of *An Eerdmans Reader in Contemporary Political Theology* (Eerdmans, 2011).

Kevin L. Hughes teaches historical theology at Villanova University in Humanities and in Theology and Religious Studies. He is the author or editor of four books, including *Constructing Antichrist: Paul, Biblical Commentary, and the Development of Doctrine in the Early Middle Ages* (CUA Pres, 2005), and his articles have appeared in *Theological Studies, Modern Theology, The Heythrop Journal,* and *Franciscan Studies.*

David Lantigua is Assistant Professor of Moral Theology and Ethics at The Catholic University of America. He was previously a Graduate Fellow at the Notre Dame Institute for Advanced Study. He is co-author with Darrell Fasching and Dell deChant of *Comparative Religious Ethics: A Narrative Approach to Global Ethics,* second edition (Wiley-Blackwell, 2011) and has published articles in *Modern Theology* and the *Journal of Moral Theology.*

Stephen Long is professor of Systematic Theology at Marquette University. He is an ordained United Methodist Minister and works in the intersection between theology and ethics. He has published numerous essays and twelve books on theology and ethics. His most recent is *Saving Karl Barth: Hans Urs von Balthasar's Preoccupation*(Fortress Press, 2014).

Daniel Wade McClain is the director of program operations for graduate theological studies at Loyola University Maryland, a former president of the Mid-Atlantic Region of the American Academy of Religion, and is completing dissertation on Bonaventure's *Breviloquium.*

John C. Nugent is professor of Old Testament at Great Lakes Christian College. He is the author of *The Politics of Yahweh* (Cascade Books, 2011), the editor of *Radical Ecumencity* (ACU Press, 2010) and

The End of Sacrifice (Herald Press, 2011), and the head editor of the three-volume Yoder for Everyone series (Herald Press, 2012–14). John also coordinates the Yoder Index project (yoderindex.com), serves as consulting editor for the *Stone-Campbell Journal*, and maintains a blog at walkandword.com.

Matthew A. Tapie is director at the Center for Catholic-Jewish Studies and Assistant Professor of Theology at Saint Leo University, Saint Leo, Florida. He is the author of *Aquinas on Israel and the Church: A Study of the Question of Supersessionism in the Theology of Thomas Aquinas* (Pickwick, 2014).

Susannah Ticciati is Senior Lecturer in Systematic Theology at King's College London. She is the author of *A New Apophaticism: Augustine and the Redemption of Signs* (Brill, 2013) and *Job and the Disruption of Identity: Reading Beyond Barth* (T&T Clark, 2005).

Melanie Webb is a PhD candidate in theology at Princeton Theological Seminary. Her dissertation, *Desiring Life: Honor, Violence, and Sexuality in Augustine's City of God*, examines the intersection of Roman and Christian virtue traditions in order to explicate Augustine's revision of traditional narratives, and with them of societal values and expectations regarding sex and sexuality, justice, and salvation. She is Senior Teaching Fellow for the Certificate in Theology and Ministry (CTM) that is offered online by Princeton Seminary's Department of Continuing Education, and is piloting CTM–Inside, a cohort of incarcerated and community lay leaders who will meet in a local prison in order to complete the certificate together.

Foreword

Stephen E. Fowl

Reading Scripture as a Political Act. This title invites us to focus our attention in specific and promising ways. In particular, we are invited to focus on the ways that reading scripture *is* a political act. Such an invitation, however, requires us to focus our attention in several respects.

For example, there already is a significant amount of biblical scholarship devoted to aspects of the Bible and politics. In this regard, there are numerous volumes that seek to display the various political forces at work in the shaping and editing of the texts that comprise the Christian canon. In their own ways, Norman Gottwald and Elisabeth Schüssler Fiorenza pioneered this type of work. With varying degrees of precision and accuracy, scholars now talk about the politics behind the formation of biblical texts, how ideological and political interests shaped (and were shaped by?) the processes that led to the production of biblical texts. In addition, there are a variety of works that seek to describe the political nature of the formation of these texts into the Christian canon.

READING SCRIPTURE AS A POLITICAL ACT

To the extent that such works have established levels of consensus, all readers are invited to recognize that the production of both specific texts and the canon as a whole is the work of human hands. This is not to say that is merely the work of human hands. Rather, it recognizes that theologians and Christians more generally have no stake in denying the obvious here. Christian attention to scripture will always depend on fairly strong convictions about the Spirit's providential role in ensuring that this fully human scripture also provides believers all they require to live faithfully before God and one another.

In addition, there are numerous volumes, typified by John Howard Yoder's *The Politics of Jesus*, that persuasively make the case that Jesus and Paul in particular offered visions of the Christian life that were ineluctably political rather than merely private and individual. The message of scripture has political implications, implications to which Christians have often been inattentive. Of course, even when believers do attend to these political implications, they often do so in ways that simply read current partisan positions back onto favored biblical characters. In this case, reading scripture is less a political act, than an occasion for scripture to become a rhetorical tool to advance political agendas determined on other grounds.

Although this volume can be seen as an heir to these two movements, it is equally important to see in *Reading Scripture as a Political Act* the convergence of recent movements both to read scripture and to think of politics, in its various forms, theologically. Efforts to reinvigorate the practice of reading scripture theologically seem to have now borne material and institutional fruit. There are now a number of journals and commentary series devoted to theological interpretation in various forms. Several groups within the Society of Biblical Literature regularly focus on theological interpretation and their sessions are well attended. It would be wrong to say that theological forms of biblical interpretation are dominant; they are not. Nevertheless, theological interpretation seems to have established itself as an academic enterprise and it is beginning to influence graduate and seminary education.

One clear, but under recognized, aspect of theological interpretation is its deep dependence on communities of interpreters. Theological interpretation thrives in community. This truth is widely recognized even if it is not always practiced. Such recognition invites further reflections on the habits and practices, on the shape and contours, of the communities who see theological interpretation of scripture to be essential to the health of their common life.

At the same time, the common life of these communities shapes their interpretation of scripture. Indeed, within the ecclesial contexts in which most theological interpretation takes place, scripture is already embedded in their liturgical, ascetic, practical and moral life. Moreover, these liturgical, ascetical, practical and moral aspects of ecclesial common life already work to constitute particular types of communities. Scholarly work on "the theopolitical imagination" has been articulating, displaying and analyzing this dynamic for some time now.

Given the great amount of overlapping concerns between those working on the "theopolitical imagination" and those advocating for a renewal of theological interpretation of scripture, it is certainly time for a more direct and directed conversation between these two spheres of work. This volume aims to get that conversation off the ground.

This volume will demonstrate that such a conversation is incredibly wide ranging. For example, readers will encounter here an analysis of the revival of spiritual interpretation of scripture and the beginnings of the monumental *Sources chrétiennes*, which ties these events to resistance to fascism in France during World War

II. They will learn that Augustine's pastoral care of women who were victims of the Visigoths' sexual violence is deeply tied to his reading of scripture. In addition, this volume contains deep analyses of biblical texts and themes that provide apt and life-giving ways of participating in such varied political practices as lament and friendship. There is much more beside these essays, too!

The richness and the diversity of these essays attest to the fact that there is much to talk about here. I see it along the lines of a very large dinner party with conversations going on with people seated next to each other, but also conversations going on across the table. It is a happy tangle of voices and views. Over time, smaller, more directed and more intense conversations can begin. It is too soon, however, to prescribe or even predict where these will go. If this initial dinner party is anything to go by, we should have high expectations.

Introduction

The broad aim of this volume is to highlight the significance of theological readings of scripture for contemporary political theology. Indeed, theological readings of scripture—especially premodern theological readings of scripture—have great potential to illuminate the sociopolitical issues at the center of political theology. Yet political theology tends to neglect this font of resources. Although divine revelation is recognized as a key concept in political theology, and biblical scholars increasingly understand scripture to contain political dimensions, scripture is often marginalized in most scholarly discussions of political theology.[1] As a corrective to this problem, the contributors of *Reading Scripture as a Political Act* attempt to demonstrate how scripture functions in the "theopolitical imagination" of theologians from the earliest Christian centuries to the present day.[2] Before describing the aim of the volume in greater detail, and specifying what we mean by the phrases "reading scripture as a political act," and "theological reading of scripture," it will be helpful to explain the rationale for this collection of essays in the

1. As Ivan Illich pointed out over four decades ago, the marginalization of scripture is itself an issue of dire political consequence. See Ivan Illich, "The Powerlessness of the Church," in *Celebration of Awareness: a Call for Institutional Revolution* (Garden City, NY: Doubleday, 1969), 95–104.
2. We borrow this term from William Cavanaugh, who uses it to speak of how theological presuppositions relate to conceptions of the political. See his *Theopolitical Imagination: Christian Practices of Space and Time* (New York: T&T Clark, 2003).

context of contemporary views of political theology and the political dimension of the Bible.

Divine Revelation as a Crucial Concept in Political Theology

The term "political theology" originated with Carl Schmitt, who argued "all significant concepts of the modern theory of the state are secularized theological concepts."[3] Since Schmitt, the concept of "political theology" has been used by scholars to refer both to a critical stance toward aspects of modern society, as well as to the relationship between religion and politics. Over the course of the twentieth century, the term became associated with theologians (especially Jürgen Moltmann, Johann Baptist Metz, and Gustavo Gutiérrez) and intellectual movements in Europe and Latin America. According to Francis Schüssler Fiorenza, the political theologies that emerged in these contexts criticized secularization and the privatization of religion in Europe and confronted the sharp contrast between elites and the poor in Latin America.[4] These thinkers and movements offered "a political hermeneutic of the Christian message, underscoring the centrality and reality of the promise of God's Kingdom."[5] Today, however, the term political theology is increasingly used to refer to theological analysis of a variety of sociopolitical issues, including war, economic injustice, racism, and the concept of religious violence.[6]

---

3. Carl Schmitt, *Political Theology: Four Chapters on the Concept of Sovereignty*, trans. George Schwab (Cambridge, MA: MIT Press, 1985), 36.
4. Francis Schüssler Fiorenza, Klaus Tanner, and Michael Welker, eds., *Political Theology: Contemporary Challenges and Future Directions* (Louisville: Westminster John Knox, 2013), 37–60 (38).
5. Ibid, 37.
6. Examples include: Vincent Lloyd, ed., *Race and Political Theology* (Stanford University Press, 2012); Schüssler Fiorenza, Tanner, Welker, *Political Theology*; James Cone, *The Cross and the Lynching Tree* (Orbis, 2013); Bustami Mohamed Khir "The Islamic Quest for Sociopolitical Justice"; and Peter Ochs, "Abrahamic Theo-Politics: A Jewish View," in *The Blackwell Companion to Political Theology*, Peter Scott and William T. Cavanaugh, eds. (Wiley-Blackwell,

INTRODUCTION

Despite the modern origins of "political theology," scholars also use the term to refer to premodern theopolitical phenomena. Eric Gregory argues that political theology is "anything to do with religion and politics."[7] It is in this broad sense of the term that scholars apply the word political theology to ancient conceptions of the civil and religious, which were frequently regarded as one and same thing—or, at least, deeply intertwined.[8] For Mark Lilla, such mixing of religion and politics is dangerous and is especially present in premodern Christianity. It was Hobbes's "great separation" that finally divorced religion and politics. For Lilla, political theology is "discourse about political authority based on a revealed divine nexus."[9] By contrast, Michael Jon Kessler suggests a definition that attempts to name that which secular and religious political theologies seem to have in common. According to Kessler, "Political theology is . . . the collection of stories we tell ourselves about our nature as humans, our aspirations for order and justice in light of the sacred, and what . . . constitutes and limits legitimate rule over our collective lives."[10] William Cavanaugh defines political theology as "the analysis and criticism of political arrangements (including cultural-psychological, social and economic aspects) from the perspective of differing interpretations of God's ways with the world."[11] Although

---

2006), 503–34; William T Cavanaugh, *The Myth of Religious Violence: Secular Ideology and the Roots of Modern Conflict* (Oxford University Press, USA, 2009).
7. Eric Gregory, "Christianity and the Rise of the Democratic State," in Michael Kessler, ed. *Political Theology for a Plural Age* (New York: Oxford University Press, 2013), 99-107 (99).
8. See Paula Fredriksen's treatment of the interrelationship of civil power and the gods in the context of the ancient Greek city and with attention to Augustine's theology in "God's and their Humans," in *Augustine and the Jews: A Christian Defense of Jews and Judaism* (New York: Doubleday Religion, 2008), 3-15.
9. Mark Lilla, *The Stillborn God: Religion, Politics, and the Modern West* (New York: Alfred A. Knopf, 2007), 23. Elsewhere, Lilla defines the term narrowly as "a doctrine that legitimates the use of public authority by appeal to divine revelation." See "A Conversation" in Michael Kessler, ed. *Political Theology for a Plural Age* (New York: Oxford University Press, 2013), 13-40 (43).
10. Michael Kessler, "Introduction," in Michael Kessler, ed. *Political Theology for a Plural Age* (New York: Oxford University Press, 2013), 1-10 (1).

3

definitions vary, scholars of political theology understand the concept to include analysis of the relationship of civil power and divine revelation.

Scholars are also increasingly attentive to how scripture has shaped modern political thought and events in important ways. The "stories we tell ourselves," at least in European and North American political contexts, have not been told in light of just any narrative, but have been shaped by the Bible. Contemporary scholars of political theology, the history of political thought, and the history of Christianity have demonstrated how the Bible has shaped the political thought of certain periods and political events, even those that are often considered wholly secular. For example, Eric Nelson has shown that early modern political thought experienced a "Hebrew Revival," in which ancient Israel was viewed as a model for republican political constitution—"the republic of the Hebrews."[12] Although Thomas Hobbes is often viewed as a secular political theorist, John Milbank and others have argued that Hobbes is in fact a political theologian since he "reads the Bible with a political horizon."[13] "A substantial part of the point of the *Leviathan*," writes Milbank, "is that he is insisting that the message of the Bible is political and not a spiritual message at all. So Hobbes's political position is not . . . an outright secular argument."[14] In *Sacred Scripture, Sacred War*, James Byrd demonstrates how biblical texts were used extensively in making the patriotic case for the Revolutionary War, and how the Bible shaped American views of war.[15] Harry S. Stout's *Upon the Altar of the*

---

11. Peter Scott and William Cavanaugh, eds. *The Blackwell Companion to Political Theology* (Oxford: Blackwell, 2004), 2.
12. Eric Nelson, *The Hebrew Republic: Jewish Sources and the Transformation of European Political Thought*, (Cambridge, MA: Harvard University Press, 2011).
13. John Milbank, "A Conversation" in Michael Kessler, ed. *Political Theology for a Plural Age* (New York: Oxford University Press, 2013), 13-40 (27). See also Matthew F. Rose, "Hobbes as Political Theologian," *Political Theology* 14, no. 1 (February 1, 2013): 5-31.
14. Milbank, "A Conversation," 27.

INTRODUCTION

Nation and Mark Noll's *Civil War as a Theological Crisis* show how scripture shaped views of the morality of the American Civil War.[16] It would not be difficult to think of more examples of how religious traditions and their scriptures continue to bear upon twenty-first century political orders.

Beyond the Political Implications of Scripture

Scholars are also aware that scripture can be interpreted politically.[17] "Many Christians," writes Richard Bauckham, "have recently been rediscovering the political dimension of the message of the Bible. This is really a return to normality, since the notion that biblical Christianity has nothing to do with politics is little more than a modern Western Christian aberration, which would not have been entertained by the Church in most periods and places of its history."[18] Richard Horsley has said that the "study of the Bible must be understood as an activity with political implications...."[19] Although an apolitical view of the Bible is indeed an aberration, and study of the Bible has political implications, these insights do not yet adequately recognize the deeply political character of the ecclesial contexts in which scripture has been read for most of history.

In order to move beyond the idea that the Bible simply has political implications, it is helpful to explain the way in which we employ the term "political act." Whereas the popular conception of "political"

---

15. James P. Byrd, *Sacred Scripture, Sacred War: The Bible and the American Revolution* (New York: Oxford University Press, 2013).
16. Mark A. Noll, *The Civil War as a Theological Crisis* (Chapel Hill: The University of North Carolina Press, 2006); Harry S. Stout, *Upon the Altar of the Nation: A Moral History of the Civil War* (New York: Penguin, 2007).
17. Richard Bauckham, *The Bible in Politics: How to Read the Bible Politically* (Louisville: Westminster J. Knox Press, 1989).
18. Ibid., 1.
19. Richard Horsley, "Introduction," in Richard A. Horsley, ed., *Paul and Politics: Ekklesia, Israel, Imperium, Interpretation* (Harrisburg, PA: Trinity Press International, 2000), 1–16 (13).

is usually taken to refer to some activity directly related to holding civil office or gaining the support of a key constituency, we use the term in the broader, classical sense of the word and with attention to its application in ecclesial contexts. By "political," we emphasize its origin in the Greek word *polis*, meaning a structured social body. According to this classical meaning, the church itself is a political entity. In the words of Thomas Aquinas, the community of the faithful "is a city."[20] Or in the words of John Yoder, the church has the "character of a *polis*."[21] Because the church is one, holy, catholic, and apostolic, it cannot be reduced to one social entity among others. Nevertheless, it is a "structured" social body that is united in common belief and practice. It is the church's political character that, in part, makes its reading of scripture a political act.

That the ecclesial context in which scripture is interpreted possesses this political character means that scripture, for most of its readers, does not function simply as a text with political implications. Rather, the act of reading scripture in and of itself—especially as this act is embedded in the church's liturgical life—possesses a character that is both political and ecclesial at the same time. Consider, for instance, martyrdom in the early church. The significance of martyrdom lies not in the spectacle of the event, but in the fact that the martyrdom was understood as a performative reading of scripture, one that reinforced the political character of the church.[22]

Indeed, as Bernd Wannenwetsch has shown, "though the political relevance of worship has oftentimes been overshadowed by other accounts of both worship and politics, it was an essential feature of the

---

20. Thomas Aquinas, *Commentary on the letters of Saint Paul to the Galatians and Ephesians* (Lander, WY: Aquinas Institute for the Study of Sacred Doctrine, 2012), 237.
21. John Howard Yoder, *Body Politics: Five Practices of the Christian Community Before the Watching World* (Scottdale, PA: Herald Press, 2001), viii.
22. Rowan Williams, "Resident Aliens: the Identity of the Early Church," in *Why Study the Past: the Quest for the Historical Church* (Grand Rapids: Eerdmans, 2005), 32–59.

original self-understanding of the church from the New Testament on and has re-emerged throughout the history of Christian theology."[23] The church's liturgy has what might be referred to as a theopolitical aim: to confess faith in Jesus Christ, the second person of the Trinity, as Lord. And scripture pervades the liturgy: "[B]iblical narratives lay behind the fundamental structures of the liturgical year, and scriptural texts [are] ubiquitous in the form of chants and readings."[24] Susan Boynton has even suggested that the reading of scripture in medieval liturgy constituted a form of interpretation that mirrored the patristic tradition: "[T]he selection and combination of biblical texts in the chants and readings of the liturgy constitute[d] a system of interpretation that parallel[ed] the readings of these same texts by patristic writers."[25]

Scholars of the "theological interpretation of scripture" have addressed the way that particular ecclesial contexts shape the practice of reading scripture. The theological reading of scripture, defined broadly, is a reading "whereby theological concerns and interests inform and are informed by reading scripture."[26] As Stephen Fowl explains, this form of reading has been the norm for the church: "Christians have generally read their scripture to guide, correct, and edify their faith, worship, and practice as part of their ongoing struggle to live faithfully before the triune God." Insofar as Christians have read scripture for the purpose of living faithfully, they have read the scriptures theologically. This struggle to live faithfully is

---

23. Bernd Wannenwetsch, *The Blackwell Companion to Political Theology*, 76–90 (76). See also Wannenwetsch, "The Political Worship of the Church: A Critical and Empowering Practice," *Modern Theology* 12, no.2 (1996): 269–99.
24. Susan Boynton, "The Bible and the Liturgy" in *The Practice of the Bible in the Middle Ages: Production, Reception, and Performance in Western Christianity*, ed. Susan Boynton and Diane J. Reilly (New York: Columbia University Press, 2011), 10-33 (10).
25. Ibid., 11.
26. Stephen E. Fowl, *The Theological Interpretation of Scripture: Classic and Contemporary Readings*, 1st ed. (Cambridge, MA: Blackwell, 1997), xiii. See also Stephen E. Fowl, *Engaging Scripture: A Model for Theological Interpretation* (Eugene, OR: Wipf & Stock, 2008).

referenced in Paul's pleading with the Ephesians to "walk" in such a way that is worthy of God's calling: "I . . . beg you to lead a life worthy of the calling to which you have been called." (Eph. 4:1). Indeed, this kind of life, which is always a life of communion in one body, is a calling from God that Paul understands in civic terms when he refers to the believers as "fellow citizens" (Eph. 2:19). Since living faithfully includes the worship of God—a sacrificial offering of our bodies to God (Rom. 12:1)—such living cannot be separated from the material reality of the political character of the church. In this sense, the theological purposes of reading scripture are also political purposes.

Although scholars have treated how the Bible has shaped political thought and political events or have addressed what they take to be the political implications of the Bible, there is general lack of attention to how Christian theologians' readings of the Bible possessed a political character, shaped their views of civil power, or enabled them to respond to the social and political problems of their day. Indeed, in recent works on Christian political theology, comment upon the Bible is often treated as prolegomena or is ancillary to exploring the thought of modern Christian theologians and the political character of Christian doctrines. Contemporary works on political theology often mention that most theologians have assumed scripture and Christianity possessed a political character. But such references are only in passing and usually occur as introductory remarks on the political aspect of Christian theological reflection in general: "[T]he political has been present in Christian theology from its very beginnings, and throughout most of Christian history church leaders and theologians have thought and taught about politics without seeing this as an entirely separate matter—of course theology would include political theology!"[27] Additionally, the *Blackwell Companion to Political Theology* provides invaluable survey of Christian political theologies in chapters mostly devoted to modern Christian theologians.[28] However, due to its broad nature, the *Companion* is limited in its treatments of political themes in the Old and New Testament. In addition to including primary texts in modern political theology, such as classic essays by Reinhold Niebuhr and John Howard Yoder, the *Eerdmans Political Reader in Contemporary Political Theology* [29] only treats the exegetical presuppositions and historical significance of liberation theology as a hermeneutic. For the most part, the *Eerdmans Reader* focuses upon the political character of Christian doctrines as these relate to important political topics (such as gender, race, 9/11). Although both volumes treat the thought of modern theologians or the political character of doctrines, they do not attend to how theologians' readings of scripture shaped their political concerns. Moreover, both books situate their study within the modern period. In these ways, the light that the theological reading of scripture has cast upon the church's pilgrim journey as it struggles to walk faithfully in the world is eclipsed. We think the focus on modern theology neglects resources in premodern Christian theological readings of scripture that can illuminate contemporary concerns in political theology.

The Sacred Page in the Theopolitical Imagination of the Church

The relationship between political theology and scripture should be treated as more than a preface to Christian political theology. Insofar as scripture is the "soul of sacred theology," it is fitting that

---

27. Elizabeth Phillips, *Political Theology: A Guide for the Perplexed* (New York: T&T Clark, 2012), 3.
28. The exception is Jean Bethke Elshtain's discussion of Augustine, and Frederick Bauerschmidt's helpful chapter on Aquinas.
29. William Cavanaugh, Jeff Bailey, and Craig Hovey, *An Eerdmans Reader in Contemporary Political Theology* (Grand Rapids, MI: Eerdmans, 2011).

Christian political theologians attend more fully to how scripture has functioned in the theopolitical imagination of the theologians of the church.[30] There is much at stake here. As Mark Noll has argued, "the political use of Scripture, even extensive use of Scripture, is no guarantee that any given political appeal will be meaningfully Christian."[31] Drawing upon the work of Derek Peterson's *Ethnic Patriotism and the East African Revival*, Noll observes that the "recent experience of African Christians . . . repeats the history of Western Christianity in putting the Scriptures to use for political witness. Sometimes it has helped, other times not."[32] It is certain that scripture will be used in politics for better or for worse. So, how should Christians interpret scripture in light of their political contexts?

Michael Kirwan's work, *Political Theology: An Introduction* (especially his chapter, "The Political Word of God"), also expresses concerns about the role of scripture in political theology. Kirwan explicitly points in the direction that this volume aims when he states that handling sacred texts is a lost art: "If there is one indispensable skill for doing political theology, it is probably the ability to handle sacred texts responsibly."[33] Kirwan then states what might be called a version of the problem of scripture and political theology: "[T]he gospel engenders and inspires political engagement, but offers no blueprint for specific political stances or options." Although the editors of this book do not agree that scripture lacks specific "political stances,"[34] Kirwan's argument that scripture does not provide a

---

30. *Dei Verbum*, Sec 6 no. 24, Second Vatican Council, available at http://www.vatican.va/archive/hist_councils/ii_vatican_council/documents/vat-ii_const_19651118_dei-verbum_en.html, accessed June 1, 2015.
31. Mark Noll, "The Peril and Potential of Scripture in Christian Political Witness," in Christian Political Witness, ed. George Kalantzis (Downers Grove, IL: InterVarsity Press Academic, 2014), 35-55 (37).
32. Ibid., 38. Derek R. Peterson, *Ethnic Patriotism and the East African Revival: A History of Dissent, c. 1935-1972* (New York: Cambridge University Press, 2014).
33. Michael Kirwan, "The Political Word of God," in *Political Theology: An Introduction* (Minneapolis: Fortress Press, 2009), 161–76 (162).

"blueprint" highlights the fact that the interpretation of scripture is crucial for any discussion of political theology.[35] Nevertheless, the resources Kirwan suggests for recovering the lost art of handing the sacred page are limited to three theological voices: Oliver O'Donovan, Jürgen Moltmann, and Karl Barth.[36]

It is at this point that this volume of essays attempts to take a next step, by exploring some of the ways that the church has read scripture politically for centuries. Analyzing particular theological readings of scripture across the ages with attention to concerns in political theology is one way of engaging the lacuna noted above. How have theologians read scripture for political purposes? In what ways have theologians understood the Bible to possess political material? What sort of approaches to reading scripture informed Christian theologians' judgments about civil power or its relationship to the church in general? In what way did these theologians apply these political readings to their political contexts? What did they understand to be the political character of the Old and New Testament and how were these texts invoked to theorize about, criticize, or support forms of civil power? What were the methodological principles by which theologians interpreted scripture politically? How did they implement such principles in relation to particular texts? Insofar as scripture is the "soul of sacred theology," it seems fitting that Christian political theology attend more fully to how readings of the sacred page function in theologians' reflections

---

34. See John Yoder's argument against this idea in his 1972 classic, *The Politics of Jesus*, 2nd ed. (Grand Rapids: Eerdmans, 1994).
35. Kirwan, "The Political Word of God," 162.
36. Ibid., 163. It should be noted that Kirwan ends the volume with a chapter on political theology and the church (177-99), which surveys what he refers to as "models of political church." Although he presents a helpful and thorough survey, each model is a summary of a contemporary theologian's view of the relation between ecclesiology and politics (e.g. John Milbank, Oliver O'Donovan, Johann Baptist Metz, David Tracy, John Yoder, William Cavanaugh). None of the models are connected to the earlier discussion on scripture or the concern to recover the lost art of reading scripture.

on the relation between the city of God and the city of man. It seems learning the lost art of how to theologically interpret the sacred page in the spirit of the theologians of the church and with attention to oppression and injustice constitutes significant political action.

Yet, this volume is not an attempt to return to the past unaware of the missteps of Christendom.[37] While we believe premodern theologians must be brought into discussion with contemporary political theology, we also want to avoid any notion that we dismiss the significance of modern theologians' readings of scripture. Therefore, the essays analyze the political character of premodern *and* modern theologians' readings of scripture with attention to how their readings relate to or address political challenges in their particular social and historical settings. In addition to treating how particular themes in the Bible, such as lament and friendship, suggest distinctive political practices, the essays in this volume attempt to highlight how scripture shaped the theopolitical imagination of Augustine, Basil of Caesarea, Bonaventure, Thomas Aquinas, Bartolomé de las Casas, John Wesley, Karl Barth, Henri de Lubac, John Howard Yoder, and others.

Collectively, these essays represent a contemporary attempt at the retrieval or *ressourcement* of the readings of scripture with attention to theopolitical issues, such as war and peace, sexual violence, capital punishment, fascism, empire, and sovereignty. The essays cover writings from ancient, medieval, early modern, and modern periods, and the contributors come from diverse ecumenical backgrounds (Roman Catholic, Episcopal, Mennonite, Methodist, Evangelical Covenant, among others), and each essay was written specifically with the aim of this volume in mind.

Rebekah Eklund's essay, "Empires and Enemies: Re-Reading

---

37. David Bentley Hart, "No Enduring City," *First Things* (August 2013): 45-51 (47).

Lament as Politics," challenges us to read the laments of scripture today in our own political settings, thereby participating in a practice that possesses an inherently political character. Lament, Eklund argues, functions symbolically and practically as a form of resistance and renarration, drawing us into a community of suffering and shared burden, and most importantly a community of witness.

Peter Dula's essay, "The Politics of Friendship in the Gospel of John," argues for the centrality of conflict in the Apostle John's account of friendship, theology, and *how* theology is done. Dula draws upon John's theological vision of the role of conflict in community, which is grounded in the Johannine experience of God in Christ.

In "Before the Eyes of Their Own God: Susanna, rape law, and testimony in *City of God* 1.19," Melanie Webb explores the function of the figure of Susanna in Augustine's "habits of thought" as he critiques Roman and Christian traditions of virtue that present suicide as assurance that a woman did not desire or consent to rape. The story of Susanna provides an alternative exemplum, one grounded in the testimony of conscience and drawn from scripture. Webb argues that Susanna's story motivates and shapes Augustine's engagement with the narrative of the rape of Lucretia.

Mark DelCogliano demonstrates the political character of the ascetic practice of fasting in "The Politics of Fasting in Basil of Caesarea." Grounded in a scriptural view of fasting, Basil constructed an ascetic practice that does not simply restore the order of the fallen world, but in fact is able to achieve a peaceful domestic, civic, and social order that recaptures the paradisical state.

Extending the theme of ascetic practice, Daniel Wade McClain argues in "Reading Genesis 1 as a Political Act," that for early Christian preachers, such as Origen, Basil, and Ambrose, Genesis 1 was significant as a resource for public formation. These preachers read Genesis 1 as a robust source for understanding the relationship of humanity to God, the world, and itself. In this manner, commentaries and sermons on Genesis 1 were crafted with education, formation, and human excellence in mind.

Travis E. Ables, in "The Apocalyptic Figure of Francis's Stigmatized Body: The Politics of Scripture in Bonaventure's Meditative Treatises," argues that a popular theological politics is receiving support, structure, and guidance in Bonaventure's mystical treatises. The treatises are Bonaventure's attempt to codify a Franciscan reading of scripture that idealizes Francis and offers a kind of *imitatio francisci*, but does so for the purpose of maintaining the popular appeal and accessibility of Francis's performance of the life of Christ.

Matthew A. Tapie's "'For He is Our Peace': Thomas Aquinas on Christ as Cause of Peace in the City of Saints," shows that scholars have overlooked an ecclesial concept of peace in Aquinas's biblical commentaries. He argues that Aquinas's approach to the sacred page allowed him to creatively nuance the theological concept of peace he inherited from Augustine and in ways that have important consequences for cultivating virtues that preserve peace.

David M. Lantigua responds to Yoder's critique of Constantinianism in "War and the Ethics of Evangelization: The Great Commission in Sixteenth-Century Political Thought." Employing Oliver O'Donovan's focus on the missionary orientation of the Church in Christendom, Lantigua identifies a Christendom legacy and tradition of social ethics that was committed to announcing the Gospel's transformative and liberating power for all peoples made in God's image against Satan's violent oppression through idolatry and the overreaching worldly assertions of church and empire.

Anthony D. Baker reads early-Anglican politics through the Bard in "The Unexceptional King: Political Theology in Shakespeare's *Richard II*." Richard's monologue at the end of the play, Baker argues, evinces "a new 'unexceptional' political theology," one that seeks to attain power for the sake of penance, and vice versa. Someone once said that if you want to understand Anglican theology, read the poets. Anthony Baker shows us that if you want to understand theological politics, read the Bard.

Kevin L. Hughes discusses "*Ressourcement* and Resistance: *La nouvelle théologie*, the Bible, and the Fathers, against Fascism." In particular, Hughes argues that the witness of Henri de Lubac's thought before the war and after suggests a continuous argument, in both word and deed, that addresses the political and cultural ills and crises of his society. For de Lubac, the recovery of spiritual exegesis was a spiritual re-armament for an underground battle, beneath the political and military maneuvers, for the soul of the church and the heart of the world. Against the rising storm of fascism, de Lubac argued that the renewal of scriptural interpretation was the necessary theological foundation for Christian resistance.

D. Stephen Long's essay, "Inhabiting Scripture: Wesley's Theopolitical Reading of the Bible," argues that reading scripture for Wesley entails a lived practice, wherein the scriptural reader encounters not only the sense of scripture, but are invited into a relationship and way of life. Wesley's General Rules and his reading of the Beatitudes show that scripture for Wesley has deep practical significance, and not just for the individual, but for the community as well. The Beatitudes, Long argues, "produce a Catholic Spirit. . . . Their purpose ultimately is to bear the fruit of the love of God and neighbor."

In "The Scriptural Logic of Barmen and the Jewish Question," Susannah Ticciatti interrogates the absence of the *Judenfrage* in the Barmen Declaration. Ticciati argues that, as a political reading of scripture, the Barmen Declaration is laudable, although today it stands in need of repair, even if the means by which it is repaired are provided by the Declaration itself. In so doing, the Declaration and Christianity's relationship to Judaism are reframed by recent theological critiques of anti-Judaism and anti-Semitism in such a way that strengthen the "universal particularism" by which Barmen responds to the local particularism of National Socialism.

John C. Nugent tackles the liberal attempt to abolish capital punishment in "The End of Sacrifice: John Howard Yoder's Critique of Capital Punishment." Nugent shows that it is Yoder's theological reading of scripture, coupled with a penetrating cultural analysis, enables him to mount a substantial theological critique of the practice of capital punishment. Yoder agrees with sociological and anthropological analyses that show that taking life is a cultic and atoning ritual act. However, liberal Christian efforts to abolish capital punishment have failed because they align not with the Gospel, but rather modern, liberal political logic. As Nugent argues, for Yoder, capital punishment can never be rejected entirely by those who have turned away from the Gospel.

In the final essay, "A Broken Body Reads Mark," Craig Hovey engages Fernando Belo's Marxist reading of Mark, and in turn proposes a new theological—indeed, eucharistic—reading of the politics of Mark. For Belo, sacramental reading necessarily reinforces that bourgeois, capitalistic rejection of material existence. Hovey challenges Belo's understanding of the sacraments, showing that a sacramental reading is the most materialist reading possible. In fact, Hovey argues, understanding Mark, a text riddled with complexity and veiled elements, requires that one read eucharistically because reading Mark entails becoming part of a community of broken bodies.

We hope the essays in this volume provoke further study of how premodern and modern theologians' readings of the sacred page shapes their understanding of politics. It is also our hope that the efforts undertaken here might assist those concerned with shaping a political theology that can articulate the liberating power of the gospel in the light of the tradition and with attention to the problems of violence and injustice.

1

Empires and Enemies

Re-Reading Lament as Politics

Rebekah Eklund

The biblical lament is a cry for God's help in the midst of distress. Save! Rise up! Hear! Especially in apocalyptic contexts, the lamenter insists—despite the available evidence—that all the nations fall under God's sovereignty and are subject to the justice of the judge of all the earth (Pss. 67:4; 82:8; 94:2; 96:10, 13; 98:9). In the midst of injustice, the lamenter challenges God to act according to God's own character, that is, to bring about justice. In this way, lament is a public expression of protest regarding the way things are, and hope in the way things will be in God's good future. When we read the laments of scripture today in our own political settings, or with our suffering neighbors, we participate in a practice that possesses an inherently political character. Indeed, lament functions as resistance and renarration: resistance to the idea that the oppressor gets the last word, and a renarration of the present injustice in light of God's inexorable promise of peace and justice for those who suffer (Rev. 21:3-4).

To investigate the claim that reading biblical lament is a Christian political practice, this essay explores the lament of the martyrs under the altar in Revelation against the backdrop of Daniel's lament, which helps to situate the martyrs' lament within the long history of Israel's laments.[1] Both Daniel and Revelation are apocalyptic texts, both use Babylon as a cipher for another political threat, both are embedded within contexts of imperial oppression and communal challenge, and both use lament to call upon God's justice to defeat the oppressor and vindicate God's suffering people. The essay concludes with a brief consideration of the relationship between *reading* biblical lament and *enacting* it through contemporary nonviolent public protests against injustice.

Enemies and Empires

The enemy is such a defining element of the biblical lament that Claus Westermann calls it one of the three constitutive elements of the lament, alongside God and the lamenter.[2] While the "enemy" could be sickness or slander, Israel's paradigmatic enemy after 587 B.C.E. is Babylon, which in turn becomes a cipher for later enemies, especially Antiochus IV (as in Daniel) and Rome (as in Revelation). The enemy of empire poses a special problem for Israel's identity as God's covenant people, as expressed so eloquently by the pseudonymous author of 4 Ezra: "And now, O Lord, behold, these nations, which are reputed as nothing, domineer over us and devour

---

1. I am grateful to Stephen Fowl, John Kiess, and Matt Moser for commenting on earlier drafts of this essay.
2. Claus Westermann, *Praise and Lament in the Psalms*, trans. Keith R. Crim (Atlanta: John Knox, 1989), 169.

us. But we your people, whom you have called your first-born, only begotten, zealous for you, and most dear, have been given into their hands" (6:57-58; cf. 3:32, 35b; 5:23-27).

As Israel's laments over time protested the domination of Egypt, Assyria, Babylon, Persia, the Seleucids, and Rome, the New Testament authors likewise appropriated lament within their own sociopolitical reality: the Roman Empire as represented by Herod the Great, Caesar Augustus, Quirinius of Syria, the colluding Sadducees and the chief priests ("We have no king but Caesar," John 19:15), Herod Antipas, Pontius Pilate, Nero, Domitian. Inasmuch as Jesus is the Messiah-King who weeps, is abandoned, and is executed as a criminal, lament in the New Testament contributes to the power-reversal inherent in the gospel: the last shall become first; the mourners shall be comforted; the martyrs who lose their lives to the empire shall be vindicated, the mighty emperor thrown down, and the slaughtered Lamb shall ascend his rightful throne.[3] The cry of lament that echoes in the New Testament protests all that is "not yet" about this good news: the last are still last; the emperor still reigns; the faithful are dragged to trial and killed; Christ has not yet returned and creation groans with longing for that day. But the lamenter also trusts in the fulfillment of what God began by taking on flesh in Jesus.[4]

Antiochus IV as Babylon: Lament as Resistance in Daniel

In the Old Testament, Daniel and his companions are the exemplars of faithfulness to God under oppression: they choose death in a fiery

---

3. Donald Juel argues that the frequent allusions in the passion narrative to the lament psalms, especially Pss. 22 and 69, "contribute to the irony" of a Messiah-King who suffers and dies a shameful death. See Juel, *Messianic Exegesis: Christological Interpretation of the Old Testament in Early Christianity* (Philadelphia: Fortress Press, 1988), 97.
4. For a detailed study of the role of lament in the New Testament, especially in relation to Jesus' laments, see Rebekah Eklund, *Jesus Wept: The Significance of Lament in the New Testament*, Library of New Testament Studies (New York: T&T Clark, 2015).

furnace rather than commit idolatry by worshiping the Babylonian king's golden image. In Daniel 7–12, Daniel receives a series of visions, one of which includes four beasts that correspond to four empires: Babylon, the Medes, the Persians, and finally the Greeks, from which spring the ten "horns" of the Seleucid dynasty. These details prompt scholars to locate the composition of Daniel's latter chapters to the crisis in Judea under the Seleucid ruler Antiochus Epiphanes IV, who in 167 B.C.E. outlawed key Jewish practices (most notably, circumcision) and desecrated the temple by replacing its holy objects with a statue of Zeus. Daniel is thus a symbol of resistance both in exile in Babylon in the sixth century B.C.E. and in occupied Judea 400 years later.

After an especially distressing vision, Daniel prays a lengthy lament, which contains a strong element of penitence for Israel's past sins.[5] First, Daniel fasts in sackcloth and ashes, which are acts of ritual mourning, and then he prays and makes confession to God (9:3-4a). Daniel pleads with God to forgive Judah, Jerusalem, and all Israel for their rebellion (9:5-11), pointing out that God's reputation is at stake, since the city of Jerusalem and the people of Israel both "bear your name" (9:18, 19; cf. 9:16b; Exod. 32:9-14). Daniel concludes with a series of imperative petitions, a common feature of lament: Hear! Forgive! Listen! Act! Do not delay! (9:19).[6]

While Daniel is still praying, the angel Gabriel arrives to explain the vision that had left Daniel appalled in the previous chapter (8:27).

---

5. Several scholars describe a shift toward penitence in post-exilic prayers: see especially Richard J. Bautch, *Developments in Genre between Post-Exilic Penitential Prayers and the Psalms of Communal Lament*, Academia Biblica 7 (Leiden: The Society of Biblical Literature, 2003); Rodney Werline, *Penitential Prayer in Second Temple Judaism* (Atlanta: Scholars Press, 1998); and William S. Morrow, *Protest Against God*, Hebrew Bible Monographs 4 (Sheffield: Phoenix Press, 2007).

6. The petition is the heart of the lament, and it typically occurs in the imperative. See, for example, Patrick Miller, *They Cried to the Lord: The Form and Theology of Biblical Prayer* (Minneapolis: Fortress Press, 1994), 86–114; James L. Mays, *The Lord Reigns: A Theological Handbook to the Psalms* (Louisville: Westminster John Knox, 1994), 28–29.

While the angel provides no easy assurance of the enemy's defeat, his answer declares that God controls and has decreed even these turbulent historical events. Every empire is under the sovereignty of the God of Israel, the judge of all the earth. By laying claim to God as the one who continues to be God of Israel despite Israel's sins, Daniel's lament "contradicts imperial claims to ultimacy," whether those of Babylon or Antiochus, and thus functions as a form of radical hope in the midst of calamity.[7] In fact, Anathea Portier-Young proposes that "the book of Daniel urges Judeans persecuted by Antiochus IV to adopt specific forms of nonviolent resistance," including "persevering in the practices of their faith even at the cost of their lives."[8] Daniel's lament is itself a practice of nonviolent resistance to oppression, as it provides a "recitation of alternative values" and a reshaping of Israel's identity as the people of God.[9] Likewise, the lament of the martyrs in Revelation renarrates the apparent triumph of the Roman Empire and represents one form of resistance to imperial demands to abandon God and worship the emperor's idols instead.

Rome as Babylon: Lament as Resistance in Revelation

If Daniel is implicitly or by application a text of encouragement to a suffering community, Revelation is explicitly an exhortation, directly addressed to seven churches in Asia Minor. Revelation's apocalyptic visions[10] encourage nonviolent resistance to the imperial cult and

---

7. Anathea Portier-Young, *Apocalypse Against Empire: Theologies of Resistance in Early Judaism* (Grand Rapids: Eerdmans, 2011), 244. Portier-Young argues that "the first Jewish apocalypses emerged as a literature of resistance to empire" (xxii). She contrasts the nonviolent resistance commended by Daniel with the armed resistance envisioned by the Apocalypse of Weeks of *1 Enoch* (ibid., 219, 313–45).
8. Ibid., 262.
9. Daniel L. Smith-Christopher, *Biblical Theology of Exile*, Overtures to Biblical Theology (Minneapolis: Augsburg Fortress, 2002), 121–22 (121); see also Portier-Young, *Apocalypse Against Empire*, 252–53. Smith-Christopher and Portier-Young discuss the penitential prayer, which is usually considered a post-exilic form of the lament.

public witness to Christ's Lordship, all in the light of God's ultimate victory over both Satan and Rome.[11] The lament of the martyrs contributes to this overarching purpose. Their cry occurs early in Revelation, after John's vision of the heavenly throne and just after the slaughtered Lamb is declared worthy to open the scroll. The "souls of those who had been slaughtered for the word of God and for the testimony they had given" cry out from beneath the altar, "Sovereign Lord, holy and true, how long will it be before you judge and avenge our blood on the inhabitants of the earth?" (Rev. 6:10).[12]

10. In terms of the function of lament in an apocalypse and in relation to Rome, Revelation has an interesting parallel in 4 Ezra, a roughly contemporaneous Jewish text. This comparison depends in part on dating 4 Ezra to ca. 100 C.E., based on 4 Ezra 3:1 as a reference to 30 years after the fall of Jerusalem in 70 C.E., and Revelation to 90–95 C.E., based on its apparent knowledge of Domitian. In the visions of both 4 Ezra and Revelation, the Roman Empire is thinly veiled as Babylon, the ancient enemy of Israel (see especially the eagle vision of 4 Ezra 11; cf. Dan. 7:3; Rev. 13:1). In both sets of visions, after a time of tumult and oppression under the eagle/beast (Rome), the lion/Messiah arises, destroys the wicked, and delivers (in the case of Ezra) the remnant of Israel or (in the case of Revelation) those who have remained faithful to Christ. Of course, they are significantly different on other points; N. T. Wright points out several important differences between Revelation and other apocalypses, including 4 Ezra; see Wright, "Revelation and Christian Hope: Political Implications of the Revelation to John," in *Revelation and the Politics of Apocalyptic Interpretation*, ed. Richard B. Hays and Stefan Alkier (Waco: University of Baylor Press, 2012), 105-24 (109–10). For analysis of the parallels between 4 Ezra 4:35-37; Rev. 6:9-11; and 1 Enoch 47:4, see David E. Aune, *Revelation 6–16*, Word Biblical Commentary 52B (Waco: Word, 1998), 391. For 4 Ezra as a theological response to the events of 70 C.E., see Karina Martin Hogan, *Theologies in Conflict in 4 Ezra: Wisdom Debate and Apocalyptic Solution*, Supplements to the Journal for the Study of Judaism 130 (Leiden: Brill, 2008). See also Bruce W. Longenecker, "Locating 4 Ezra: A Consideration of its Social Setting and Functions," *Journal for the Study of Judaism in the Persian, Hellenistic and Roman Period* 28, no. 3 (1997): 271–93; and Michael E. Stone, "Reactions to Destructions of the Second Temple: Theology, Perception and Conversion," *Journal for the Study of Judaism in the Persian, Hellenistic and Roman Period* 12, no. 2 (1981): 195–204.
11. See Michael J. Gorman, *Reading Revelation Responsibly: Uncivil Worship and Witness: Following the Lamb into the New Creation* (Eugene, OR: Cascade Books, 2011); N. T. Wright, "Revelation and Christian Hope: Political Implications of the Revelation to John," in *Revelation and the Politics of Apocalyptic Interpretation*, 105–24; Stefan Alkier, "Witness or Warrior? How the Book of Revelation Can Help Christians Live Their Political Lives," in ibid., 125–41; Brian K. Blount, *Can I Get a Witness?: Reading Revelation through African American Culture* (Louisville: Westminster John Knox, 2005).
12. The cry "How long?" is a common complaint in lament psalms regarding the apparent delay of God's vindication. The Greek phrase ἕως πότε ("how long") appears in the LXX in Pss. 6:4; 12:2-3; 73:10; 78:5; 79:5; 81:2; 88:47; 89:13; 93:3. Cf. Luke 18:7, "And will not God grant justice to his chosen ones who cry to him day and night? Will he delay long in helping them?"

The martyrs have presumably lost their lives in one of the waves of imperial persecution.[13] When they cry out, they address God as δεσπότης (NRSV: Lord), a relatively rare word in the New Testament. Although δεσπότης can refer to God in the LXX and in Jewish and Christian literature (for example, Luke 2:29; Acts 4:24), it is also "a regular Greek translation of two Latin terms for the Roman emperor, *dominus* and *princeps*."[14] Here, as perhaps also in Luke-Acts, the slaughtered souls address God as the true δεσπότης, not the emperor, just as Jesus is the true Lord (κύριος).[15]

Additional symbols undergird the martyrs' lament with political force. The martyrs' lament occurs when the Lamb opens the fifth seal, after the first four seals have unleashed the famous four horsemen of conquest, war, famine, and plague. As symbols of war, horses represent the might of Rome, but John repurposes them: "Those thundering hoofs that once heralded the irresistible power of Roman armies are now signaling the inevitable doom of the empire."[16] The sword (μάχαιρα) of the second horseman is another "symbol of imperial authority" (see Rom. 13:4).[17] Even the altar under which the martyrs cry out may function as an allusion to Rome's authority and

---

13. The first great wave of persecution occurred under Nero (64–68 C.E.) and a more scattered persecution may have taken place under the reign of Domitian (81–96 C.E.), although scholars split over whether any real evidence exists for the persecution of Christians during Domitian's reign. No evidence exists that Christians before Constantine actively revolted against Roman rule; instead, some of them simply refused to participate in the imperial cult. See, for example, David A. deSilva, *Honor, Patronage, Kinship and Purity* (Downers Grove, IL: InterVarsity Press Academic, 2000). This kind of Christian resistance in the first century is assumed rather than specifically narrated in Revelation and in other NT books (for example, Rev. 2:12-13; Heb. 10:32-34). For other early Christian documents, see George Kalantzis, *Caesar and the Lamb: Early Christian Attitudes on War and Military Service* (Eugene, OR: Wipf and Stock, 2012).
14. Aune, *Revelation 6–16*, 407.
15. For the title "Lord" in Luke-Acts, see C. Kavin Rowe, *World Upside Down: Reading Acts in the Graeco-Roman Age* (Oxford: Oxford University Press, 2009), 103–15.
16. Allan Boesak, *Comfort and Protest: Reflections on the Apocalypse of John of Patmos* (Philadelphia: Westminster, 1987), 63.
17. Justo González, *For the Healing of the Nations: The Book of Revelation in an Age of Cultural Conflict* (Maryknoll, NY: Orbis, 1999), 38.

its blasphemous claims to divinity. While most interpreters take the altar in 6:9 as a heavenly altar, David May argues that it is a Roman altar, meant to evoke the "monumental altar to Zeus at Pergamum," where the first martyr mentioned in Revelation died (2:13).[18] Even if the altar is meant to be the heavenly altar and not an earthly, Roman one (cf. Rev. 8:3-5; 9:13; 14:18), the blood of the martyrs and the motif of their sacrifice, combined with the symbolism of the altar, is surely evocative of the power of Rome to bear the sword. Perhaps the ambiguity is deliberate, or at least fortuitous; the heavenly altar connects the sacrifice of the martyrs to the death of Christ, as does the application of the verb σφάζω (slaughter) to both the Lamb and the martyrs (Rev. 5:6, 9, 12; 6:9), whereas the earthly Roman altar reminds the reader of the blasphemous pretentions of Rome and her imperial idols, and who it was who shed the blood of those now crying out for justice.

The martyrs petition God to judge and to avenge their blood on "the inhabitants of the earth," a phrase always used in Revelation of the enemies of God and the church.[19] In verse 11, they receive an initial response (the passive suggests a divine response): they are given white robes as signs of their purity or their cleansing by Jesus' blood (see Rev. 7:14) and told to remain, or rest, a little while longer (see 4 Ezra 7:75). In the rest of the book of Revelation, the martyrs and their lament appear again and again: through the angelic visions, the churches are assured that God hears and will answer the martyrs'

---

18. David M. May, "Interpreting Revelation with Roman Coins: A Test Case, Revelation 6:9-11," *Review and Expositor* 106 (2009): 445-65 (458). May suggests that "Satan's throne" in Rev. 2:13 is another reference to the altar at Pergamum. The concept of souls under the heavenly altar has parallels in Judaism: Aune cites *'Abot R. Nat.* 12 ("the souls of all the righteous are in safekeeping under the throne of glory") and *'Abot R. Nat.* 26 ("He who is buried in the land of Israel is as though he were buried under the altar; for the whole land of Israel is fit to be the site of the altar. And he who is buried under the altar is as though he were buried under the throne of glory") (Aune, *Revelation 6–16*, 405). An altar (θυσιαστήριον), probably a heavenly one (although it is sometimes ambiguous), also appears in 8:3-5; 9:13; 11:1; 14:18 (cf. 15:5); 16:7.
19. Aune, *Revelation 6–16*, 410.

plea for justice (8:4-5; 10:6-7; 16:4-6; 17:1-6; 18:4, 8; 19:2). God's vindication of the suffering faithful culminates in Rev. 20:4, when the seer writes, "I also saw the souls of those who had been beheaded for their testimony to Jesus and for the word of God. . . . They came to life and reigned with Christ a thousand years."[20]

Babylon v. God: God Wins

In Romans 13, Rome is the government ordained by God; in Revelation 13, it is the beast that derives its authority from Satan. If the gospels (and Paul) portray a Rome who might be converted to the way of Christ, Revelation has no such optimism. Revelation aligns Rome with the enemies of God—indeed, with the great Adversary himself—and depicts the decisive downfall of the great empire. In this way, Revelation boldly reframes the current political reality of Christians in Asia Minor living under the threat of persecution: as God's enemy, Rome's coming destruction is certain. The lament of the martyrs in 6:9-11 plays a key role in this reframing, because Revelation depicts the fall of Rome as God's answer to the lamenters' cries. Indeed, Scott Ellington proposes that the movement from lament to response to praise in Revelation "lend[s] to the book of Revelation as a whole the tone of a lament prayer as the unfolding vision moves from a cry in the midst of suffering to a shout of triumph as God answers the prayer of lament."[21]

In chapter 18, toward the end of the book, an angel sings a dirge over the proleptic/promised fall of Rome (presented, of course, as Babylon): "Alas, alas, the great city, Babylon, the mighty city! For in one hour your judgment has come" (Rev. 18:10). Unlike the

---

20. On the thousand-year reign as a reward to the slaughtered souls of Rev. 6, see Robert H. Mounce, *The Book of Revelation*, The New International Commentary on the New Testament (Grand Rapids: Eerdmans, 1977), 354–55, 359.
21. Scott A. Ellington, *Risking Truth: Reshaping the World through Prayers of Lament* (Eugene, OR: Pickwick, 2008), 172.

anguished dirge sung over the fall of Jerusalem in the book of Lamentations, this is a triumphant dirge, which concludes with the multitude of heaven shouting "Hallelujah! Salvation and glory and power to our God, for his judgments are true and just; for he has judged the great whore who corrupted the earth with her fornication, and he has avenged on her the blood of his servants" (Rev. 19:1-2). Several key words link the description of Babylon's fall to the martyrs' cry: servants and fellow-servants (δούλων, 19:2; σύνδουλοι, 6:11), and the action of God to judge and avenge the blood of God's servants (ἔκρινεν and ἐξεδίκησεν, 19:2; κρίνεις and ἐκδικεῖς, 6:10; αἷμα in both).[22]

In the last few chapters of the book, the judgment on historical Rome and the end of history merge in a characteristically apocalyptic way, so that the final defeat of the empire includes the defeat of the devil and death itself and the descent of a new Jerusalem from heaven. As Richard Hays points out, "the politics of 'Babylon, the mighty city' (18:10) is judged and supplanted by God's new *polis*, the New Jerusalem, in which God dwells with his people and wipes away all tears (21:1-4)."[23]

God and the Lamenter

To return to Westermann's famous "triangle," the lament involves the one who cries out, the enemy, and God—the One who hears the lament. The biblical laments of Old and New Testaments depend on a particular God, who created and reigns over all the nations and who made specific promises. The lamenter cries out to God from within a

---

22. Heil notes an additional connection between servants (1:1) and fellow servants (6:11), and points out that the recipients of the letter can likewise expect to face death for their testimony; John Paul Heil, "The Fifth Seal (Rev. 6:9-11) as a Key to the Book of Revelation," *Biblica* 74, no. 2 (1993): 220-43 (221).
23. Richard B. Hays, "Faithful Witness, Alpha and Omega: The Identity of Jesus in the Apocalypse of John," in *Revelation and the Politics of Apocalyptic Interpretation*, 69-83 (82).

defined relationship (covenant, fidelity to Christ) and invokes God's character as the grounds for his appeal. God has promised to help Israel: *rise up, then, and help!* God is a just God: *deliver justice!* In the Old Testament, the lamenter cries out to God for redemption because God has promised to be the God *of Israel*, the one who will bless and protect her, who will shelter her from her enemies, the one who carried her out of Egypt and settled her into a place of rest and safety, a land of milk and honey. The fundamental problem of every lament—whether the symptom of that problem be sickness, slander, or exile—is a rupture in that relationship, a threat to the integrity of God's own character and promises.

Of course, God is sovereign over the entire created world and all the nations, not just Israel, a point made with equal clarity by Genesis and Job. The prophets excoriate those who commit injustices and trample the poor, and the nations are not exempt from God's judgment (for example, Amos 1–2). Abraham appeals to God's responsibility for all the nations when he bargains with YHWH for the fate of two wicked cities: "Shall not the Judge of all the earth do what is just?" asks Abraham regarding Sodom and Gomorrah (Gen. 18:25). In 4 Ezra, a document probably composed ca. 100 C.E., Ezra frequently invokes the relationship between God and Israel, but he also challenges God to act justly toward the entire creation (4 Ezra 3:3-8, 20-23; 6:54; 7:62-69, 116-121).[24]

The Revelation martyrs likewise call upon God as the sovereign judge of all the earth ("Sovereign Lord, holy and true . . ."). Rather than naming the covenant as the factor that should motivate God to act, they invoke a different relationship, the one forged between God and those redeemed by Christ (Rev. 1:5b-6). Unlike Daniel, Revelation uses lament not to reframe past disobedience but to urge

---

24. Ezra's most strident complaint is a reworking of Psalm 8: "But what is man, that you are angry with him; or what is a mortal race, that you are so bitter against it?" (4 Ezra 8:34).

patient endurance and faithful witness to the Lamb who was slain.[25] Although the author of Revelation chastises those who have lost their first love, and urges repentance for those who have tolerated evildoers, the key of lament here is protest rather than penitence: the suffering of the churches is never construed as punishment for rebellion or disobedience. The martyrs do not narrate their oppression as the result of disobedience to the covenant; rather, their suffering is due to their *faithful* witness. Just as the Lamb was slaughtered (σφάζω, 5:6, 9, 12), so too can those who witness to the Lamb expect to be slaughtered (σφάζω, Rev. 6:9).

Their lament represents anguished longing but also hope, which is the twin impulse of lament in the New Testament and in the church, where lament is longing for God's kingdom, inaugurated in Christ, fully to come; and confident hope that it is already breaking into the world and that nothing will hinder its arrival. In his letter to the churches in Rome, Paul assures Christians in Rome that nothing in all creation, not even the sword of the empire that slaughters them (σφάζω again, Rom. 8:36), will be able to separate them from the love of God in Christ (Rom. 8:35-39).

Reading and Embodying Lament as Resistance

None of this, of course, necessarily leads to a new kind of politics. The reading of Revelation—and the reading of lament—has not always occasioned thoughtful engagement with the world and its injustices. On the other hand, at least some of those who have read Revelation and other lament texts from their own contemporary contexts of suffering and oppression have found in those texts calls to resistance. Brian Blount, for example, consciously reads Revelation

---

25. For the emphasis on witness in Revelation, see Blount, *Can I Get a Witness?*, 46–67. See also Hays, "Faithful Witness," 77–79. For the theme of patient endurance (ὑπομονή) in Revelation, see Rev. 1:9; 2:2, 3, 19; 3:10; 13:10; 14:12; compare Rev. 2:13.

through the lens of African-American experience, and he argues that the author of Revelation not only hears and joins in on the lament of the people, but he also "tries to turn that lament into transformative behavior," that is, into "nonviolent resistance against the great power that afflicts them."[26] Blount claims that lament and resistance are closely linked: "[L]ament breeds fury at the oppressions and the people who caused them, and—in John's scenario at least—it drives those who lament to resist."[27] But lament, he says, is risky business. The hearers of Revelation must decide whether to lament and thereby "do everything that lament requires," which includes joining "the resistance of the Lamb," or to "accommodate [themselves] to the ways of Rome and the draconian things it does."[28] That's the choice; there is no lukewarm option (Rev. 3:16). For Blount, there is no *violent* option either, at least not on Revelation's terms. Vengeance belongs to God.

Likewise, in the context of South Africa in the 1980s, Allan Boesak identifies those who cry "How long?" with those currently suffering under apartheid.[29] Denise Ackermann writes from the same context, and she too identifies the power of lament to redefine reality and create change, through its combination of complaint and petition with trust in God's power, goodness, and justice: "The combination of lament and praise [in the lament psalms] has powerful political implications. When lamenting people assume the power to define reality and to proclaim that all is not well, things begin to change. . . . The lamenters' voices become subversive. They are, in fact,

---

26. Brian Blount, "Breaking Point: A Sermon," in Sally A. Brown and Patrick D. Miller, eds., *Lament: Reclaiming Practices in Pulpit, Pew, and Public Square* (Louisville: Westminster John Knox, 2005), 145-53 (146).
27. Ibid., 149.
28. Ibid., 150.
29. Boesak, *Comfort and Protest*, 69–72. Boesak dedicates his commentary to "all those who, true to their faith, have struggled and fought with us; gone to jail and shared pain and bread with us. They are seeing the power of the beast. They shall see the victory of the Lamb."

celebrating God's ability to act in this world, to right the wrongs far beyond conventional notions of the possible."[30]

It is worth asking, then, what kinds of resistance might arise from lament today. James Cone and Brian Blount have identified the spirituals, the blues, and modern rap music as acts that participate in both lament and resistance.[31] Others focus on lament as penitence for national sins like slavery or apartheid.[32] I choose to explore a different example: public nonviolent protests against injustice. These kinds of protests are sometimes associated with the term lament (in a colloquial sense). And like the apocalyptic laments of Daniel and Revelation, they often participate in resistance to oppression. Since biblical lament is typically spoken, written, or read, actions like gathering in silent protest hardly seem to qualify as lament. On the other hand, other ritual actions often accompany the biblical lament: for example, tearing the clothes, putting ashes on the head, and fasting (Dan. 9:3).[33] Might protest movements participate in the ethos of the biblical lament, without using speech?

The women's peace initiative in Liberia offers one interesting test case. During the horrific civil war in Liberia in the 1990s, thousands of Muslim and Christian women gathered every day for weeks to

---

30. Denise Ackermann, "On Hearing and Lamenting: Faith and Truth-Telling," in H. Russel Botman and Robin M. Petersen, eds., *To Remember and To Heal: Theological and Psychological Reflections on Truth and Reconciliation* (Cape Town, South Africa: Human & Rousseau, 1996), 47-56 (116).
31. James H. Cone, *The Spirituals and the Blues: An Interpretation* (New York: The Seabury Press, 1972); Blount, *Can I Get a Witness?*, 91–117. See also Carol Antablin Miles, "'Singing the Songs of Zion' and Other Sermons from the Margins of the Canon," *Koinonia* 6, no. 2 (1994): 151–75.
32. Ackermann, "On Hearing and Lamenting," 52; Soong-Chan Rah, "The American Church's Absence of Lament," http://sojo.net/blogs/2013/10/24/american-churchs-absence-lament (accessed June 2, 2015). Ackermann and Rah, among others, raise the pressing question of how one can lament from a position of relative power and comfort, rather than from a position of oppression or suffering. See also Blount, "Breaking Point," 148–53.
33. Gunkel, *The Psalms: A Form Critical Introduction*, trans. Thomas M. Horner (Philadelphia: Fortress Press, 1967), 5–7, 13. James Mays notes that even the individual laments were adopted and used in corporate worship: "psalms written for ceremonies centering on individuals came to be used by the community" (James L. Mays, *Psalms*, Interpretation [Louisville: John Knox, 1994], 11).

sit in the fish market along the president's daily route to demand peace.³⁴ They wore white T-shirts and white headscarves. Over time, they were instrumental in jumpstarting the stalled peace talks. On the surface of it, these actions bear a striking resemblance to the biblical lament. They protested injustice and cried for justice, much like the martyrs' cry in Revelation. Their white shirts and scarves and their visible gathering in the fish market could be analogous to the visible marks of fasting and ashes.³⁵ Norman Gottwald and Derek Suderman, among others, have argued that even individual lament psalms have a public function: the community, and not just God, is meant to hear the lament.³⁶ The prayer of the martyrs of Revelation is not private but is recorded and sent to churches throughout Asia Minor. When the women gathered in protest along a well-traveled road, and again outside the building hosting the stalled peace talks, their communities, both potential friend and foe, witnessed their actions.

In this way, the silent cries of the Liberian women may reflect lament as a form of challenge to God to enact God's justice, and a form of hope that God will do so. Leymah Gbowee, one of the initiators of the women's peace movement there, explains her decision to begin protesting with a simple lament, an invocation and a petition: "Please God, end the war."³⁷ Her decision to launch the

---

34. The story is told in Leymah Gbowee's memoir *Mighty Be Our Powers: How Sisterhood, Prayer, and Sex Changed a Nation at War: A Memoir* (New York: Beast, 2011), and the documentary *Pray the Devil Back to Hell* (produced by Abigail Disney, 2008).
35. Other modern protest movements often don visible symbols of their protest: the Madres of the Plaza de Mayo in Argentina also wore white scarves; the women of the Black Sash in South Africa wore black sashes as a symbol of mourning over the constitutional rights denied to black South Africans.
36. Norman Gottwald, "Social Drama in the Psalms of Individual Lament," in Randall Heskett and Brian Irwin, eds., *The Bible as a Human Witness to Divine Revelation* (New York: T&T Clark, 2010), 143–52; W. Derek Suderman, "Are Individual Complaint Psalms Really Prayers? Recognizing Social Address as Characteristic of Individual Complaints," in *The Bible as a Human Witness*, 153–70. See also Nancy C. Lee, *Lyrics of Lament: From Tragedy to Transformation* (Minneapolis: Fortress Press, 2010), 99.
37. Gbowee, *Mighty Be Our Powers*, 25. Of course, this analysis relies on Gbowee's own description of the movement.

Christian Women's Peace Initiative arises from a dream in which a voice speaks to Gbowee commanding her: "Gather the women to pray for peace!" Gbowee and the other women pray, "Jesus, help us. You are the true Prince of Peace, the only one who can grant us peace."[38] Once joined by their Muslim sisters, they begin every day of their silent protest in the field with Christian and Muslim prayers.[39] Gbowee writes, in language reminiscent of Ackermann's reflections on lament and empowerment in South Africa, "God's hands were under our effort. . . . You can tell people of the need to struggle, but when the powerless start to see that they really can make a difference, nothing can quench the fire."[40] This movement explicitly evokes God's commitment to peace as its motivating impulse, and narrates its efforts as a participation in God's design for peace. This coheres with the heart of lament as a cry for *God's* justice and an unwavering belief in God as the agent of true and lasting justice and peace.

If we return to the question of the relationship being claimed by the lamenter, the Liberian women's peace movement appears to operate out of two contexts. For Gbowee and the specifically Christian women, their actions laid claim to Jesus as the Prince of Peace. Yet unlike the Revelation martyrs, they do not claim that their suffering results from their faithfulness to Christ.[41] Instead, especially once they are joined by their Muslim sisters, their prayers appeal to the God of the whole earth, who loves justice and hears the pleas of *all* those who suffer. Thus, like the lamenter described in the first paragraph of this essay, they challenge God to act according to what they believe to be true about God's own character, as One committed to justice and peace.

---

38. Ibid., 122, 123.
39. Ibid., 136, 138.
40. Ibid., 151.
41. Nor, of course, do they explain their suffering as the result of disobedience to God, as in the case of Daniel.

When the church laments as the church, whether in speech or action, it affirms the most basic trust of the biblical lamenter: that there is a God who hears and who wipes away all the tears, a God who defeated death and evil and invites us into abundant resurrection life, the God before whom all earthly powers are already disarmed. What this looks like in practice is difficult to prescribe in advance but surely deserves our attention. Which actions best witness to the victory of the slain Lamb while still crying out "How long?" to God? Which ones yield the greatest anger at injustice, the most courage, the greatest solidarity with others who suffer, and the most hope? Which ones allow us to express our outrage and anguish at the "not yet" of the kingdom of God while still embracing and celebrating its "now"?

Lamenting is only one practice of resistance and hope. But it may be a practice that encourages and flows into other Christian practices like peacemaking and bearing one another's burdens and offering hospitality to strangers. It might help awaken us to the suffering of brothers and sisters that we might not see otherwise, because it forces us to see what is *not yet* set right in this world. It might be the prayer that uses the laments already in scripture to give voice to anger and grief in the midst of distress, the prayer that undergirds and shapes actions like truth and reconciliation commissions and silent public protests. Indeed, I suggest that lament is a necessary element of the church's life in these in-between times, both as a witness *against* injustice and as a witness *to* God's justice and peace—to the Christian hope in the God who redeems everything, even the worst of evils. Whether in speech or in action, the lament of the church today joins in equal measure with the anguished cry of the martyrs—*How long, Lord?*—and the final longing, hopeful plea of Revelation: *Come, Lord Jesus!*

The Politics of Friendship in the Gospel of John

Peter Dula

In his preface to *The Community of the Beloved Disciple*, Raymond Brown worries about the unattractive picture of the early church that he presents in the book: "In the reconstruction of community history I shall concentrate on relationships to other groups and on a life-situation that reflects both loves and hates, and so this book is not an overall Johannine theology with neatly balanced pros and cons. (It may very well be more interesting because it shows a frank picture of church life, 'warts and all.') Consequently, I hope that for most readers this will *not* constitute their maiden voyage into troubled Johannine waters."[1]

---

1. Raymond Brown, *The Community of the Beloved Disciple* (New York: Paulist Press, 1979), 7.

Brown may be right that there are better introductions to the Gospel of John than his remarkable book.[2] But I worry about his wariness concerning the place and role of conflict in John's Gospel. In what follows, I argue that this "frank picture of church life," in which conflict is a persistent feature is not just more interesting. Rather, it is essential to John's account of friendship, his account of theology, and to his account of *how* theology is done. I find in John a remarkable theological vision of the role of conflict in communal or political relationships, one made possible by the Johannine experience of God in Christ.[3]

Friendship in Contemporary Theological Ethics

That John is a theorist of friendship is well known, but I think that contemporary theological ethics have been ill equipped to spot the originality of John's account of friendship. In part, this has to do with the lingering influence of Anders Nygren's rigid isolation of *agapē* from *eros* and *philia*.[4] While few of his conclusions are still accepted in scholarly circles, his thesis "continues to exercise a subtle gravitational pull in theological discussions of love that tends to distort theological reflection."[5] Under that gravitational pull, the scholarly task has not been understood as developing an account of friendship from the Gospels but rather to sort out just how Greco-

---

2. See Raymond Brown, *An Introduction to the Gospel of John*, ed. Francis Maloney (New Haven: Yale University Press, 2003).
3. The author wishes to acknowledge grant support from the Louisville Institute for the research and writing of this paper.
4. Nygren, *Agape and Eros*, trans. A. G. Herbert (New York: MacMillan, 1932). Among the most influential recent defenders of *philia* against Nygren are Paul Waddell, *Friendship and the Moral Life* (Notre Dame, IN: University of Notre Dame Press, 1990); Gilbert Meilaender, *Friendship: A Study in Theological Ethics* (Notre Dame, IN: University of Notre Dame Press, 1981) and Stanley Hauerwas and Charles Pinches, *Christians Among the Virtues* (Notre Dame, IN: University of Notre Dame Press, 1997).
5. David H. Kelsey, *Eccentric Existence: A Theological Anthropology*, 2 vols. (Louisville: Westminster/John Knox, 2009), 2:736.

Roman accounts of friendship were received by Christianity, especially by Augustine and Aquinas. Such a turn is in many ways appropriate; the ancient discussion of friendship is a profound one. But I see at least two issues with it. First, especially in the case of Aristotle, because his account is so emphatic about the similarities and wary of difference between friends, it reinforces a tendency to write conflict out of the relationships between friends. Theologians of friendship such as Hauerwas and Pinches as well as Meilaender clearly recognize this.[6] But they do not turn to the Gospels to develop an alternative. Second, just insofar as these theorists turn to the classical tradition *instead* of the Gospels, they inadvertently reinforce Nygren's suggestion that the Gospels really are about a narrowly defined *agapē* and provide no account of *philia*, let alone one capable of competing with Aristotle or Cicero. The two issues are linked. Because they don't turn to the Gospels, these thinkers miss the opportunity to develop a conflictual account of friendship. The reverse is also true. They don't turn to the Gospels because they have difficulty recognizing friendship in the antagonistic relationships portrayed there.

In fact, in the Fourth Gospel, friends sometimes look like, and sometimes are, enemies. Friends and enemies are not discrete categories of persons but things that each of us may be at different times. It is this feature of John's account of friendship that makes it so original. The Johannine community's experience of betrayal and denial makes clear that friends can become enemies. Its experience of reconciliation in Christ makes clear that enemies can become friends. This is easy to miss if under the influence of Nygren's "subtle gravitational pull" because the friend/enemy distinction is essential

---

6. As Hauerwas and Pinches put it, "Aristotle comes close to requiring that the constancy [friends] share protects us from one another's difference" (*Christians Among the Virtues*, 41). Meilaender suggests something similar when he pleads for "a little more openness" in Aristotelian friendship's "contented exclusivity" (*Friendship*, 16).

to Nygren's *eros/agapē* distinction. Enemy love is a central defining feature of *agapē*, and one that decisively distinguishes it from *philia*, dependent as the latter is on mutuality.[7] In the enemy, all the characteristics of *agapē* come together such that one knows better than anywhere else that it is true *agapē*.[8] In what follows, I hope to complicate the too easy dualisms between *agapē* and *philia* and between friends and enemies as well as to encourage a more hopeful account of conflict not just in friendship but theology itself. In order to do so, I begin by reading the friendship of Jesus and Peter in the Fourth Gospel in light of a passage that seems most problematic from the perspective of the agapists, John 15:12–17.

The Greatest Love

At the heart of this passage, we find these famous words of Jesus: "This is my commandment, that you love one another as I have loved you. No one has greater love than this, to lay down one's life for one's friends. You are my friends if you do what I command you. I do not call you servants any longer, because the servant does not know what the master is doing; but I have called you friends."[9] Perhaps the most obvious question provoked by this passage is this: Why is dying for one's friends instead of for one's enemies, or for "the world" as John 3:16 has it, the greatest kind of love? Though the question occurred to Aquinas[10] as well as many others, a distinguished

---

7. Throughout this paper, unless otherwise specified, I will use *philia* and *agapē* as they are used in the theological ethics literature. That is, I will use them as if they denote distinct kinds of love. Much recent NT commentary, however, argues that in actuality they had become synonymous. See Liz Carmichael, *Friendship: Interpreting Christian Love* (New York: T&T Clark, 2004), 36–39 and Raymond Brown, *The Gospel According to John I–XII* (Garden City, NY: Doubleday, 1966), 497–99.
8. Nygren, *Agape and Eros*, 101. See also Gene Outka, *Agape: An Ethical Analysis* (New Haven: Yale University Press, 1977), 280.
9. John 15:12–15. All citations of scripture are from the NRSV.
10. Thomas Aquinas, *Commentary on the Gospel of John: Chapters 13–21*, trans., Fabian Larcher, OP

list of modern commentators is dismissive. Bultmann and Barrett, for example, agree that the line means that the greatest way to show love to your friends is to die for them.[11] That is, it is meant to compare degrees of love for friends, not to compare love of friends with love of enemies, strangers, neighbors, etc.

Yet, that conclusion sits uneasily with the widespread conviction that the Fourth Gospel is relatively uninterested in love of neighbor let alone enemy love: "If you love those who love you, what reward do you have? . . . And if you greet only your brothers and sisters, what more are you doing than others?"[12] seems the direct opposite of John. David Rensberger summarizes the consensus as follows: "With a purity of focus unmatched in any of the Synoptics, John has seen the essence of Jesus' ethical intention in the single commandment, 'Love'; yet he reduces the scope of this commandment in a way that all but undermines the intention of the historical Jesus, making it read 'Love *one another.*' Not 'your enemies'; not even 'your neighbor as yourself'; but only 'one another.'"[13] The common explanation for the Johannine retreat from radical love directs us to consider the context of the Johannine community's bitter conflicts with the synagogue. Given that context, it becomes understandable how "love *one another*" (13:34-35) within the community takes precedence over the command to love the enemy. Again Rensberger summarizes it well, "The sect, under intense pressure from the outside, needed to

---

and James A Weisheipf, OP (Washington, DC: Catholic University Press of America, 2010), 107.
11. Bultmann, *The Gospel of John: A Commentary*, trans. G. R. Beasley-Murray (Philadelphia: Westminster Press, 1971), 542, n. 4. C. K. Barrett, *The Gospel According to John* 2nd ed. (Philadelphia: Westminster Press, 1978), 476-77.
12. Matt. 5:46-47.
13. David Rensberger, *Johannine Faith and Liberating Community* (Philadelphia: Westminster Press, 1988), 124. Nygren put it this way: love "now becomes particularistic; it loses something of its original all-embracing scope and is limited to those who bear the Christian name . . . not a love directed to those outside" (*Agape and Eros*, 114). See also Raymond Brown, *The Gospel According to John XIII–XXI* (Garden City, NY: Doubleday, 1970), 613.

forge its own internal bonds even more strongly.... The hatred from without must be balanced and opposed by the love within the sect itself."[14] This is sometimes (though not in Rensberger) accompanied by a tone of condescension to John. The gospel's elevation of love within the community over love of neighbors, strangers and enemies, or of *philia* over *agapē*, might be understandable given the context, but it remains a disappointment, a "sectarian" failure of nerve.

Others have attempted to find a space for love of enemies in John. They sometimes point out that those critical of John's account of love are dependent upon an argument from silence. To say that John does not want us to love our enemies is like saying that "because he does not mention that husbands should love their wives therefore he does not believe it!"[15] Others insist that "love one another" be set within the larger context of mission. This community of love is also sent into the world "as the Father sent me"[16] and in doing so manages to helpfully complicate the academic category of sectarian. Sharon Ringe argues that "At issue is not whom to have as a friend, but how to be a friend."[17] As such, it is about the qualities identified as constitutive of friendship, not about excluding enemies and strangers from the circle of those to whom we can extend those qualities.

I think there is something to all these perspectives. But more can be said, and so in what follows I pursue another angle. These discussions tend to assume that when we say that "one another" in John 13 or

---

14. David Rensberger, "Love of One Another and Love of Enemies in the Gospel of John," in *The Love of Enemy and Nonretaliation in the New Testament*, ed. Willard Swartley (Louisville: Westminster/John Knox, 1992), 297-313 (305). See also Johannes Nissen, "Community and Ethics in the Gospel of John," in *New Readings in John: Literary and Theological Perspectives*, eds., Johannes Nissen and Sigfred Pedersen, (New York: T & T Clark, 2004), 194-212 (211).
15. William Klassen, "Love Your Enemies: Some Reflections on the Current Status of Research," in *The Love of Enemy and Nonretaliation*, 1-31 (18-19).
16. Victor Paul Furnish, *The Love Command in the New Testament* (Nashville: Abingdon, 1972), 147–48. See also Rensberger, *Johannine Faith*, 144-50.
17. Sharon Ringe, *Wisdom's Friends: Community and Christology in the Fourth Gospel* (Louisville: Westminster John Knox Press, 1999), 68.

"you" in John 15 means other Christians, we have said all we need to say. They assume further, that we know all we need to know about what is meant by "friends." John 15 is not understood as providing a distinct account of friendship so much as applying a preconceived (usually Aristotelian) account of friendship to the church. So as a way of prying open this discussion let's begin by being specific about the "one another" and the "you" and then see if that helps discern a particular account of friendship implied in John 15.

Perhaps the most curious thing about Jesus' remarks about friendship in John 15 is that his words were addressed to a group that was not going to act very friendly. All abandoned him. Peter cut off the guard's ear and then denied Jesus three times. There is, of course, a reconciliation scene in John 21, but he did not then *become* Jesus' friend. The one who denied Jesus three times was already declared "friend" as were the ones of whom Jesus said, "You will be scattered, each to his own home and you will leave me alone" (16:32). What sort of thing must Jesus think friendship is if he used it so confidently of these people? In other words, the central clue to understanding "as I have loved you" is "you." Who are these people?

Peter in the Fourth Gospel

That question is more easily approached via another question: Who is Peter in the Fourth Gospel? The question is crucial, because Peter is a representative of, and spokesperson for, the apostles. If we know who he is, then we know who these "friends" are. Thirty years ago, Arthur Maynard identified two basic and conflicting views of Peter in the Fourth Gospel.[18] On one view, represented by Raymond Brown and Oscar Cullman, John clearly acknowledges Peter's privileged role. Any negative portrayals of Peter in the Gospel are not intended to

---

18. Arthur Maynard, "The Role of Peter in the Fourth Gospel," *New Testament Studies* 30 (1984): 531-48 (531).

deny that unique position but to minimize it, to deny its exclusivity in order to make room for the special role of the 'Beloved Disciple.' The opposing view argues that "not only is there a strong anti-Petrinism in the Gospel, but that it is a major theme" which works to shift the basis of authority from Peter to the Beloved Disciple.[19] Maynard described these positions as in opposition but in fact they share a great deal in common. For the scholars on both sides of this question, Peter is understood to be contrasted negatively with the Beloved Disciple and to represent a community, the Apostolic church, subordinate to, and in tension with, the Johannine community. He has a low Christology; he refuses to allow Jesus to wash his feet; he attacks the servant in the garden; he denies Jesus three times; and he finishes second-place in the race to the tomb. For all these reasons and others,[20] scholars find a negative view of Peter, especially in relationship to the beloved disciple. At issue is whether that negativity minimizes Peter's leadership position or displaces it, whether it makes room for the Beloved Disciple alongside Peter or replaces Peter with the Beloved Disciple.

That account of Peter has been challenged in recent years. Bradford Blaine and Kevin Quast have both made compelling arguments in defense of Peter. Their primary strategy is to emphasize the positive things Peter does and to place the negative things in the best possible light. They argue that in the majority view, Peter's failures are overemphasized and his accomplishments are slighted.[21] Moreover, his failures are arguably the by-product, so to speak, of his successes. In the foot-washing scene, for example, "even in his misunderstanding he reveals his attachment to Jesus."[22] And our

---

19. See, for example, Graydon F. Snyder, "John 13:16 and the Anti-Petrinism of the Johannine Tradition," *Biblical Research* 16 (1971): 5–15.
20. Maynard provides a long list of Peter's failures. See Maynard, "The Role of Peter in the Fourth Gospel," 543–44.
21. Bradford Blaine, *Peter in the Gospel of John* (Atlanta: Society of Biblical Literature, 2007).

reasonable dismay at his denials in John 18 should not blind us to the simple fact that he is there, still following Jesus. He may be the only disciple to deny Jesus but he is also "the only disciple *in a position* to deny him."[23] So Quast offers re-readings of key moments in the portrayal of Peter and concludes: "Peter is commended to the Johannine reader as leader, spokesman, witness, disciple, and pastor."[24]

The argument of this paper depends upon a third way of reading Peter. If the standard readings outlined by Maynard view Peter in a negative light because of his range of mistakes, sins and misunderstandings, and the revisionist reading views Peter in a positive light because of his accomplishments, I suggest we view Peter in a positive light not in spite of the negative things he does but precisely because of them. (This may not be an argument with Blaine and Quast so much as an alternative way to frame the conclusions of their findings.) In other words, Blaine and Quast are right to rehabilitate Peter in the face of the scholarly consensus that sees only rivalry and subordination, but wrong in thinking that to do so they need to minimize the extent of Peter's failures.[25] What if the negative portrayal of Peter is not just a tool in the quarrel over authority between two Christian communities, but is doing theological work in the sense that putting *this* person, who did specific and sometimes terrible things, at the heart of the community, tells us something indispensable about what the Fourth Gospel thinks the church is and who the Fourth Gospel thinks God is?

---

22. Quast, *Peter and the Beloved Disciple* (Sheffield: Sheffield Academic Press, 1989), 163.
23. Blaine, *Peter in Gospel of John*, 96.
24. Quast, *Peter and the Beloved Disciple*, 164.
25. Blaine's "Conclusion" opens with "This study has argued that Peter is portrayed very positively in the Gospel of John" (*Peter in Gospel of John*, 183-96 [183]).

Peter's Denial

Of all Peter's failures, I will focus only on the most egregious, his denial of Jesus. As many have noted, John 18 seems to go out of its way to underscore the gravity of the denial. There are a number of ways it does this. First, unlike the Synoptics, John interrupts the account of Peter's denial with Jesus' testimony before the high priest, an interruption that draws attention to the contrast between Jesus' "I have spoken openly to the world. . . . I have said nothing in secret" (18:20) and Peter's desperate attempts to hide and conceal. Second, in a Gospel where the two most important words are arguably "I am," here in chapter 18, again in contrast to the Synoptics, Peter's denial is twice a simple "I am not."

Both these devices are not isolated to chapter 18. Read within the overall context of the Gospel's larger preoccupation with the theme of confession and denial, we can see how the lies of John 18 have echoes and parallels throughout the Gospel, perhaps most importantly, the story of the blind man in John 9. One curious aspect of John 9 is that Jesus is absent from the story for longer than any other point in the Gospel. Rensberger explains this absence as follows: "[T]he blind man's] attitude before the Pharisees is daring to the point of insolence, in obvious contrast to the behavior of his own parents and that of Nicodemus in 7:50-51. Indeed, its nearest parallel is Jesus' demeanor before the high priest in 18:19-23. Perhaps this very parallel explains why Jesus can be absent from the central episodes of the story: his role is taken over by the blind man himself."[26]

This is an astute observation and deserves further development. For if it is plausible to say that the blind man is here being identified with Jesus, then it follows that in chapter 18 Peter is being identified with

---

26. Rensberger, *Johannine Faith*, 43.

the blind man's parents. Rensberger notes this but much later and as an aside, "Like Jesus and like the blind man (and in sharp contrast to the denial of Peter), they are to give uncompromising testimony when called before the Jewish authorities."[27] But Rensberger might have gone on to add that John 9, like John 18, is a trial scene that includes three denials (9:16, 21 and 29-34).[28] Moreover, as in John 18, the denials are placed in alternating sequence with the blind man's confessional repetition of "I am." In John 9:9, "[H]e kept saying, 'I am the man'" echoes Jesus in 9:9 but also points to Jesus' repeated "I am" in 18:5, 8, and throughout the gospel, and forms a striking contrast with Peter's twice-repeated, "I am not" (18:17, 25). In other words, the power of contrasting Jesus and Peter in John 18 is not only to subordinate Peter to the beloved disciple but to identify Peter with the Crypto-Christians—those who refused to publicly confess belief in Jesus for fear of being expelled from the synagogue.[29]

This suggests an *intensification* of the scholarly consensus. If the conventional thesis is that Peter is subordinate to the Beloved Disciple and that he represents an inferior community, the Apostolic Christians, then this reading shows Peter not only as "subordinate." Peter is forcefully, if subtly, identified with the crypto-Christians themselves. Conversely, the crypto-Christians are identified with Peter.

Arguably, the Gospel of John goes even further. As Jeffrey Staley recreates the scene in John 18, Peter becomes identified with the police who arrested Jesus.[30] Verse 18 and 25 recreate the scene of 18:5 such that he is not simply identified with the police but with

---

27. Ibid., 90.
28. This is arguably also true of John 7 see, Stephen Motyer, "Bridging the Gap: How Might the Fourth Gospel Help Us Cope with the Legacy of Christianity's Exclusive Claim over Against Judaism?," in *The Gospel of John and Christian Theology*, eds. Richard Bauckham and Carl Mosser (Grand Rapids: Eerdmans, 2008), 143-67 (158).
29. See Brown, *The Community of the Beloved Disciple*, 71–73.
30. Jeffrey Staley, *Reading with a Passion* (New York: Continuum, 1995), 102–3.

Judas as all the verbs employed to describe the police in 18:18 and 25 are there in 18:5. Further reinforcing the identification, we can now hear Peter's repeated "I am not" as contrasting not just with Jesus before the high priest but with Jesus' three "I am's" (18:5, 6, 8) in the garden. Staley even remarks that Peter's three denials should be placed alongside his three previous misunderstandings (13:6-11, 13:36-38 and 18:10-11) concluding that Peter is "placed alongside Judas and Jesus' antagonists as . . . epitomes of failure."[31]

If Rensberger and Staley's readings are plausible, then we have found throughout John's Gospel confirmation of what has been called the "negative" portrait of Peter, a portrait that at crucial moments seems to identify him with the community's enemies. Now we can revisit the question of friendship in John 15: What does it mean to say of *this* person, Peter, "I have called you friends"? What does it mean to say, "Greater love has one than he lay down his life for friends like Peter"?

It means, for starters, that John puts conflict at the heart of his account of friendship. Friends are many of the things Aristotle said about them, but friendship is also prone to brokenness and division. Friends misunderstand, abandon and deny one another just when they need each other most. That Peter is friend raises the possibility that friends and enemies may cease to be discrete categories. They are not necessarily or even often separate segments or classes of people. They are more like stages in relationships. The Old Testament might have prepared us for this. David and Saul were friends. Cain and Abel were brothers. Our friends and family are also our enemies. Moreover, this isn't accidental. If this kind of love is best, then this kind of betrayal and denial are worst. The problem that John's Jesus seems acutely aware of is not the problem friendship theorists worry

---

31. Staley, *Reading with a Passion*, 93.

about—that we can fall in and out of friendship in the sense that we lose touch, fall out of contact, get bored with each other,[32] but that we can careen from love to hate. *This* kind of love is best because this kind of betrayal is worst: "Greater love has no one than he lay down his life for his friends" is "greater love has no one than he lay down his life for friends who abandon and deny him."

This seems fairly straightforward. Anyone who works in community mediation or victim-offender reconciliation would find it obvious. Gail O'Day, one of the few John commentators to note this, writes, "The history of the church and of individual communities of faith suggests that to love one another may be the most difficult thing Jesus could have asked. There are many circumstances in which it is easier to love one's enemies than it is to love those with whom one lives, works, and worships day after day."[33] Yet it is not a commonplace observation. While it may be obvious that friends and enemies are often the same people, it is rarely remarked upon either in the literature on friendship or in the literature on Peter in the Fourth Gospel. Most contemporary theological and philosophical accounts of friendship are relatively frictionless. It is not that they deny the reality of conflict, but that they rarely mention it, let alone put it at the heart of their accounts.[34] Yet at the same time, writers on friendship such as Gilbert Meilaender, argue that friendship is a school of virtue: "Friendships are to school us in love; they are a sign and a call by which God draws us toward a love more universal in scope"[35]

---

32. See for example, Gilbert Meilaender, *Friendship*, 53–67.
33. Gail O'Day, "John," *The Women's Bible Commentary* ed. C. A. Newsom and S. H. Ringe (Louisville: Westminster John Knox, 1992), 293-304 (302). This seems to me exactly right. But O'Day overlooks the fact that while it may be easier to love enemies than friends and colleagues, our friends and colleagues can become enemies. Perhaps especially when those friends are connected through a revolutionary social movement.
34. Accounts of marriage emphasize conflict. But texts on friendship, such as Meilaender's, deliberately exclude marriage from their purview.

Paul Waddell says something similar. Moreover, he is clear and articulate about the importance of difference and strangeness. But dependent as he is on Aristotle's *Nicomachean Ethics*, he says nothing about conflict. It is essential to Waddell's account that "Friendship repositions us by drawing us out of ourselves, by pulling us beyond the confines of our narrow world into the sometimes vastly different world of the other."[36] But the ways that drawing and pulling often happen through a process of conflict and reconciliation is not acknowledged. Friendship may be a school, but it is not a school of hard knocks. In what follows, I want to say a bit about why this acknowledgment of conflict might have seemed more important to the Johannine community than it does to us.

The Theopolitics of Friendship in the Johannine Community

The church gathered around John at the time the Gospel was composed was thoroughly Jewish and in conflict with, and persecuted by, the synagogue because of its Christology.[37] Persecuted communities, like revolutionary social movements, tend to be tightly knit. It is as if, as Rensberger suggests, the internal bonds increase in a way commensurate with the external hostility. But precisely for this reason their internal conflicts tend to be much more severe. What is true for anarchists, Marxists, feminists and civil rights activists is also true for churches. Any history of the civil rights movement, the power struggles of the Southern Christian Leadership Conference and the dissolution of the Student Non-violent Coordinating Committee alongside their extraordinary achievements might, I suspect, demonstrate this.

---

35. Meilaender, *Friendship*, 17.
36. Waddell, *Friendship and the Moral Life*, 145–46.
37. For a helpful summary of the issues, see James D. G. Dunn, "Let John Be John: A Gospel for Its Time," in Peter Stuhlmacher, ed., *The Gospel and the Gospels* (Grand Rapids: Eerdmans, 1991), 293-322 (305–6).

But on what grounds would John put conflict at the heart of his account of friendship? If I am right to read John 15:12-17 and the story of Peter together, what could have produced such an account of friendship? I am tempted to say that the answer to that question is twofold, one "political," one "theological," but nothing is more important than recognizing that the two emerge together. It is not enough to say, as I did above, that it is straightforward or obvious. For the question is why John chooses to make the obvious explicit and why most accounts of friendship choose to repress it. Why, in Russell Jacoby's terms, do we project our fear and hatred on to the distant stranger in order to avoid reckoning with our antipathy to the near friend?[38]

Theologically, this account of friendship follows from their perception of God. To understand, as Maynard and Sanders do, the negative aspects of Peter as 'subordination' or 'depreciation' is wrong—and disastrously so—because of the kind of God it implies. Peter is both the one who "retains a certain prominence [in the Fourth Gospel] as a spokesman for the Twelve"[39] and the one who is most impulsive, takes the most risks, makes his mistakes so grievously and so publicly. Peter is at the heart of this because he is the one who becomes the enemy. What kind of God would make Peter a subordinate?

God is a reconciling God. But that doesn't mean a bland liberalism in which God's mercy exists without judgment. It means God's mercy is God's judgment. Both those who view Peter negatively and those who view him positively send a clear if subtle message to the church about who is subordinate and superior in our congregations. It suggests that, if you are a grievous sinner in need of forgiveness and

---

38. Russell Jacoby, *Bloodlust: On the Roots of Violence from Cain and Abel to the Present* (New York: Free Press, 2011).
39. Raymond Brown, et al., *Peter in the New Testament* (Minneapolis: Augsburg, 1973), 132.

radical transformation, then you are a second-class Christian. It places the partisans of the Beloved Disciple uncomfortably close to those in John 8 condemning the woman caught in adultery.

The Johannine community's perception of God emerges hand in hand with the politics of the community. I have thus far ignored the issue that governs most accounts of Peter in the Fourth Gospel—authority in the church. Maynard and Snyder argue, "This Gospel apparently came from a community that wanted nothing to do with the primacy of one man, not even Peter!"[40] Brown writes that for Matthew and Luke/Acts "continuity with Peter and the Twelve was becoming an important factor in church identity and self-security."[41] As I read it, John affirms that but at the same time, redefines what it should mean. The argument in John affirms identity in Peter, but does so in order to cast a skeptical eye on security. In other words, John should not be read, as Maynard and Snyder do, as using Peter's repeated failures as arguing against the church finding its identity in him. Rather, we should read John as using Peter's failures to specify just what kind of identity the church should claim. Brown writes that the churches coped with the "teaching gap" that resulted from the deaths of Peter, Paul and James by "stressing that the officials who succeeded the apostles should hold on to what they were taught without change"[42] in contrast to the Johannine community's invocation of the Paraclete and its accompanying relative anti-institutionalism—but also, we might add, in contrast to John's theology of conflict. In other words, the Johannine community's pneumatology and anti-institutionalism has everything to do with their faith that conflict could be productive and transformative.[43]

---

40. Maynard, "The Role of Peter," 546.
41. Brown, *Community of the Beloved Disciple*, 86.
42. Ibid., 87.
43. For a summary account of transformative conflict see John Paul Lederach, *Preparing for Peace: Conflict Transformation Across Cultures* (Syracuse, NY: Syracuse University Press, 1995), 17-19.

In one of the most perceptive passages in his book, Rensberger explains how this works. He argues that the story of the blind man in John 9 is one of "progressive christological enlightenment" achieved "not in reflective encounter with Jesus, as Thomas and the Samaritan woman do but in the process of *confrontation* with the Pharisees."[44] Here too, the blind man stands in for the Johannine community and remains an exhortation to the community: "[L]et what has happened to you bring you into conflict with the rulers, with Moses himself if need be; for in this *process* your enlightenment will be completed, and at its end you will meet the one who granted you your sight and know him for who he is."[45]

For Rensberger, this is an argument against reading John's theological pronouncements as "a demand for conformity to a preordained dogma." Such readings, which find in John a tone of authoritarianism, turn John into a Pharisee. But the story of the blind man should instruct us instead that "[F]or the Johannine community, the truth about Jesus came, not at the beginning, nor even simply at the end, but out of the midst of this process of confession, rebuke, and stubbornly continued confession itself."[46] John 15 writes this process into the church itself.

Conclusion

In his wonderful little book, *Friendship and Ways to Truth*, David Burrell glosses one of the Fourth Gospel's most famous lines, "I am the way, the truth and the life" (John 14:6) with, "What Jesus' words presume, without asserting, is that this *way* will be constituted by personal encounters. The way to truth will entail meeting others and journeying with them. For whatever truth is, it is not something we

---

44. Rensberger, *Johannine Faith*, 46.
45. Ibid.
46. Ibid.

start with but something we discover. . . . [I]f truth is to be had, it will only be had in a tradition, within a community, in the company of friends."[47] I think Burrell is exactly right and I have tried to argue that John's gospel shows us how this might be true *if* we also let it teach us its particular account of friendship, one in which friends and enemies, insiders and outsiders, are not discrete categories, but instead are fluid.

By refusing to flinch before ugly conflictual personal encounters and friends that are also enemies, John may offer hope to conflict-ridden communities and relationships. John confronts us with a socio-historical context that included a profound and hard-earned awareness of conflict with the synagogue, the crypto-Christians, the Apostolic Christians, *and* a theological context that included a profound and hard-earned awareness of the power of Jesus to reconcile. Though it was surely hard for them, as it is for us, what if we assumed that they were able to refuse to see these as mutually exclusive? That they had no choice but to refuse in light of what had happened in Christ?

My hunch is that only a community that practices genuine conflict and reconciliation and are the kind of people who allow friends to be enemies and enemies to be friends and to go back and forth can recognize this dimension of the story. The reverse is also true. A community shaped by this story can allow for fluidity between friends and enemies. This is a community that can anticipate reconciliation because it has experienced reconciliation and continues to tell the story of that experience. They can anticipate reconciliation because what they saw happen in the life, death and resurrection of Jesus convinced them that this is the way God works. From this perspective, the reconciliation scene in John 21 does not add

---

47. David Burrell, *Friendship and the Ways to Truth* (Notre Dame, IN: University of Notre Dame Press, 2000), 2.

anything. It simply makes explicit the community's hope.[48] It reinforces that hope, but it doesn't create it.

Then this portrait of Peter is not just meant to teach us something about Peter but about the power of God in communities that recognize that God is a God of reconciliation. That this is not obvious to us may suggest something not just about the depth and intensity of our conflicts but about how little we ourselves believe in that kind of God.

---

48. The community's hope is already evident in 10:16 and 17: 20-21. See Brown, *Community of the Beloved Disciple*, 90.

3

"Before the Eyes of Their Own God"

Susanna, rape law, and testimony in City of God 1.19

Melanie Webb

In his *City of God*, Augustine sets out to address pastorally the pressing social and ecclesial concerns in the aftermath of the sack of Rome (410 C.E.), specifically through appeal to and revision of both Roman and Roman Christian virtue traditions. Captives of the Visigoths had been released on the shores of Hippo, among whom were women raped during the sack of Rome. While Augustine's *City of God* is often read from the perspective of Augustine's role as an iconic theologian/philosopher of the fifth-century Christian church, this chapter presents a reading from the perspective of Augustine's role as the bishop of a Christian community in Hippo. He is reassuring his flock that the depredations of 410 C.E., and others like them, were not a consequence of the community's religious promiscuity, and especially reassuring women in the community that they need not feel the burden and shame associated with rape.

Although late ancient Roman law distinguished among adultery, elopement, and rape, a woman's will, or initiative, did not play any part in defining these categories.[1] In other words, rape was not clearly or consistently distinguished from other forms of illegitimate sexual activity.[2] A woman who had a sexual encounter not approved by her *pater familias* was subject to capital punishment by him.[3] In the received Christian martyrologies, as well as within stories from the Roman virtue tradition, the only indubitable testimony that women did not in any way desire or consent to rape was suicide; the women who arrived in Hippo had obviously refused to kill themselves.

Augustine indicates in 1.16 that it is to these women that he refers.[4] How could North African society receive these women in such a way that they might not, as Augustine puts it in *City of God* 2.2, repent of their very lives?[5] Augustine writes of them as follows: "They have, to be sure, the glory of chastity within, the testimony of conscience; but they have [it] before the eyes of their own God and they do not require more, where there's nothing more that they might rightly do."[6] How did such a view become imaginable to Augustine?

---

1. Antti Arjava, *Women and Law in Late Antiquity* (Oxford: Oxford University Press, 1996), 38; Gillian Clark, *Women in Late Antiquity: Pagan and Christian Lifestyles* (New York: Oxford University Press, 1993), 36–38; Judith Evans-Grubbs, "Abduction Marriage in Antiquity: A Law of Constantine (CTh IX. 24. 1) and Its Social Context," *The Journal of Roman Studies* 79 (January 1, 1989): 59–83; Kyle Harper, *From Shame to Sin: The Christian Transformation of Sexual Morality in Late Antiquity* (Cambridge, MA: Harvard University Press, 2013), 43; 169; Jill Harries, *Law and Empire in Late Antiquity* (Cambridge: Cambridge University Press, 1999), 153–71.
2. Elaine Fantham, "*Stuprum*: Public Attitudes and Penalties for Sexual Offenses in Republican Rome," in *Roman Readings: Roman Response to Greek Literature from Plautus to Statius and Quintilian* (New York: De Gruyter, 2011), 115–43 (119).
3. Judy E. Gaughan, "Power of Life and Death: Pater *and* Res Publica," in *Murder Was Not a Crime: Homicide and Power in the Roman Republic*, Ashley and Peter Larkin Series in Greek and Roman Culture (Austin: University of Texas Press, 2010), 23–52 (32–38).
4. This argument is informed by Augustine's review in *City of God* 2.2 of his goals for book 1.
5. Augustine, *De ciuitate dei* 2.2. Unless noted otherwise, translations are my own.

This chapter will explore how scripture forms Augustine's mind, not only in terms of his values but also his patterns of thought. Crucial to Augustine's response is his use of scriptural exemplars. In his description of these women, although he does not cite it, Augustine seems to allude to the story of Susanna, which is included as the last chapter of the book of Daniel in the Septuagint.[7] While bathing in her garden, Susanna was approached by two elders of the city and presented with the following choice: have sex with us, or we try you for adultery. She refused, was tried and convicted of adultery, and then was condemned to death—but she called out to God and proclaimed her innocence to him. The (other) elders of the city only recognized her innocence once the prophet Daniel, prompted by the Holy Spirit, testified on her behalf and cross-examined the two witnesses, proving their account false.[8] Susanna's chastity was, like that of the refugees from Rome, called into question, and her own testimony was not sufficient to secure her position under society's gaze.

Susanna was a fixture in the "habits of thought" of late ancient Christians.[9] In the ancient world, the transmission of stories,

---

6. Augustine, *De ciuitate dei* 1.19.
7. Augustine mentions Susanna in: *Contra Cresconium* 4.56.66; *Contra Iulianum opus imperfectum* 4.37; *Contra litteras Petiliani* 2.23.53; *De bono coniugali* 8.8; 26.35; *De opere monachorum* 5.6; *De sancta uirginitate* 20; *De sermone Domini in monte* 2.32; *Enarrationes in Psalmos* 3.4; 21[22](2).6; 34(2).5; 125.8; 137.2; *Epistulae* 140; 262; *In Iohannis euangelium tractatus* 36; *Retractiones* 2.22; *Sermones* 96; 156; 196; 318; 343; 350; 359; *Sermones nouissimi* 13D(=159A); *Quaestionum in heptateuchem Exodi*, 78.
8. Different versions of Susanna's narrative circulated at different times. By 250 C.E., for liturgical use an account known as the Theodotion version had taken precedence over that found in the Septuagint. Kathryn A. Smith notes three ways in which the Theodotion account differs: "First, there is a lengthier discussion of Susanna's beauty, the Elders' lust and their conspiracy to seduce Susanna; Daniel's character is given greater prominence; and, at Verse 46–47, Daniel forcefully dissociates himself from the community's guilty verdict (the result of the Elders' false testimony) and Susanna's imminent execution" (Kathryn A. Smith, "Inventing Marital Chastity: The Iconography of Susanna and the Elders in Early Christian Art," *Oxford Art Journal* 16, no. 1 (1993): 3-24 [22 n. 35]).
9. I owe the concept "habit of thought" to Kathryn A. Smith, whose magisterial article on the

particularly exemplars, was as imagistic as it was textual.[10] Robin Jensen writes, "Christians encountered their scriptures in pictures as much as they read them or heard them proclaimed by lectors or preachers."[11] Whenever Susanna is remarked upon, then, late ancient Christians would have recognized the themes and dynamics of her story not only from its theological and liturgical presentation[12] but also from its representation in the art of their day.[13] A third-century prayer called *Commendation of the soul* contains a petition featuring Susanna as a chaste woman delivered from false testimony, as Daniel was delivered from the lions' den and Jonah was delivered from the whale's belly. In many visual representations, Susanna is depicted standing before the eyes of her own God, in the posture of the orant—arms open, head raised slightly in prayer. Like the *Commendation of the soul* itself, the iconography of Susanna invites the viewer to identify with her and to adopt her posture before

iconography on Susanna shaped my reading of this portion of Augustine's *City of God.* See: Ibid., 21.
10. See: Harriet I. Flower, *Ancestor Masks and Aristocratic Power in Roman Culture* (Oxford: Clarendon Press, 1996); Harriet I. Flower, *The Art of Forgetting: Disgrace & Oblivion in Roman Political Culture*, Studies in the History of Greece and Rome (Chapel Hill: University of North Carolina Press, 2006); Paul Zanker, *The Power of Images in the Age of Augustus*, trans. Alan Shapiro, Jerome Lectures 16 (Ann Arbor: University of Michigan Press, 1988).
11. Robin Jensen, "Visual Narratives, Picturing the Text," *Liturgy* 29, no. 4 (2014): 45-55 (45).
12. For a sample of Susanna's mention in other late antique Latin theological works, see: Tertullian, *De corona* 4.14; Cyprian, *Ad Quirinium* 3.20; *Epistula* 43.4; Ambrose, *De Abraham* 2.6.36; *De Iacob et uita beata* 2.7.33; *De Ioseph* 5.26; *De fuga saeculi* 9.53; *De Nabuthae* 11.46; *De Tobia* 20.78; *Explanatio Psalmorum* xii, psalmus 37, 45.6; ps. 38, 7.3; *Expositio psalmi* cxvii, 3.44, 17.25, 20.35; *Exposito euangelii secundum Lucam* 10. 933; *De officiis* 1.3, 1.18, 3.14; *De uirginibus* 1.8, 2.4; *De viduis* 4.24; *Exhortatio uirginitatis* 13.87; *De spiritu sancto* 3.6; *Epistula* 34.5; Hieronymus, *Liber interpretationis hebraicorum nominum* 56.19, 66.2; *Commentarii in Ezechielem* 2.6.428; *Commentarii in Danielem*, prol., 4.12-13; *Aduersus Heluidium de Mariae uirginitate perpetua* 4; *Aduersus Iouinianum* 1.25; *Apologia aduersos libros Rufini* 2.33; *De uiris inlustribus* 63.30; *Epistulae* 1.9 and 65.2; Zeno of Verona, *Tractati* 1, 36, and 40.
13. Indeed, after Eve, Susanna is the biblical woman most commonly featured in early Christian funerary art. See the list provided at Robin Jensen, "Compiling Narratives: The Visual Strategies of Early Christian Visual Art," *Journal of Early Christian Studies* 23, no. 1 (2015): 1-26 (13). I am grateful to Robin Jensen for generously sharing the page proofs of her article, which was given as the 2014 NAPS Presidential Address. Her lecture provoked the initial idea for the argument of this chapter.

God.[14] As with the orants painted on catacomb walls, the women to whom Augustine refers have adopted Susanna's assertive piety in their posture before God.

In contrast to the Roman virtue tradition, which held up Lucretia as the quintessential chaste matron, Augustine refers throughout his writings to Susanna as the primary exemplar of marital chastity.[15] Both Lucretia's and Susanna's stories were circulated prominently in Augustine's day. Investigating the traces of Susanna in *City of God* 1, I argue that Augustine's prior internalization of Susanna's story and the themes associated with it enables him to advance a twofold claim in response to rape: 1) chastity is not compromised through rape any more than it is compromised through false accusations of adultery; and 2) a woman's testimony of conscience is sufficient data for shaping society's view of her chastity in the aftermath of rape (just as it should also be in the aftermath of false accusations of adultery). In order to undermine the prevailing Roman and Roman Christian view that, in situations of rape, suicide testified to an otherwise compromised chastity, Augustine describes the secure position of these women as "before the eyes of their own God."[16]

In the first section of the essay, I explore Susanna's place in the "habits of thought" of Augustine and, then, of his readers. In the second section, I lay out the twofold claim regarding rape that Augustine implicitly derives from engagement with Susanna's narrative, associating rape with false accusations of adultery and arguing that women's testimony of conscience is sufficient to assure her chastity in the eyes of her society, as well as in the sight of God.

---

14. André Grabar comments that the orant is an "image-sign" for piety, a virtue that Christian art sought to inculcate in its viewers. André Grabar, *Christian Iconography: A Study of Its Origins*, trans. Terry Grabar, Bollingen Series 35 (Princeton, NJ: Princeton University Press, 1968), 10.
15. See especially: Augustine, *De bono coniugali* 8.8; 26.35; *De sancta uirginitate* 20.
16. Augustine, *De ciuitate dei* 1.19.

Habits of Thought

I will begin with Augustine's allusive association of women raped in the sack of Rome with Susanna, including her relationship to Lucretia, whose story Augustine treats at length *City of God* 1.19. Next, I briefly examine Susanna's place within the habits of thoughts of Augustine's readership. Both in Roman Christian funerary art and Latin theology, Susanna is specially positioned before God as both chaste and triumphant.

Susanna and Lucretia—Augustine's habits of thought

While Susanna is not identified by name in *City of God*, the themes of chastity, suspicion, testimony, and standing before the eyes of God invoke the emblematic moments of her narrative. Whether or not he presumed that his audience would recognize her in the contours of his discussion of the social status of living women who were raped in the sack of Rome, I suggest that his familiarity with her narrative and his high regard for her inclined him to respond in his local setting to a widespread crisis in a unique and compelling way.

Elsewhere in his writings, Augustine presents Susanna as the quintessential exemplar of marital chastity in *Holy Virginity* 20.20 and *On the Excellence of Marriage* 8, both of which date to ca. 401 C.E. Here, Susanna is mentioned by name, but her story is not recounted—indicating that Augustine was confident his readership would immediately recognize the significance of his reference to her and her applicability to the point at hand. He gives extended attention to Susanna's story in Sermon 343 (delivered 397 C.E.), juxtaposing her with the two Josephs—the one who resisted the advances of Pharaoh's wife and the one who remained faithful and welcomed Mary without accusing her of adultery. In Sermon 343, Augustine introduces Susanna as one who "remained chaste, [though] about to die unless someone had been present who saw what evaded the ones judging."[17] Susanna's story is, for Augustine, a challenge to see what is hidden.

That Augustine is familiar with the *Commendation of the soul* is evidenced by his quotation from it in his second exposition of Psalm 21[22], which was preached on a Good Friday.[18] When preaching on the darkness of Christ's condemnation on the cross, Augustine unmistakably invokes the prayer said by Christians when facing death. Central to this prayer is Susanna's deliverance from false accusation, *de falso crimine*.[19] Augustine also recites lines from the *Commendation of the soul* in letter 140.11 as he wrestles with Jesus' cry of Psalm 21[22] from the cross. Associating the *Commendation of the soul* so closely with the death of Christ has at least two effects: 1) each figure mentioned in the prayer is presented as a type of Christ; and 2) Christians who seek to be like Christ, even at the moment of death, are given the prayer as a promise of deliverance that also increases endurance. In this prayer, Susanna is delivered "from false witnesses," *a testibus falsis*.[20] Augustine also mentions Susanna in passing in sermon 359, delivered in 411. Across the decade, she was a figure prominent in Augustine's "habits of thought." When he comes, then, in 413 C.E., to draft the first book of his *City of God*, we find that these patterns of association position him to support women who refused to kill themselves in response to rape, challenging his

---

17. Augustine, *Sermo* 343.1.
18. Augustine, *Ennarationes in Psalmos* 21(2).6.
19. Catherine Brown Tkacz, *The Key to the Brescia Casket: Typology and the Early Christian Imagination*, Collection Des Etudes Augustiniennes, Série Antiquité 165 (Notre Dame, IN: University of Notre Dame Press, 2002), 122. Tkacz notes that the key phrase regarding Susanna's deliverance in both the Old Latin and Vulgate versions of Dan. 13 is given as *falsum testimonium*, but Augustine uses the extrascriptural phrase *de falso crimine*, which appears only here in his extant works. The *Commendation of the soul*, however, uses exactly this phrase to describe Susanna's deliverance. On these grounds, Tkacz argues that Augustine knew the *Commendation of the soul*.
20. Augustine, *Epistula* 140.11.

predominantly male readership to reconsider their society's assumptions.

In *City of God*, Augustine's discussion of women raped in the sack of Rome, and his representation of them as so many Susannas, comes at the conclusion of his lengthy engagement with Lucretia. Lucretia was a Roman matron whose modesty aroused the evil lust of the king's son Sextus Tarquinius, who subsequently raped her. Because Tarquinius had threatened to leave the dead body of Lucretia's slave upon hers in her own bed and then tell her husband that he had taken vengeance for honor when he found them together, she did not scream or resist, and Tarquinius's lust was victorious over her resolute chastity.[21] The next morning, she gathered her kinsmen and requested vengeance before killing herself, despite their insistence that she bore no guilt. Her suicide became the impetus for the overthrow of the Etruscan dynasty and the founding of the Roman Republic (sixth century B.C.E.).[22]

Embedded in Lucretia's story and its rhetorical deployment is an insidious social commentary on the value of women's lives, and the role of the specific virtue of chastity in determining their fates.[23] In Augustine's treatment however, there is a polemic against the traditional view that self-slaying was how women could, through the movements of their bodies, make their will to chastity known

---

21. For an astute discussion of whether, given contemporary categories of Roman law, Lucretia might be said to have "consented" to Tarquin's advances, see: Diana C. Moses, "Livy's Lucretia and the Validity of Coerced Consent in Roman Law," in *Consent and Coercion to Sex and Marriage in Ancient and Medieval Societies*, ed. Angeliki E. Laiou (Washington, DC: Dumbarton Oaks Research Library and Collection, 1993), 39–81 (68–70).
22. Livy, *Ab urbe condita* 1.58.1–11.
23. Lucretia's story was rhetorically useful for not only motivating women to chastity (or, at least, away from adultery) but also motivating men to steel themselves for suicide. See: Quintilian, *Institututio Oratoria* 5.11.10. In addition, Seneca exhorts men to marry a woman like Lucretia. As Kathy Gaca notes, "he repeatedly censures breaches of marital infidelity, especially adultery by wives, and he idealizes Lucretia as the kind of faithful Roman woman a man should marry." Kathy L. Gaca, *The Making of Fornication: Eros, Ethics, and Political Reform in Greek Philosophy and Early Christianity* (Berkeley: University of California Press, 2003), 87.

in anticipation or aftermath of rape.[24] Augustine wanted neither political nor religious martyrdom in response to rape.

Susanna's story poses a striking contrast to Lucretia's. Refusing forced intercourse with the two elders, she was falsely accused while still living. The elders, threatening to secure a death sentence for Susanna, relied on the city to carry out the deed that Tarquinius promised but Lucretia accomplished. Susanna's testimony was legitimated not by her suicide but by the intervention of Daniel. In both narratives, societal perception drives injustice. In Lucretia's story, the injustice is exposed by Lucretia's corpse, which is carried through the streets to motivate the Latin people to overthrow the Tarquin dynasty; in Susanna's story, the injustice is exposed by Daniel's intervention in the trial.

Indeed, Susanna's story invites engagement with Deuteronomic law. Her plea to God is in keeping with Deuteronomic law, that a woman is to cry out when threatened within the city walls.[25] Yet, also in keeping with Deuteronomic law, the testimony of two witnesses results in her condemnation.[26] The author of Susanna's story deploys Susanna's steadfast piety to explore the implications of the Deuteronomic law codes regarding rape and testimony. The resolution to Susanna's story comes when the (other) elders of the city finally heed her testimony, yet they only do so once the prophet Daniel testifies on her behalf and cross-examines the two witnesses to draw out the inconsistencies in their story, thus proving it to be false. Deuteronomic law is then applied such that the sentence they sought for her through their false testimony is transferred to them, and they are to be executed.[27]

---

24. I discuss Augustine's polemic against his Roman and Roman Christian predecessors and contemporaries in Melanie Webb, "'On Lucretia Who Slew Herself': Rape and Consolation in Augustine's *De Ciuitate Dei*," *Augustinian Studies* 44, no. 1 (2013): 37–58.
25. Deut. 22:24.
26. Deut. 19:17.

The author of Susanna's story demonstrates that the Mosaic Law, when wisely engaged, conduces to justice even for a people in exile and in the face of false accusations. Augustine enacts this pattern of thought in approaching the entrenched moral problem of (false) accusation with the intent of death in his own society. While the treacherous elders expected that the other elders would execute Susanna, Augustine's readership was steeped in the values of a Roman society that put the knife in the hands of women who had been raped. Augustine could expect that his elite male Christian readership would recognize, in this cluster of themes, Susanna's narrative.

Susanna and the Habits of Thought of Augustine's Readers

Augustine invokes emblematic moments from Susanna's narrative in order to associate women who were raped, and are falsely suspected of being unchaste, with her. These moments became emblematic of Susanna's story not only in textual but also visual exegesis.[28] Even though Jerome decided, in his influential Latin translation of the Hebrew scriptures and in his commentary on the book of Daniel,[29] not to treat as canonical the story *Susanna and the Elders* from the Septuagint, its legacy as a formative narrative of exemplary chastity and the triumph of truth over false witness endured in the iconography of Susanna.[30]

---

27. Deut. 19:19.
28. Robin Jensen, "Towards a Christian Material Culture," in *The Cambridge History of Christianity*, ed. Margaret M. Mitchell and Frances M. Young, vol. 1: *Origins to Constantine* (Cambridge: Cambridge University Press, 2008), 568–85 (573).
29. Hieronymus, *Commentarii in Danielum*, prologue. See: Elizabeth A. Clark, *The Origenist Controversy: The Cultural Construction of an Early Christian Debate* (Princeton, NJ: Princeton University Press, 1992), 173. Rufinus severely criticized Jerome for this exclusion. Perhaps Rufinus's response was motivated by the importance of Susanna in the early Christian imagination, as demonstrated and perhaps informed by her prevalence in Christian art. Hieronymus, *Commentarii in Danielum*, prologue.
30. For a now classic discussion of the role of images in the late ancient diffusion of Christian themes, see: Averil Cameron, *Christianity and the Rhetoric of Empire: The Development of*

Susanna's story was visible particularly within funerary art. Catherine Tkacz demonstrates how, in the case of the Brecia Casket at least, the *Commendation of the soul* supplies the cast of biblical figures for the artistry that will surround one in death.[31] The figures with whom the living, once dead, wish to be associated indicate which exemplars were the most cherished. For noble Roman Christian women, Susanna was the exemplar of choice, featured in catacombs of the second and third centuries C.E. as well as on sarcophagi of the fourth and fifth centuries C.E.—though, in fact, the choice available for those designing their final resting place was predetermined by "a relatively limited range of formal elements," which artisans and their clientele combined in order to create "what is simultaneously an interrelated corpus of copious material (both pagan and Christian) and one in which many figurative images allude (at different levels) to narratives that may range from myth and oral tradition to scriptural texts."[32] Roman Christian clients chose the elements of Susanna's story, in part, because this was the funerary vocabulary in which they were immersed and, in part, because she embodied the values which they held most dear. The position of Susanna's story in early Christian theology and its iconography resembles the position of Lucretia and other chaste Roman matrons whose noble status is preserved on and in stone. The similarity of Susanna's and Lucretia's narratives, and the commitment to marital

---

Christian Discourse, Sather Classical Lectures, vol. 55 (Berkeley: University of California Press, 1991), 150–54.

31. Tkacz, *The Key to the Brescia Casket*, 130–37. As Paul Zanker and Björn C. Ewald write, "the ways in which the living speak of the dead is connected with their own sense of identity, their ideals, values, and expectations." Paul Zanker and Björn C. Ewald, *Living with Myths: The Imagery of Roman Sarcophagi*, trans. Julia Slater, 1st ed., Oxford Studies in Ancient Culture and Representation (Oxford: Oxford University Press, 2012), 175.
32. Jaś Elsner, "Image and Rhetoric in Early Christian Sarcophagi: Reflections on Jesus' Trial," in *Life, Death and Representation: Some New Work on Roman Sarcophagi*, ed. Jaś Elsner and Janet Huskinson, Millennium-Studien, Bd. 29 (New York: De Gruyter, 2010), 359–86 (359).

chastity asserted by each, perhaps accounts in part for Susanna's inclusion in early Roman Christian art.

The most emblematic scene from Susanna's narrative is when the two elders approach her and she cries out to God. In this scene, Susanna is depicted standing between two trees, in an orant posture—sometimes with elders near or behind each tree, sometimes without the elders. Other moments that became emblematic are Susanna's encounter with Daniel in the court, sometimes with elders accusing her and sometimes with the elders being judged by Daniel or stoned by soldiers.[33] The latter two scenes, focusing on judgment before a human court, pertain clearly to the themes of Augustine's discussion. Here, I want to focus on the first, the scene of prayer.

The orant (*orans*) figures prominently in early Christian funerary art. Sarah Spence notes the dual meaning of *orans* as both "speaking" and "praying," and comments that "[the *orans*] appears in early Christian art as a signal or invitation to interpret, [and] is used . . . to insist that all paintings are to be treated as a combination of oratory and prayer and so point out that the audience must not watch passively but must actively participate by interpreting."[34] Susanna's frequent posture as an orant invites the reader both to identify with her and to seek to interpret, that is, be a truthful witness. As an orant, Susanna's prayer is directed to God but, as a speech, it provokes everyone to respond: "The viewer becomes Susanna's judge; her pious chastity is clearly indicated by her placement entirely within the space created by the trees and by her cry/prayer for help."[35]

---

33. Of the 23 instances in which Susanna appears in an entry categorized as "early Christian" or "late antique" in the Index of Christian Art (http://ica.princeton.edu), 18 depict Susanna in the orant posture in her garden; five depict Susanna at trial or in an encounter with Daniel; and four depict the elders being judged or punished. See also Catherine Brown Tkacz, "Susanna as a Type of Christ" *Studies in Iconography* 20 (1999): 101–53; and Tkacz, *The Key to the Brescia Casket*, 81.

34. Sarah Spence, *Rhetorics of Reason and Desire: Vergil, Augustine, and the Troubadours* (Ithaca: Cornell University Press, 1988), 64.

It is precisely this image of Susanna to which Ambrose appeals in his discussion of modesty in the influential treatise *On the Duties of the Clergy* (ca. 391). In 1.18, Ambrose writes of Susanna: "Susanna was silent amid the dangers and considered the loss of modesty more serious than that of life. She did not deem that the safety of modesty was to be guarded from danger."[36] Ambrose seems to imagine Susanna in the orant posture, flanked by the two elders, her arms and hands open to God.[37]

Representations, and descriptions of Susanna in the orant posture honed the interpretative apparatus involved in engaging her story not only for the purposes of closely engaging scripture, but also for truthful and careful engagement with the circumstances of one's own life and social relationships. Furthermore, the posture of prayer assumed by the orant reflects the posture of the viewer in her own standing before God. For this reason, the orant invites the viewer into the painting and the complex of meanings represented there. In some cases, the identification is so close that it is difficult to tell whether a given representation was actually intended to represent Susanna, or rather mirrored the viewer herself. One striking example is the portrayal of Susanna as an orant on a sarcophagus from the fourth century.[38] The detail with which her facial features are cut

---

35. Smith, "Inventing Marital Chastity," 12.
36. Ambrose, *De officiis* 1.18.68; translation my own. "tacebat in periculis Susanna et grauius uerecundiae quam vitae damnun putabat. nec arbitrabatur, periculo pudoris tuendam salutem."
37. Susanna is represented in this way on the following: Rome: Cemetery, Domitilia (Catacomb, first half of the fourth century), Rome: Cemetery, Nuova, Via Latina (Catacomb, fourth century), Rome: Cemetery, Petrus and Marcellinus (Catacomb, ca. 340-360), Thessaloniki: Cemetery, Hypogeum (Catacomb, second half of the fourth century—first half of the fifth century), Brescia: Church, S. Giulia (Casket, third quarter of the fourth century) [body, front, zone 3: Susanna is in orant posture, flanked by two trees and two elders; body, back, zone 1: Susanna is in orant posture, flanked by two trees], Arles: Museum, Musée de l'Arles antique (Sarcophagus, late-fourth century), Barcelona: Museum, Museo Arqulógico Provincial (Sarcophagus, fourth century), Gerona: Church, S. Feliú (Sarcophagus, fourth century), Rome: Museum, Camposanto Tedesco (Sarcophagus, third quarter of fourth century), and Rome: Museum, Musei Vaticani, Museo Pio Cristiano (Sarcophagus, second third of the fourth century).

indicates that the deceased, or her family, wished her face to be transposed to Susanna's body—and therefore into Susanna's place. She is also depicted holding a scroll, invoking Susanna's education in the Mosaic Law as well as the literacy of the deceased.[39] While common in Roman funerary art, the practice is rare in Roman Christian iconography,[40] making it all the more remarkable in this instance. In addition, in this sculpture, the deceased survives with the virtue and position before God of Susanna.

As Augustine engages the social implications of the refusal of women raped in the sack of Rome to kill themselves, I propose that he is constructively appropriating the iconographic and theological representation of Susanna in order that these women not be compelled to repent in shame of their very lives.[41]

Susanna and Augustine's Revision of Roman Rape Law

Being among the "limited range of formal elements" used in Christian funerary art from the earliest centuries through late antiquity, we can be confident that the currents of Susanna's story predisposed Augustine to support life without shame for women raped in the sack of Rome, and to expect his readers to grasp the implications of his argument. By reading Augustine's description, at *City of God* 1.19, of the enduring chastity of the women raped in the sack of Rome as an allusion to Susanna's story, I argue that Augustine advances a twofold claim in response to rape: 1) chastity is not compromised through rape any more than it is compromised through false accusations of adultery; and 2) a woman's testimony of

---

38. Arles: Museum, Musée de l'Arles antique (Sarcophagus, late-fourth century) and Barcelona: Museum, Museo Arqulógico Provincial (Sarcophagus, fourth century). The sarcophagus in Arles depicts Susanna holding an open scroll. For a discussion of Susanna's depiction on the Arles sarcophagus, see Smith, "Inventing Marital Chastity," 15–16.
39. See Dan. 13:2-3. Tkacz, "Susanna as a Type of Christ," 74–75.
40. Jensen, "Compiling Narratives," 15.
41. Augustine, *De ciuitate dei* 2.2.

conscience is sufficient data for shaping society's view of her chastity in the aftermath of rape (just as it should also be in the aftermath of false accusations of adultery). Let us take each claim in turn.

Rape as a False Accusation of Adultery

Augustine recognizes that society's response to rape parallels society's response to adultery. As he writes of Lucretia in her determination to demonstrate her chastity through death: "Whence she thought that that punishment, witness of her own mind, was to be brought before the eyes of humans, to whom it was not possible to demonstrate her conscience. Indeed she blushed to be thought an accomplice of the deed, if, what another had done against her shamefully, she herself bore patiently."[42] Rape disrupts Lucretia's sociality; prior to rape, she would never have been suspected of adultery but, after rape, she is resituated under society's suspicions—there could never again be certainty about her status as faithful wife of Collatinus. Her death secures what she can no longer have in life: recognition of her chastity. Augustine attributes to the Romans a refusal to implicate Lucretia in adultery, yet his own reading of Lucretia's narrative accents the fear and violence inflicted on her by Roman society. In this section, I will argue that Augustine undermines both Roman and Roman Christian responses to rape by using Susanna's story to insist that his readers, based on women's own testimonies, respond to rape as they would to a false accusation of adultery.

Augustine characterizes Lucretia's fear regarding how she would be seen as the "infirmity of shame." It is an internalized weakness fostered within and by her society such that, when she was raped, she knew—despite her kinsmen's pleadings—that she would have to demonstrate her conscience to the eyes of humans (*ad oculos*

---

42. Augustine, *De ciuitate dei* 1.19; translation my own.

hominum). It is essential to understand shame (*pudor*), as the Romans experienced it, in order to grasp how rape and adultery might provoke similar affective responses.[43]

Robert Kaster describes Roman shame as "the pain experienced at seeing oneself devalued."[44] That is, one sees oneself seen by others. For the maturation of each emotion, there are a variety of scripts, "little scenarios that [the Romans] play out—as sequences of cause and effect, of perception, evaluation, and response."[45] Kaster spins out a taxonomy of shame-scripts, one of which is shame as a result injury. He treats rape[46] as a subset of injury and recognizes the tension that arises in such cases between injury and blame. Defining an offense as an injury absolves the one injured of responsibility. In situations of rape, however, "the act is commonly conceived by our sources (exclusively male) as causing raped persons (usually but not exclusively female) to experience [shame] as a result of the rapists' actions, because they see themselves being devalued, and often even being regarded (against the facts) as in some sense blameworthy."[47] In other words, both rape and adultery were expected to stir a woman to shame, which in turn provided her with a scripted response that makes shame (*pudor*) yield chastity (*pudicitia*).

Augustine writes with confidence that women's fear of being devalued is a valid reaction to their society's response to rape. Indeed,

---

43. The Latin word *pudor* indicates both "shame" and "modesty," suggesting that one cannot be modest without some experience of shame. In the emotional world of the Romans, if a woman is modest (*pudor*), she will be stirred to shame (*pudor*) by illicit sexual encounters. Though I provide only "shame" parenthetically, I repeat the Latin term *pudor* (and, later, *pudica* and *pudicitia*) in the text as a way of retaining the foreign and multivalent implications inherent in this term.
44. Robert A. Kaster, *Emotion, Restraint, and Community in Ancient Rome* (Oxford: Oxford University Press, 2005), 12.
45. Ibid., 29.
46. There is no single Latin term for the English word "rape." The phrase *stuprum per uim inlatum* translates literally as "illicit sex carried out through force," and that is what Kaster discusses. Augustine uses *stuprum* as shorthand for the entire phrase.
47. Ibid., 35–36.

Lucretia's shame occurs not during the rape but after. Livy scripts among her final words the insistence that "never in any time to come will an unchaste woman live by the example of Lucretia."[48] For Lucretia, death is her witness. Her image, as reflected back to her in the eyes of men, is distorted beyond recognition and repair, and she rejects it wholly. Like Susanna, she sees herself being seen as an adulterer. Though the accusation against Lucretia is as false as that against Susanna, Lucretia subjects herself to death. Unlike Lucretia, though, Susanna was confident in what could not be seen by the eyes of men because God saw her. Yet, she faces the trouble that Lucretia assumes is inevitable: that her accuser will be believed regardless of her prior demonstration of virtue. In sermon 343, Augustine notes that "Against [their] mistress, Susanna's household had believed the lying elders. And although her life, unafflicted and unbesmirched prior to the events, seemed to offer sufficient testimony of chastity, nonetheless it seemed impious not to believe those elders"[49] Disregard for both Lucretia's and Susanna's history of chaste living characterizes human suspicion. Augustine identifies such disregard as the result of a fear of being impious, of not listening to the men entrusted with the spiritual care of the community. Yet, social position is not a reliable indicator of character.

Trusting Women's Testimony of Conscience

Given that Livy presents death as the most reliable witness that a woman's chastity endures after rape, how else might the parameters for testimony in situations of rape be sketched? At the conclusion of *City of God* 1.19, Augustine writes of the women of his own day: "But this is not what those Christian women did who suffered in the same way and yet are still alive." Augustine states vividly

48. Livy, *Ab urbe condita* 1.58.10.
49. Augustine, *Sermo* 343.1.

what these women have not chosen: "[B]ecause enemies out of lust (*concupiscendo*) committed rape against them, they (have) not out of shame (*erubescendo*) committed homicide against their own selves."[50] Shame (*pudor*) and blush (*erubescentia*) often appear as synonyms, with blushing being the outward sign of inward shame. Augustine here parallels lust (*concupiscendo*) and shame (*erubescendo*) as driving forces or motives that lead to these dual acts of violence—rape and homicide. The societal suspicions that befall women who suffer rape could only be satisfied when the blush poured forth in blood. Rape and homicide are vividly aligned in Livy's own text, and Lucretia completes what Tarquinius began. As Tarquinius says, "Silent, Lucretia. I am Sextus Tarquinius; in my hand is a sword; you will die if you let go your voice."[51] And, so it comes to pass, that once she lets go her voice, she dies.

For Augustine's mentor, Ambrose, silence is precisely what marks chastity: "Silence, also, in which there is rest for the rest of the virtues, is the chief act of modesty. . . . Susanna was silent in danger, and considered the loss of modesty more serious than that of life."[52] It would seem, then, that as Ambrose reads the Susanna story, her cry is not the cry commanded in Deuteronomy—a cry meant to be heard by others—but a cry of personal address to God. Her cry constitutes silence, which in turn constitutes modesty. Ambrose does not depart too far from the text, though; Susanna's cry was after all like silence, insofar as it went unheeded by the judging elders, who had power of life and death over her, until Daniel spoke. Here, Ambrose promotes not Daniel's attentiveness but Susanna's silence(/ing). In a sermon

---

50. Augustine, *De ciuitate dei* 1.19: "quoniam hostes in eis concupiscendo stupra commiserant, illae in se ipsis homicidia erubescendo committerent."
51. Livy, *Ab urbe condita* 1.58.2: "Tace, Lucretia, inquit. Sextus Tarquinius sum ferrum in manu est moriere si emiseris uocem."
52. Ambrose, *De officiis* 1.18.68. Ambrose, *De officiis* 1.18.68: "Silentium quoque ipsum, in quo est reliquarum virtutum otium, maximus actus verecundiae est. . . . Tacebat in periculis Susanna et gravius verecundiae quam vitae damnum putabat."

on Luke's gospel, though, we find a suggestion of the view that Augustine was to develop; comparing Susanna and Christ's trials, Ambrose says, "it can be seen that, before wicked judges, one may be unwilling, as opposed to unable, to defend oneself."[53]

Augustine insists that these women's testimony of conscience is enough—no defense needs to be launched. If these women do bring their testimony to others, however, then they are to be believed. He asserts that "within themselves, indeed, by the testimony of conscience, they have the glory of chastity (*gloriam castitatis*)." For his contemporaries, Augustine insists on the "testimony of conscience" in place of death, Daniel, or silence. This is particularly striking given the uneven standards for women's testimony in the Theodosian Code, the fifth-century compilation of the legal prescripts of Christian emperors. An edict attributed to Constantine reports (falsely!) that "the ancients" prevented girls, or young women, "from conducting suits in court and from giving testimony and from all matters pertaining to courts" in order to (re)enact such a standard in 326.[54] Though another statute issued two years later states that women were indeed able to plead their cases in person, the Christian 'Ambrosiaster,' commenting on legal practices, claims that a woman "cannot teach nor be a witness nor stand surety nor act as a judge."[55] From these passages, Antti Arjava suggests that "it is possible that in the fourth and fifth centuries women were despised as witnesses, perhaps in documents if not generally in court."[56] And this is in

---

53. Ambrose, *Expositio Euangelii secundum Lucam* 10.97. I owe this reference, and translation, to: Tkacz, *The Key to the Brescia Casket*, 75.
54. *Cod. theod.* 9.24.1 (1 April, 326), as translated in Judith Evans Grubbs, *Women and the Law in the Roman Empire: A Sourcebook on Marriage, Divorce and Widowhood* (New York: Routledge, 2002), 181.
55. Ps. Aug., *quaest.* 45.3, I owe this reference and translation to Arjava, *Women and Law in Late Antiquity*, 236–37.
56. Ibid., 257.

general, on cases relating to the murder of sons or husbands or perhaps the theft of property or other injury to her person.

In situations of rape, the stakes were very high. If a woman did bring forth a charge of *per vim stuprum* (illicit sex through force), she had to be confident that her rapist could not mount a defense by arguing that she had consented; if it was determined that she had, then she could in turn be charged with adultery, if she was married, or *stuprum* (illicit sex), if she was not—and, if she was married, her husband would have to divorce her or face prosecution.[57] As Jane Gardner says: "The social and legal consequences of failure may have been a deterrent to bringing prosecutions for rape."[58] This is, of course, only for citizen, that is, elite and some free(d), women—a prostitute, entertainer, or slave could not bring charges of rape (*stuprum per vim inlatum*) since she could not, according to the law, be violated.[59]

So, both the legal and the exemplarity traditions underwrote a set of situations in which a woman would legitimately fear being viewed as blameworthy for rape. Augustine says of these women: "They intend no more than to do right, lest they deviate (*deuiant*) from the authority of divine law when they wrongly avoid (*deuitant*) the scandal of human suspicion."[60] That is, for Augustine they would be doing so not for love of Christ, as Ambrose suggests, but in order to

---

57. Patrick Laurence, "Les Femmes Dans Le Code Théodosien: Perspectives," in *Le Code Théodosien: Diversité Des Approches et Nouvelles Perspectives*, ed. Sylvie Crogiez-Pétrequin and Pierre Jailette (Rome: École fraçaise de Rome, 2009), 264.
58. Elaine Fantham writes, "we find no instances of *stuprum* that do not involve intercourse with male or female citizens, because the Romans would not have seen anything improper in such acts. . . . For *stuprum* ostensibly blurs the distinction between rape and seduction, or even between the isolated act and the continued relationship." See Fantham, "*Stuprum*," 118. See also: Jane Gardner, *Women in Roman Law & Society* (London: Croom Helm, 1986), 91.
59. Arjava, *Women and Law in Late Antiquity*, 202–5; 208–10; Suzanne Dixon, *Reading Roman Women: Sources, Genres and Real Life* (London: Duckworth, 2000), 50–52; Laurence, "Les Femmes Dans Le Code Théodosien: Perspectives," 262–63.
60. Augustine, *De ciuitate dei*. 1.19.

avoid the scandal of human suspicion. As a bishop, Augustine himself was involved in arbitration in the courts of Hippo; but here, in the *City of God*, he is speaking into the court of public opinion before whose eyes these women must now live. He wants there to be no offense, no scandal as they seek to move forward from the atrocities they have survived.

How are these women to view themselves? It is significant that Augustine shifts the language of the virtue in question from *pudicitia*--chastity, which he has used exclusively in book 1 until the very end of chapter 19, to *castitas*-chastity, employing a term philologically unrelated to shame (*pudor*). That is, Augustine goes to the root. The Roman edifice of *pudicitia*-chastity is built on shame, which Augustine seeks to expose as centrally infirm and unstable. While *pudicitia*-chastity sprouts from shame, the glory of *castitas*-chastity is rooted in the testimony of conscience. In this way, *castitas*-chastity takes its nourishment from conscience, which literally means, "knowledge (*scientia*) with (*con*)." And in this case, it is a knowing with God, indeed, with one's own God (*dei sui*). As far as I can tell, this is one of the only places where Augustine describes God as *sui*, one's own. He appropriates God to these women, and in so doing insists that God is not the property of his male readership—something consistently overlooked by his (many male) translators as well.[61]

Augustine wants his readers to see that, rooted in the testimony of conscience, a woman's chastity is not compromised through rape any more than it is compromised through false accusations of adultery; society is to offer to these women the stability available to Susanna once her name was cleared by Daniel. But Augustine does not adopt

---

61. Among English translations, I have only found the term *sui* in the phrase, from 1.19, *coram oculis dei sui*, translated by George E. McCracken in the Loeb edition: Augustine, *Augustine: City of God, Volume I, Books 1-3*, trans. George E. McCracken (Cambridge, MA: Harvard University Press, 1957).

the dynamics of false accusations of adultery into situations of rape. Rather, he intensifies the Susanna narrative: "They have, to be sure, the glory of chastity within, the testimony of conscience; but they have [it] before the eyes of their own God and they do not require more, where there's nothing more that they might rightly do."[62] First, like Susanna, these women do not believe that they must make their conscience known to the eyes of men; they have the testimony of their own conscience. When approached by the elders, "she defied what she heard, because she feared one whom she did not see, but to whose divine eyes she herself was visible. Just because she did not see God did not mean that she was not seen by God."[63] Second, they live before the eyes of their own God—this redounds to glory. It is notably not the glory of *pudicitia*-chastity but of *castitas*-chastity—it does not take its coordinates from the realm of shame, that is, the sight of men but from the vision of God. This distinction seems more pronounced in *City of God* than in Augustine's writings on Susanna, insofar as he is contrasting Christian women who have not killed themselves after being raped and the exemplary Roman matron Lucretia, who is renowned for her *pudicitia*-chastity. Because he has so closely associated *pudicitia*-chastity with shame in the previous paragraph, it is significant that he shifts the language he uses to refer to the stable virtue of these women.

In the eyes of their own God, these women have the glory of *castitas*-chastity. Notably, *castitas*-chastity is a virtue of both women and men, yet glory was traditionally reserved for men. Seneca, in his treatise *On Marriage*, encourages women to pursue *pudicitia*-chastity at home and men to pursue glory in politics, rhetoric, and war.[64]

---

62. Augustine, *De ciuitate dei.* 1.19.
63. Augustine, *Sermo* 343.1. Augustine, *Sermo* 343.1: "contemnebat quod audiebat, quia timebat quem non uidebat, cuius tamen diuinis oculis erat ipsa conspicua. neque enim quomodo illa deum non uidebat, sic non uidebatur a deo."

Here, before the eyes of civil and ecclesial leaders, Augustine attributes to Christian women the security of the ultimate Roman social status, glory, for a virtue, *castitas*-chastity, which both men and women pursue.

By rooting the "glory of chastity" in the "testimony of conscience," Augustine sets aside the need for Lucretia's claim "death is my witness" and replaces it with Susanna's standing before God.[65] Not silence but true self-testimony is the outward sign of chastity for Augustine. How, then, are Augustine's readers to view these living women? They are to coordinate their vision with the vision of God: "They have, to be sure, the glory of chastity within, the testimony of conscience; but they have [it] before the eyes of their own God and they do not require more, where there's nothing more that they might rightly do."[66]

Conclusion

In 409 C.E., the priest Victorianus, disturbed by the violence of Visigothic and Vandal raids, wrote to Augustine with a request for a "lengthy work" (*prolixo opere*). He wanted Augustine to respond to questions such as "even if we sinners merited these punishments, why are the servants of God also killed by the sword of the barbarians and the handmaids of God taken captive?" and to address pagan accusations that such ills had befallen the provinces only after (and therefore as a result of) the rise of Christianity.[67] Augustine wrote

---

64. Seneca, *De Matrimonia* (78-79 Haase), as found in Gretchen J. Reydams-Schils, *The Roman Stoics: Self, Responsibility, and Affection* (Chicago: University of Chicago Press, 2005), 168–69.
65. Augustine's association of women in his own day with Susanna is not unique. Jerome refers, in a letter to Principia, to chaste women as "many Susannas" (*multae susannae*). Hieronymus, *Epistula* 65.2.
66. Augustine, *De ciuitate dei* 1.19: "habent quippe intus gloriam castitatis, testimonium conscientiae; habent autem coram oculis dei sui nec requirunt amplius ubi quid recte faciant non habent amplius."
67. *Epistula* 111.3; Augustine, "Letter 111: Augustine to Victorian," in *Letters 100–155*, ed.

in response that "such evils deserve lengthy groans and weeping (*prolixi gemitus et fletus*) rather than lengthy books (*prolixi libri*)."[68] As he responds to Victorianus's despair about the terrors enacted in Gaul, Spain, and Italia by Visigoths and Vandals alike, Augustine asks, "Can we, then, be even better than Daniel himself, of whom God says through the prophet Ezekiel to the prince of Tyre, Are you wiser than Daniel?" He then quotes at length from Daniel's prayer, including: "[O]pen your eyes (*aperi oculos tuos*) and look at our destruction and that of your city, Jerusalem, upon which your name is invoked."[69] In 413 C.E, as he writes the first books of *City of God*, Augustine aims to assuage the suspicion that has risen regarding women who suffered rape during the sack of Rome. While Susanna's fate was allayed by Daniel's claim of a word from God given especially to him, Augustine argues for the validity of these women's own testimonies, or witnesses, of conscience in the court of public opinion concerning them. Of Susanna's situation, Augustine writes: "The household believed one thing, the Lord saw something else."[70] Such is the situation that these formerly captive women now find themselves in. Augustine gives his audience a glimpse of what God sees, so his readers can conform their vision to God's.

Given that the first words of *City of God* are "the most glorious city of God,"[71] any conferral of glory is worth attending to carefully. These women are the first persons to whom Augustine attributes the glory to be anticipated in the vision of God, which all citizens of the heavenly city will enjoy. On sarcophagi and in catacombs in which Susanna appears, as an orant or otherwise, she is displayed among the

---

Boniface Ramsey, trans. Roland J. Teske, The Works of Saint Augustine. vol. 2/2. (Hyde Park, NY: New City Press, 2003), 89.
68. *Epistula* 111.1; Augustine, "Letter 111," trans. Teske, 88.
69. Augustine, *Epistula* 111.4; Augustine, "Letter 111," trans. Teske, 90.
70. Augustine, *Sermo* 343.1.
71. Augustine, *De ciuitate dei* 1.prologue.

panoply of other biblical figures who anticipate bodily resurrection; one comes to expect that her virtue will endure not only in paint and stone but also in flesh and blood. Both Augustine's consistent regard for Susanna's distinctive virtue and her frequent inclusion in artistic representations of exemplary figures may have shaped his proclivity for imagining a resurrected community in which women are fully themselves. Indeed, her story is about life after near-death, and she survives because she was "seen by God."[72] By envisioning an eschatological community constituted by women and men, Augustine presents to his readers the imaginative resources to recognize the virtue and value of the living women in their current communities.[73]

---

72. Augustine, *Sermo* 343.1.
73. I am indebted to Ellen Charry, Geddes Hanson, Sarah Stewart-Kroeker, Jessica Wright, and the editors of this volume for their thoughtful and critical feedback on this chapter. Jessica Wright also assisted me with Latin translations. Any deficiencies that remain are entirely my own.

4

The Politics of Fasting in Basil of Caesarea

Mark DelCogliano

Manifold are the benefits of fasting according to Basil of Caesarea. It is "the mother of health," bringing physical well-being to the infirm and preserving bodily health for the fit.[1] It is also "a good guardian of the soul," producing spiritual health, purifying the soul of sin, and equipping the soul with weapons most effective for spiritual warfare.[2] And yet, even though Basil recognizes that fasting brings such personal and individual advantages, he actually views the benefits of fasting primarily in social and political terms, and more specifically in terms of the eradication of disorder and the establishment of good order in the domestic and civic realms. In fact, Basil is so optimistic about fasting's power to bolster social and

1. *Iei1* 7. See also *Iei1* 9 and *Iei2* 7.
2. *Iei1* 6. See also *Iei1* 1 and *Iei2* 1–2.

political order that he sees it enabling its corporate practitioners to achieve a profound peace that is modeled on and in a way recaptures the paradisiacal state. It is thus a political practice that procures salvation.

The best resources for Basil's views on fasting are three extant homilies, two of which focus on fasting itself, whereas the third is against drunkenness.[3] While these three homilies cannot be dated any more precisely than to the entire span of Basil's presbyteral (363-370 C.E.) and episcopal (370-378 C.E.) ministries,[4] they are linked thematically and liturgically. The homilies on fasting rail as much against drunkenness as they do against gluttony, and the common thread running through all three is the need for self-control in the face of over-indulgence, whether in eating or in drinking. The two homilies on fasting were preached during Lent, seemingly on one of the Sundays before the five-day fast each week (Mondays through Fridays) that was practiced for seven weeks in Basil's era and area during this liturgical season.[5] These homilies are exhortations to his congregation not to "drown themselves in drink"[6] the day before the

---

3. *Iei1* = *Homilia de ieiunio I* (CPG 2845) [traditionally numbered homily 1]; *Iei2* = *Homilia de ieiunio II* (CPG 2846) [homily 2]; and *Ebr* = *Homilia in ebriosos* (CPG 2858) [homily 14]. The authenticity of these homilies has not been doubted since Julian Garnier's edition of Basil's *opera omnia*, published in 1721–1730 by the Maurists; on this edition, see Paul Jonathan Fedwick, *Bibliotheca Basiliana Vniversalis* (Turnhout: Brepols, 1993) i, 272–89 (hereafter=*BBV*). The Maurist edition remains the latest. De Sinner's reprint of the Maurist edition in 1839 is considered the best from a technical standpoint; see Fedwick, *BBV* ii, 291–94. In this reprint edition, the homilies are printed in vol. ii, pp. 1–14, 14–22, and 171–182. When the Maurist edition was reprinted by J. P. Migne, errors were frequently introduced, but these remain the most accessible editions of these three homilies; see PG 31.163–184, 185–198, and 443–463. The translations quoted here are mine, taken from Susan R. Holman and Mark DelCogliano, *St. Basil the Great: On Fasting and Feasts*, Popular Patristics Series 50 (Yonkers: St. Vladimir's Seminary Press, 2013), 55–71 (*Iei1*), 73–81 (*Iei2*), and 83–95 (*Ebr*).
4. See Paul Jonathan Fedwick, "A Chronology of the Life and Works of Basil of Caesarea," in Paul Jonathan Fedwick, ed., *Basil of Caesarea: Christian, Humanist, Ascetic. A Sixteenth-Hundredth Anniversary Symposium* (Toronto: Pontifical Institute of Medieval Studies, 1981), 3–19 (9–10). Jean Bernardi, *La prédication des pères cappadociens* (Paris: Presses universitaires de France, 1968), 72–76, dates *Iei1* and *Iei2* to 371, and *Ebr* to 372, but his arguments are unpersuasive.
5. See *Iei1* 7, *Iei2* 4, and 7. According to later Orthodox practice, from the second to the sixth week of Lent a strict fast is kept from Monday to Friday, in which one abstains from meat, fish,

five-day fast but rather to observe the "true" fasting taught by the holy scriptures. The homily against drunkenness seems to have been preached shortly after Easter—perhaps even on Easter Monday—in response to some members of his congregation having celebrated the festival with excessive drinking and public debauchery.[7] This homily is a plea to them not to end their Lenten fast with such shameless self-indulgence and to prepare for Pentecost in a far more appropriate manner. It should come as no surprise, then, that these three homilies often appear together in the manuscripts, and were even assigned for Lenten reading, underscoring their thematic and liturgical connections.[8]

The problem with self-indulgence, as Basil sees it, aside from its negative personal and individual effects,[9] is that it results in social and political disorder in both the private (domestic) and the public (civic) spheres. Basil is particularly disturbed that self-indulgence results in an upsetting of the customary social order, its hierarchies, its gender roles, its boundaries, and its norms.[10] For example, Basil

---

eggs, dairy, wine, and oil. On Saturday and Sunday wine and oil are permitted. It is not clear if this was the precise practice in Basil's time, but it was probably something along these lines.

6. See *Iei1* 10, *Iei2* 4, and 7.
7. See *Ebr* 1 and 8.
8. See the contents of the Greek corpora in Fedwick, BBV ii, 1–125. For example, Paris Bibliothèque Nationale de France gr. 763 has the three homilies in a row. In the manuscripts *Iei2* often precedes *Iei1*, though *Ebr* is generally the third in the series. On the manuscript evidence for these homilies, see BBV ii, 1063–67 and 1082–91. On the reading of these homilies during Lent, see Fedwick, "A Chronology," 9 n. 37 and BBV ii, 1082 n. 59 and 1087 n. 66.
9. Two examples: "What is easier for the stomach? To pass the night with plain fare? Or for it to lie there weighed down by an abundance of food? Or rather, not for it to lie there, but for it to be constantly upset, bloated, and grumbling?" (*Iei1* 4 [58]); "No one experiences a hangover from drinking water. No one's head hurts if it is saturated with water. No one needs another's feet if he spends his life drinking water. No one trips over his own feet, no one loses the use of his hands, if he imbibes water. For digestive problems, which are the necessary consequence of self-indulgence, produce terrible maladies in the body" (*Iei1* 9 [65]).
10. Basil was also surely aware that extreme asceticism could lead to similar social and political disruptions. At the Council of Gangra (whose exact date remains disputed, with conjectures ranging from 340 to 355 C.E.) Basil's one-time mentor, Eustathius of Sebasteia, was censured for spearheading such ascetical fanaticism. Anna Silvas, *The Asketikon of St Basil the Great* (Oxford: Oxford University Press, 2005), 19–20, gives a succinct account of the social and

poses a rhetorical question to those who have indulged in drinking to the point of drunkenness: "How will you rule your household servants when you yourselves are enslaved to foolish and harmful desires as if you were prisoners of war? How will you reprove your children when you live a life that is deaf to reproof and devoid of regulation?"[11] Self-indulgence reverses the customary hierarchies, making the master an enslaved prisoner and the parent an unruly child; domestic disorder reigns.

In another example, Basil describes a drinking party at which drunkards perversely mock the expected social hierarchies and norms by creating a façade of order in disorder:

> As soon as the day breaks they immediately adorn the places for their *symposiums*, or drinking parties, with multicolored carpets and floral wall hangings, and display eagerness and diligence in the preparation of the vessels, arranging the *psykters*, the *kraters*, and the *phiales*, as if assembling them for a kind of procession or sacred festival. Thus they conceal their indulgence through a variety of vessels and sufficiently prolong their time for drinking by the alteration and exchange of vessels. At these drinking parties there are *symposiarchs* who preside, as well as head cup-bearers and table-waiters: they bring about a semblance of order in disorder and organization in chaos. And so, just as the presence of bodyguards boosts the dignity of civic leaders, so too the attendants stationed around the wine as if it were a kind of empress conceal its ignominy with the greatest possible zeal. In addition, garlands, and flowers, and perfumes, and incense, and innumerable other trifles create even more preoccupation for those who are perishing. Then as the drinking proceeds, quarrels, arguments, and

---

political disorder created by Eustathius and his followers: "the disparagement of marriage, the unilateral adoption of celibacy by ascetic-minded spouses; the subverting of parent-child, slave-master relationships; the provocative stance of ascetics with regard to the local church; their commandeering of church funds for distribution to the poor; their wearing outlandish clothing; women behaving as if the ascetic life emancipated them from sexual differentiation, shown by their cropped hair and male attire." Basil's own ascetic program in general, and his understanding of the role of fasting in the church in particular, would seem to steer a middle course between the equally disruptive tendencies of ascetic extremism and laxity in the form of over-indulgence, a rhetorical position that is implicit in the homilies under consideration here.
11. *Ebr* 8 (94).

disputes break out over who gets more to drink since they aspire to surpass each other in drunkenness. But the devil presides at these games, and sin is the reward for victory. For whoever pours out more undiluted wine carries away the victory prize from the others. Truly, *they glory in their shame* [Phil. 3.19]. For while they vie with each other, they inflict harm on themselves. What could I say that would get through to those who have become so shameless? Everything brims with irrationality, everything brims with confusion. The defeated get drunk, the victorious get drunk, the attendants mock them. The hand falls limp from exhaustion, the mouth can take no more, the stomach bursts, but the evil does not diminish. The wretched body, having lost its natural tone, is dissipated in every way, unable to withstand the violence brought on by excess.[12]

The drinkers' *symposium* is a mirror image of a religious procession, a sacred festival, or the retinue of a dignitary: the objective of the detailed planning and organization that goes into these is diametrically opposed to that for the *symposium*. The sham "order" of the *symposium* is aimed at maximizing the drunkenness of the participants. It establishes an arena for a contest in which one wins by being defeated. It is a descent into irrationality, confusion, and disorder. In this context, Basil brings up a specific instance of the reversal of civic norms brought on by drunkenness when he bemoans how a soldier who should make his enemies tremble with fear is defeated by wine and becomes a public laughingstock:

> What a pitiful spectacle for Christian eyes! A man who is in the prime of life, vigorous in body, pre-eminent in the military ranks, is carried home on a stretcher, able neither to stand up nor to walk on his own feet! A man who ought to make his enemies tremble with fear sparks the laughter of boys in the forum! He has been stricken, but not by a sword; he has been slain, but not by enemies. A man-at-arms at the very pinnacle of his life has become a casualty of wine, ready to suffer according to the whim of his enemies. . . . O man, you have turned your drinking party into a battlefront. You remove the young men from

12. *Ebr* 6 (90-91).

battle, leading them by the hand as though they were wounded, in that you brought death to the flower of youth with wine. And you invite him to a meal as a friend, but you send him away dead, in that you have snuffed out his life with wine.[13]

The implication here is that the city is imperiled when those entrusted with its order and security overindulge in drinking, when disorder disrupts civic expectations and norms.

In a final example, Basil seems to have another specific incident in mind when deploring the disorder brought on by self-indulgence. On Easter day several women were caught drinking, dancing erotically, and singing obscene songs in front of the martyrs' shrines, attracting a crowd of young men, who ogled them and ached to do more than ogle:

> Lewd women, who forget the fear of God and scorn the everlasting fire, on that day when they were supposed to be sitting in their homes in remembrance of the resurrection, reflecting on that day when the heavens will be opened and the judge will appear to us out of the heavens, as well as the trumpets of God, and the resurrection of the dead, and the just judgment, and the repayment to each according to his deeds—lewd women, instead of pondering these things in their mind, purifying their hearts of wicked thoughts, washing away their past sins with tears, and preparing themselves to meet Christ on that great day of his appearing,[14] instead of doing these things they shook off their yoke of slavery to Christ, ripped the veils of modesty from their heads, despised God, despised his angels, acted shamelessly at the sight of every male, tousling their hair, *dragging their garments in trains and at the same time tinkling with their feet* [Isa. 3.16 LXX], incited frenzied dancing with their lascivious eyes and boisterous laughter, enticing young men to commit every form of licentiousness with them, formed bands of dancers in the martyr's shrines in front of the city and made the holy places a workshop for their own obscenity. They defiled the air with their obscene ditties, defiled the earth with their unclean feet, stomping on it while dancing, and drew a crowd of young men into a circle of

13. *Ebr* 7 (91-92).
14. See Acts 2:20; Jude 1:6; Rev. 6:17, 16:14.

spectators around themselves: they were truly insolent and totally carried away, omitting no excess of insanity.[15]

Here is but one example of the boisterous celebrations at the martyrs' shrines which bishops throughout the Christian world denounced again and again.[16] According to Basil, these women rejected not only their religious obligations on the most important Christian solemnity of the year, but also the social norms that governed female behavior: they removed their veils, tousled their hair, drank, danced and sang in public, even in places marked off as holy, laughing boisterously, and tempted innocent young men to acts of licentiousness.[17] These women also upset the social order by causing a ruckus in a public space, to say nothing of distracting the young men from whatever they were supposed to be doing. That these women were drinking is clear not only from the context of this passage, from the opening section of the homily against drunkenness, but also from what immediately follows: "Drunkenness is the demon of our own choosing, entering souls through pleasure. Drunkenness is the mother of wickedness, the antithesis of virtue."[18] Basil is obviously

---

15. *Ebr* 1 (83-84).
16. The difference here, of course, is that the rowdy celebration took place on Easter, not on the festival day of a martyr. For the problem in Cappadocia, see Vasiliki M. Limberis, *Architects of Piety: The Cappadocian Fathers and the Cult of the Martyrs* (Oxford: Oxford University Press, 2011), 16 and 25; Brouria Bitton-Ashkelony, *Encountering the Sacred: The Debate on Christian Pilgrimage in Late Antiquity* (Berkeley: University of California Press, 2005), 37–39. On Augustine's response to the problem, see Peter Brown, "Enjoying the Saints in Late Antiquity," *Early Medieval Europe* 9 (2000): 1–24.
17. Note that Basil doesn't spare the young men either: "Let me apply what I have said to the men. Has one of them leered? Has one of them ogled? *Whoever looks upon a woman in order to lust has already committed adultery* [Matt. 5.28]. If accidentally encountering women is so dangerous for those whose eyes wander around carelessly, how much more dangerous is it to meet with women deliberately to watch them behaving disgracefully from drunkenness, making erotic gestures, and singing dissolute songs? Merely hearing these songs can produce every kind of frenzy for pleasure in licentious people! What will they say? How will they defend themselves? From such spectacles they round up a swarm of innumerable evils. Haven't they have looked for this reason, that they might rouse lust? So then, according to the inescapable verdict of the Lord, they are liable to the condemnation of adultery" (*Ebr* 8 [94]).
18. *Ebr* 2 (84).

quite disturbed that drunkenness has caused the contravening of so many expectations of the religious and social order.

One of the main problems with the self-indulgence of drinking, according to Basil, is the unbridled, frenzied sexual activity that it prompts, in such a way that sexual boundaries are crossed. He repeatedly compares gluttons and drunkards to irrational beasts in heat whose lust knows no limits in mating. For example, Basil writes: "For self-indulgence and drunkenness and every variety of rich food is swiftly accompanied by every kind of bestial licentiousness. Thus men became *horses in heat* [Jer. 5.8] because of the sting of lust which self-indulgence produces in the soul."[19] In another place he even opines that drunkards are worse than irrational beasts:

> How do you differ, O man, from irrational brutes? Isn't it by the gift of reason, which you received from the one who created you, that you became the ruler and lord of all creation? So whoever has deprived himself of his wits through drunkenness *is compared to senseless beasts and becomes like them* [Ps. 49.12 (48.13 LXX)]. In fact, I would say that those in a drunken state are even more irrational than beasts. For all quadrupeds and beasts have the impulse to mate at appointed times, but those whose soul is seized by drunkenness and whose body is filled with unnatural heat are driven at every opportunity and at every hour to impure and disgraceful intercourse, and to pleasures.[20]

In the manner of irrational beasts, or so Basil thinks, self-indulgence, and in particular drunkenness, leads the unmarried to have sex outside of marriage and the married to have sex with those not their spouses. Probably referring to the incident on Easter mentioned earlier, Basil writes:

> [M]en and women jointly form mixed bands of dancers, hand their souls over to the demon of wine, and thereby wound each other with the arrows of passion. The giggling on the part of both sexes, their appalling

19. *Iei1* 9 (68-69).
20. *Ebr* 3 (85).

ditties, and their obscene gestures inflame lewdness. Tell me, do you giggle and delight in licentious delights, even though you should be weeping and groaning over your past actions? Do you sing obscene ditties, discarding the psalms and hymns that you were taught? Do you move your feet, and leap around like a madman, and dance with those who ought not dance, even though you should be bending your knees in adoration? For whom should I lament? For the unmarried maidens? Or for those constrained by the yoke of marriage? After all, the former have returned without their virginity, but the latter have not returned their conjugal chastity to their husbands. Even if one way or another some of them avoided sinning with their body, nonetheless they welcomed corruption into their souls with open arms.[21]

Basil also suggests that self-indulgence, and, again, in particular drunkenness, leads to homosexual acts: "Inversions of nature arise when people are drunk; they seek the male in the female and the female in the male."[22] This in fact makes drunkards even worse than beasts, who at least know with whom to mate.[23] Basil appears to attribute the "slip" into homosexual intercourse to the confusion and misperception of the senses that results from drunkenness.[24] It seems

---

21. *Ebr* 8 (93). Basil also writes that "fasting also recognizes limits for marital relations" (*Iei1* 9 [69]), implying that self-indulgence neglects these limits.
22. *Iei1* 9 (69). See the next n. too.
23. "A lack of self-control with respect to pleasures is quick to arise from wine, like water suddenly welling up from a spring, and undiluted wine is swiftly accompanied by the malady of lasciviousness. This malady demonstrates that every madness which beasts have for females takes second place to the lust of drunkards. For irrational brutes recognize the boundaries of their nature, but drunkards seek the female in the male and the male in the female" (*Ebr* 4 [86]).
24. "And not only does this produce brutish irrationality in them, but also the perversion of their senses shows that the drunkard is worse than every beast. For what beast's vision and hearing is as distorted as a drunkard's? Don't they fail to recognize their closest kin and frequently run up to strangers as if they were intimate friends? Don't they frequently jump over shadows as if they were streams or gullies? Their ears are filled with sounds like the roaring of the billowing sea. The ground seems to rise uphill and the mountains appear to circle around them. Sometimes they cannot stop laughing, sometimes they are pained and wail inconsolably. Now they are courageous and undaunted, now terrified and cowardly. They find sleep onerous, insufferable, suffocating, and in fact bordering on death, but when awake they are in more of a stupor than when asleep. For their life unfolds in a dream: they have neither coat nor anything to eat the next day, yet in their drunkenness they rule like a king and lead armies, build cities, and distribute goods. It is the wine seething in their hearts that fills them with such fantasies and such great delusion" (*Ebr* 3 [85-86]).

that Basil thinks that men and women can become so drunk that they simply have no idea with whom they are having sex, mistakenly seeking the "male in the female and the female in the male," as he puts it. Moving on from Basil's quaint views on sex, his words and his analyses of the various situations mentioned here make it clear that for him the inevitable result of self-indulgence, whether excessive eating or drinking, is disorder, whether in the household or in the city, whether by transgressing traditional hierarchies and boundaries or by upsetting social norms and expectations.

Given this situation, Basil thinks that fasting is necessary not only for stemming domestic and civic disorder but also for achieving a peaceful social and political order in the private and public spheres. He thinks this not least of all because he interprets the scriptures as inculcating a universal obligation to fast. The command to fast antedates the Law (here Basil is thinking of the obligation to fast on the Day of Atonement); in fact, it is "as old as humanity" as "it was legislated in paradise" when God commanded Adam not to eat from the tree of the knowledge of good and evil in Gen. 2:17.[25]

Basil does not locate the scriptural basis for the obligation for fasting solely in the story of Adam and Eve. He goes through the history of fasting in the scriptures to demonstrate that it has been an obligation from the beginning that was practiced by the greatest saints. "All the saints," writes Basil, "received fasting as a kind of paternal inheritance, observed it as such, and handed it on, father to child. And so, through a chain of succession, this asset has been

---

25. *Iei1* 3 (57). Basil also uses Noah to prove that there was no self-indulgence in paradise (presumably with the exception of the eating of the forbidden fruit). First, he interprets Gen. 9:3 (the concession of an omnivore diet to humanity after the flood) to mean that "the enjoyment of meat was conceded only when the hope of perfection was lost" (*Iei1* 5 [59]). Second, he views Noah's drunkenness after planting the vineyard as proof that humanity had no previous experience with wine and did not know that it needed to be consumed in moderation: "And so, the invention of drinking wine is more recent than paradise, and thus the dignity of fasting is ancient" (*Iei1* 5 [59]).

preserved even for us."[26] Prominent fasters include Moses, who through fasting ascended the mountain and received the Law, whereas through gluttony and drunkenness the Israelites devolved in idolatry and the tablets of the Law were shattered. Fasting also allowed Moses to receive the Law a second time.[27] Samuel was granted to Hannah when she joined fasting to her prayer.[28] Samson's mother only conceived him when she fasted, and Samson performed so many mighty feats as long as he fasted, but his downfall occurred when he was seized by drunkenness and fornication.[29] Through fasting, Elijah saw the Lord, restored a child to life, and shut the heavens for three and half years.[30] Elisha enjoyed the hospitality of the Shunamite woman and received the prophets with fasting.[31] By fasting, the three young men in the fiery furnace made their bodies impervious to fire.[32] By fasting, Daniel escaped the mouth of the lions and saw visions.[33] By fasting, Lazarus gained rest in the bosom of Abraham.[34] The life of John the Baptist, writes Basil, "was a single continuous fast."[35] Paul's fasting "when boasting over his afflictions brought him up to the third heaven."[36] And finally, Jesus—"the principal example among those already mentioned"—fasted not only "to fortify the flesh that he assumed for our sake" against the devil's assaults, but also to instruct us to fast "in order to prepare and train ourselves for struggles with temptation."[37] Basil also gives the negative example of Esau's failure to fast even

26. *Iei*1 5 (59).
27. *Iei*1 5, *Iei*1 9, and *Iei*2 6.
28. *Iei*1 6 and *Iei*2 6. See 1 Sam 1:11.
29. Ibid.
30. Ibid.
31. *Iei*1 6. See 2 Kgs. 4:8-41.
32. *Iei*1 6.
33. *Iei*1 7 and 9. See Dan. 6:17-25.
34. *Iei*1 9.
35. Ibid., 66.
36. Ibid. See 2 Cor. 11:27 and 12:2.
37. *Iei*1 9 (66).

for a single meal causing him to lose his birthright.[38] In each of these positive and negative examples, someone fasted and received some personal benefit or it enabled them to benefit another or others. The point Basil wants to make here with these various examples, particularly with the example of Jesus, is to show that everyone is obligated to fast.

But Basil also provides two corporate examples of fasting in which the practice brings social and political benefit: the Israelites fleeing Egypt and the Ninevites. When the Israelites fled Egypt, as long as they fasted on manna and water from the rock they were successful in escaping the Egyptians but when self-indulgent by remembering the fleshpots they failed to realize their hopes as a people for the promised land.[39] "The Ninevites," writes Basil, "would not have escaped the destruction with which they were threatened if the irrational animals had not fasted along with them."[40] According to Basil, the civic fasting orchestrated by the Ninevites required not only human but also jumentous participation in order to be successful. These two examples accord with Basil's idea that corporate fasting brings social and political benefits, even if he is using them as scriptural evidence for the obligation of fasting.

As these two final examples show, Basil thinks that the obligation to fast is not merely incumbent upon individuals, but that all members of a household or city should fast: only in this way can corporate fasting can bring about peace and order in the domestic and civic realms. "Fasting," writes Basil, "brings about the orderliness of a city, the tranquility of the forum, the peace of households, the security of possessions."[41] In regard to the household, Basil writes, "Fasting is the expansion of households, . . . the pedagogue of youth,

38. *Ieil* 6.
39. *Ieil* 9.
40. Ibid., 67. See Jonah 3:4–10.
41. *Ieil* 11 (71).

an adornment for seniors, . . . and a safe housemate for married couples."[42] He also says, "Fasting protects children, chastens the young, makes seniors venerable. For grey hair is more venerable when it is adorned with fasting. It is an adornment very well suited for women: it restrains those in their prime, guards the married, nourishes virgins. Such is how fasting is practiced privately in homes."[43] Fasting, then, when practiced by all the members of the household, contributes to its overall well-being and order: children are properly raised and kept safe, seniors are accorded the respect they deserve, unmarried women and virgins observe traditional sexual boundaries, and harmonious relations flourish between husbands and wives.

On the subject of how fasting helps maintain order within a marriage, Basil writes: "A husband does not suspect treachery in his marriage when he observes his wife living with fasting. Nor is a wife consumed with jealousy when she observes her husband embracing fasting."[44] Basil sees fasting as the guardian of martial fidelity if both spouses practice it. Fasting on the part of the members of the household also contributes to the maintenance of its provisions through its lack of consumption.[45] It also affords rest to the household servants, bringing about peace in the whole house; there is harmony between the master and mistress and their servants.[46] And so, a fasting

---

42. *Iei1* 7 (63).
43. *Iei2* 5 (77).
44. *Iei1* 7 (63).
45. "Who has suffered the loss of his household possessions when fasting? Count what's in your house today, and count it after the fast. Nothing will be missing from your household possessions because of fasting. No animal bemoans death: an implacable stomach neither sheds the blood of animals nor issues an order for their slaughter. The butcher puts down his knife and the table is content with plants" (*Iei1* 7 [63-64]).
46. "The sabbath was given to the Jews, it says, that *your donkey and your manservant* might rest [Exod. 20:10]. Let fasting be for your household servants a rest from their perpetual labors, seeing that they serve you for the whole year. Give your meat cook a rest. Give your tablesetter a holiday. Stay the hand of your winepourer. Give some time off to your pastry chef, who makes a variety of desserts. Give your household some quiet from the endless clamor, from

household eradicates disorder brought on by unruly and imperiled children, disrespected elders, unfaithful spouses, sexually promiscuous daughters, and overworked servants, creating an order characterized by peace, harmony, and good relations that maintains societal norms and expectations, anti-consumerism, and the non-exploitation of the household staff.

Basil also points out the benefits that fasting brings to the public and civic spheres. He states that everyone in the city is obligated to fast; no one, no profession, no economic status, no location, is exempted. "The summons to fast," writes Basil, "has been announced to the whole world. There is no island, no mainland, no city, no people, no remote place which does not hear the summons. Rather soldiers, and travelers, and sailors, and merchants all likewise hear the announcement and receive it with great joy. No one should remove himself from the register of those who fast, in which all peoples and all ages and all ranks of dignity are counted."[47] In one passage, Basil directly addresses the various members of the household and the city, reminding each not to despise fasting:

> Are you rich? Do not mock fasting, deeming it unworthy to welcome as your table companion. Do not expel it from your house as a dishonorable thing eclipsed by pleasure. Never denounce yourself to the one who has legislated fasting and thereby merit condemnation to bitter penury caused either by bodily sickness or by some other gloomy condition. Let not the pauper think of fasting as a joke, seeing that for a long time now he has had it as the companion of his home and table. But as for women, just as breathing is proper and natural for them, so too is fasting. And children, like flourishing plants, are irrigated with the water of fasting. As for seniors, their long familiarity with fasting makes a difficult task easy. For those in training know that difficult tasks done for a long time out of habit become quite painless. As for

the smoke and cooking aromas, and from the servants who run up and down to cater to your stomach as if it were an imperious lady" (Iei1 7 [64]).
47. Iei2 2 (74).

travelers, fasting is an expedient companion. For just as self-indulgence necessarily weighs them down because they carry around what they have gorged themselves with, so too fasting renders them swift and unencumbered. . . . Take fasting, O you paupers, as the companion of your home and table; O you servants, as rest from the continual labors of your servitude; O you rich, as the remedy that heals the damage caused by your indulgence and in turn makes what you usually despise more delightful.[48]

"Hence one finds," says Basil, "the benefit of fasting in every pursuit and in every bodily state, and it is equally suitable for everything: homes, fora, nights, days, cities, deserts . . . in so many situations fasting graces us with something that is good in itself. . . ."[49] Basil furthermore thinks that the social and political order generated by fasting is possible only if all participate in the practice (much like in Nineveh, though Basil does not make the connection). The "good in itself" with which corporate fasting graces the social or political body is order and peace. In a key passage, Basil explains how corporate fasting creates a "good order" (*eutaxia*) in the city and a "profound peace" (*eirēnē batheia*) throughout the world; as he gives his explanation apparently he has in mind the incident on Easter that I mentioned above in mind, but he goes beyond it:

> But how is it [fasting] practiced in our public life? It disposes every city as a whole and all its people to good order, quiets shouting, banishes fighting, silences abuse. What teacher's arrival settles down the uproar of boys as abruptly as the advent of fasting quells the tumult of the city? What reveler carries on when fasting? What band of lascivious dancers is formed by fasting? Silly giggling and obscene ditties and erotic dancing abruptly leave the city, banished by fasting as if by a stern judge. Now if all were to take fasting as the counselor for their actions, nothing would prevent a profound peace from spreading throughout the entire world. Nations would not rise up against one another, nor would armies clash in battle. If fasting prevailed, weapons would not be wrought, courts

48. *Iei2* 2 (74-75) and 7 (79).
49. *Iei2* 7 (79).

of justice would not be erected, people would not live in prisons, nor would there ever be any criminals in the deserts, any slanderers in the cities, or any pirates on the sea. If all were students of fasting, they would never hear *the voice of the taskmaster* [Job 3.18] mentioned in the book of Job.[50]

A quelling of rowdiness, a silencing of revelry, a cessation of hostilities, an end to crime: these are just some of social and political benefits of corporate fasting both within the city and between cities. Here Basil paints a picture of eschatological peace reminiscent of Isa. 2:1-4 and 11:6-9 (though there appears to be no direct borrowing).

Basil's conviction that the benefits of fasting are primarily social and political is rooted in a scriptural view of fasting, which teaches that true fasting is abstaining from vice. In this regard he does not fail to evoke Isa. 58:3-9, writing: "Do not define the good derived from fasting only in terms of abstaining from food. For true fasting is being a stranger to vice. *Loose every bond of wickedness* [Isa. 58:6]. Let your neighbor grieve you; forgive him his debts [Matt. 6:12]. Do not *fast only to quarrel and fight* [Isa. 58:4]."[51] Similarly, he says elsewhere: "True fasting is being a stranger to vice, controlling the tongue, abstaining from anger, distancing oneself from lust, evil speech, lying, perjury. The absence of these vices makes fasting true, and so shunning these vices makes fasting good."[52] And so, if vice leads to social disorder, then the practice of true fasting—self-control not only in matters of food and drink, but also in vice—creates a virtuous society and consequently social and political order.[53] Basil makes this explicit connection in one passage: "Nor would our life be

---

50. *Iei2* 5 (77-78).
51. *Iei1* 10 (69). See also *Iei1* 1.
52. *Iei2* 7 (80). Cf. "if you wish to make your mind strong, subdue your flesh through fasting" (*Iei1* 9 [67]).
53. Note that fasting, when understood as not eating, cannot be practiced continually, but fasting, when understood as self-control in matters of food and drink as a way of supporting the avoidance of vice and the cultivation of virtue, can.

so lamentable and sorrowful if fasting were to preside over our life. For it is clear that it would have taught all people not only to control themselves with regard to food, but also to completely avoid and be utterly estranged from avarice, greed, and every kind of vice. When these are extirpated, nothing can prevent us from passing our life in profound peace and tranquility of soul."[54] Here the "profound peace" (*eirēnē batheia*) and "tranquility of soul" in which life is passed when true fasting is practiced is social and political, not simply personal, just as in the passage cited above.

Finally, the peaceful social and political order in the domestic and civic spheres that can be gained by fasting is for Basil a kind of recapturing of the paradisiacal state. It is clear that for Basil fasting is crucial to salvation: "see how fasting conveys to God and how self-indulgence forsakes salvation."[55] For fasting reverses the original sin: "If Eve had fasted from the tree, we would not need this fasting now.... We have been injured by sin; let us be healed by repentance. But repentance is futile without fasting.... Make satisfaction to God through fasting."[56] Thus, there is a kind of symmetry: just as the first sin occurred by breaking the command to fast, the repentance for the sin must be done by fulfilling the obligation to fast. Accordingly, this means that fasting is also the way to return to paradise, from which humanity was expelled because of that first transgression: "It is because we did not fast that we were banished from paradise. So let us fast that we may return to it. Don't you realize that Lazarus entered paradise through fasting? Do not imitate the disobedience of Eve."[57] Basil also comments that "fasting is likeness to the angels [and]

54. *Iei2* 5 (78).
55. *Iei1* 5 (60).
56. *Iei1* 3 (57).
57. *Iei1* 4 (57-58).

companionship with the righteous"[58]—something which would seem to be a foretaste or prefiguration of the heavenly life.

Yet, Basil does not make an explicit connection between the order achieved through fasting and the order of the paradisiacal state. Nonetheless, the connection is there: the peaceful order of paradise is Basil's model for social and political order. Throughout his corpus, Basil recognizes the harmonious relations between God, humanity, and all creation that characterized the world before the fall.[59] And so there is in his thought at least the implicit idea that the "profound peace" of the "good order" in the domestic and civic realms is somehow paradisiacal. It seems that for Basil the different results of fasting (that is, the return to paradise and the creation of social and political order) are but different aspects of the same reality, which in this life is never fully achieved but always to be pursued. The practice of true fasting in this fallen world is thus fuelled by an eschatological hope, for Basil says that God created human beings to practice virtue "to bring about upon the earth a reflection of the good order [*eutaxia*] in heaven."[60] As we have seen, fasting, the true fasting taught by the scriptures, is fundamental to, or rather is, this practice of virtue, which when practiced collectively brings about on the earth a "good order" and "profound peace" in domestic and civic realms that "reflects" [*skiagraphein*] the "good order in heaven." For Basil, then, fasting is replete with political ramifications of eschatological and soteriological importance.

---

58. *Iei2* 6 (78).
59. See e.g. *Homilia dicta in Lakizis* 8 (This homily is traditionally numbered 26).
60. *Quod rebus mundanis adhaerendum non sit* 5 (traditionally numbered homily 21), translation taken from Mark DelCogliano, *St. Basil the Great: On Christian Doctrine and Practice*, Popular Patristics Series 47 (Yonkers: St. Vladimir's Seminary Press, 2012), 170.

5

Contemplating Genesis 1 as a Political Act in Late Antiquity

Daniel Wade McClain

"In truth the most difficult of sciences is to know one's self."[1]

In contemporary popular culture, the political significance of the Genesis 1 creation narrative is usually associated with battles over public school curricula. This essay argues that readers can more fully appreciate the profound political significance of the Genesis narrative when we consider its reception among late Antique interpreters.

1. Basil, *Homélies sur l'Hexaéméron*, 2nd ed. (Paris: Éditions du Cerf, 1968), 9.6; hereafter, *Hexaemeron*. The English translation is Basil, *Exegetic Homilies*, trans. Agnes Clare Way (Washington, DC: The Catholic University of America Press, 1963). For the reader's sake, I have cited all ancient texts according to their paragraph or section number, which correspond to both the respective critical editions and translations as noted.

For early Christian preachers, such as Origen, Basil, and Ambrose, Genesis 1 was significant as a resource for ascetic formation, for coming to terms with the place of humanity with God and within the world. Early Christian commentary on Genesis 1 was concerned with education, formation, and human excellence. To the extent that politics in the ancient world was conceived of as a skill or practice of living well in community, Genesis 1 was, for these authors, a political text. However, the "politics of Genesis," for these authors, can only be understood if one first comes to terms with the ascetical value that they saw at work in both the text and the world itself. Indeed, by drawing upon both the creation narrative of Genesis 1 as well as the ascetic legacy imparted by Moses, who was considered the paragon of contemplative ascent, early Christian preachers constructed a tradition of contemplation and formation intended to conform the hearer and reader to God.

Genesis 1, then, was one site of development for the burgeoning tradition of ascetic, contemplative formation. This development was related directly to the broader Christian enterprise of theological inquiry and education. The order of the six days of creation (the hexaemeron), the relationship of humanity to the rest of creation and to the Creator, and the fall, all bore on the way in which early Christians understood themselves, their communities, and their relationship to God.

In this essay, I trace this tradition of ascetic contemplation through four commentaries on Genesis 1. A close reading of these commentaries shows that each author read Genesis 1 as a text of moral consequence. I will first examine Philo of Alexandria's *De opificio mundi*. Philo was the first to see Genesis 1's moral significance. Second, I will highlight the way in which Origen's homily on Genesis 1 is entirely concerned with the spiritual and moral life of man precisely because Origen began with the ultimate beginning,

Christ. Third, I will show how for Basil of Caesarea, more than Philo and Origen, Genesis 1 is fecund as a source of not only moral formation, but also ecclesial formation. It is thus because Basil took the christological importance of Genesis from its cosmic origin to its ecclesial and eschatological conclusion. Finally, Ambrose of Milan amplified the christological frequency of Genesis 1 even more than Basil by seeing Christ even in God's Sabbath rest. This enabled Ambrose to uncover a liturgical significance in the making of man, thereby contributing to the ecclesial, and therefore political, application of the text.

Cosmology as a Way of Life

It should be noted that the relevance of Genesis 1 for formation, whether political or ecclesial, precedes the late Antique commentarial tradition. Jean Daniélou believed that the historical occasion of Genesis 1 was itself political and educational. Daniélou adopted the historical-critical approach of the documentary hypothesis to locate Genesis 1 in the fifth century B.C.E. However, rather than demythologizing the text, Daniélou employed the historical-critical stance for theological ends. True, the Priestly source's cosmology bears striking resemblance to the cosmologies of its Canaanite, Egyptian, and Babylonian counterparts.[2] However, the text distinguishes itself from these counterparts precisely in the way it frames Elohim in relation to the cosmos. Near Eastern pagan accounts divinize nature—primordial forces lack coherent explanation, and people cower before and attempt to placate these primordial forces and the gods they birth. "Cosmogony, in reality, is a theogony," an account of the melodrama and violence of the gods

---

2. For instance, the P account adopts a tri-partite division of the earth; a firmament that hangs over the celestial luminaries; and a juxtaposition of a "primordial chaos" to the orderly arrangement that comes to prevail over the chaos.

and nature, and the sometimes unintentional, or at least accidental, losses that humanity suffers in the crossfire.³ The approach of Genesis 1, on the other hand, is not one of cosmology as such. Rather, Genesis 1 pushes against its contemporaries in its understanding God's relationship to the cosmos and, most especially, the people called to be God's people.

Genesis 1, therefore, emerges as an "anti-polytheistic polemic."⁴ It replaces theogony or divine struggle, with Elohim, a God-creator. All of the forces of nature are demythologized and subordinated to God, their creator. The Lord not only reigns supreme over natural forces, but calls these "good." Their goodness is a result of the source; God, is the beginning, the origin of all things, "the principle, *bereshith*. . . ."⁵ For the first readers of Genesis 1, this God is the God of the covenant, who had called his people out of the desert, and was recalling them once again, now out of Babylon. This God had as his first action the creation of the world itself. Nothing precedes this God. Anything that is his creation, is his subject, and is therefore good.⁶ Genesis 1 reminded the Israelites that the God of the covenant was also the God of the cosmos. In this manner, the theological rhetoric of Genesis 1 itself is also a political rhetoric; it distinguishes the polity of the Israelites, not by some virtue of their own, but rather by means of a quality inherent to Yahweh, who elects a particular people.

Likewise, commentaries on this text related rather than dichotomized the cosmological and political qualities of the text. According to J. C. M. Van Winden, the fundamental context of early Christian interpretation of Genesis 1 was the philosophical formation that scriptural interpreters received.⁷ In contrast to Genesis

---

3. Jean Daniélou, *In the Beginning: Genesis I-III*, trans. Julien Randolf (Baltimore: Helicon, 1965), 29.
4. Ibid., 30.
5. Ibid., 33.
6. Ibid., 34–35.

1, and then the Gospel of John, both of which located the source of the world in a non-material principle, the Greek concept of ἀρχή placed a premium on material causation.[8] Jewish and Christian commentaries negotiated this philosophical problem through commentaries on Genesis 1, thereby coordinating a conversation between inchoate Christian theological doctrine and Greek cosmology.[9] And since many Christian theologians adopted the Neoplatonic doctrine of an orderly cosmos, Genesis 1 commentaries critically appropriated the shape and character of this order in their understanding of the scriptural account.[10]

Precisely in the same way that ancient philosophy was convertible with a way of life,[11] the interpretation of Genesis participated in a very practical conversation about how to live as people called by

---

7. J. C. M. Van Winden, OFM, "In the Beginning: Some Observations on the Patristic Interpretation of Genesis 1:1," *Vigilae Christianae* 17 (1963): 105: "The basic problem of Greek philosophy is that of the ἀρχή."
8. On ἀρχή (beginning) in Gen. 1:1 see Van Winden, "Some Observations," 105-6.
9. James Adam said in his Gifford Lectures, "It is difficult to overstate the influence which the dialogue [of the *Timaeus*] exercised on religious thought and speculation. . . . The *Timaeus* did more than any other literary masterpiece to facilitate and promote the fusion of Hellenism and Hebraism out of which so much of Christian theology has sprung." James Adam, *The Religious Teachers of Greece*, Gifford Lectures at Aberdeen 1904/06 (Aberdeen: University of Aberdeen, 1908), 373-74; cited in Jaroslav Pelikan, *Classical Culture and Christian Theology: The Metamorphosis of Natural Theology in the Christian Encounter with Hellenism* (New Haven: Yale University Press, 1993), 96.
10. David T. Runia, *Philo of Alexandria, On the Creation of the Cosmos According to Moses*, Philo of Alexandria Commentary Series (Leiden: Brill, 2001), §13 [49]See Thomas O'Loughlin, *Teachers and Code-breakers: the Latin Genesis Tradition, 430-800* (Turnhout: Brepols, 1999), 273: "One of those shared desires of those who wrote within the Genesis tradition was that they should be good *discipuli* to their patristic teachers and hand on without corruption what they had received. In actual writing this manifested itself in the claim that they did not change what they had received, but with *breuitas*, and a concern for their students, had repeated the opinions of the Fathers. But they wrote in a new social and academic situation and for a different audience. . . ." See Robert L. Wilken, *The Christians as the Romans Saw Them*, 2 ed. (New Haven: Yale University Press, 2003), 85-87. On rejection of Greek religion, see Pelikan, *Classical Culture and Christian Theology*, 23-25; on acceptance of the philosophers' critique of polytheism, see 77-78.
11. See Pierre Hadot, "Philosophy as a Way of Life," in *Philosophy as a Way of Life: Spiritual Exercises from Socrates to Foucault*, ed. Arnold Davidson (Oxford: Blackwell, 1995), 264-76; and Pierre Hadot, *What is Ancient Philosophy?* (Cambridge, MA: Harvard University Press, 2002), 55-58.

the Creator God. Cosmological conversation and reflection were significant for the unfolding of Christian teaching about God's work and the life of the Church. This was especially true for developing distinctly Christian practices of learning through reading, hearing, and expositing scripture. Prior to Augustine of Hippo, Jewish and Christian authors had begun the arduous task of constructing a tradition of reflection and contemplation on Genesis 1 in which moral formation played a key role.

Philo and the Propaedeutic Law

The first author that we know of to note explicitly the formational and political significance of Genesis 1 was Philo of Alexandria. His *De opificio mundi* is the earliest extant commentary on the hexaemeron, written around 30–40 C.E.[12] A contemporary of Christ's, Philo would bequeath a tradition of interpretation to Christian theologians who shared his preoccupation with Genesis 1. The most noteworthy aspect of this tradition for our purposes is the emphasis in Philo's commentary upon Genesis 1 as legal and ethical prolegomena. By way of his commentary, Philo sought to assimilate Greek philosophical thought to the wisdom of the original philosopher and lawmaker, Moses:[13] "If you consider the other lawgivers, you will find that some drew up the regulations as just in an unadorned and naked fashion, while others enclothed their thoughts with a mass of verbiage and so deceived the masses by concealing the truth

---

12. *De opificio mundi*, in *Philonis Alexandrini opera quae supersunt*, vol. 1, ed. L. Cohn, P. Wendland, and S. Reiter (Berlin: Reimer, 1896). English translation from David T. Runia, *Philo of Alexandria, On the Creation of the Cosmos According to Moses*, Philo of Alexandria Commentary Series (Leiden: Brill, 2001).
13. See S. Sandmel, "Philo Judaeus: An Introduction to the Man, his Writings, and his Significance," in *Aufsteig und Niedergang Der Römische Welt*, vol. II.1, ed. Hildegard Temporini and Wolfgang Haase (Berlin: Walter De Gruyter, 1984), 5-6, and 12; and Norman Bentwich, *Philo-Judæus of Alexandria* (Philadelphia: The Jewish Publication Society of America, 1910), 104.

with mythical fictions. Moses surpassed both groups."[14] By situating cosmological contemplation within commentary on the law, Philo helped establish interpretive patterns that would have consequence for the entire tradition of Genesis commentaries. Most notable among these was his argument that conformity to the Mosaic law entails first conformity to the cosmological order elaborated in Genesis 1.

Despite his engagement with the *Timaeus*, the result of Philo's investigation into law and cosmology yields a distinctive account of order. For Philo, cosmic order *qua* order reflects God. While cosmology precedes ethics (the Torah), it is thus only because both the order of the cosmos and the order of the law share the same source. Indeed, both emanate from the same hierarchy. Thus, Genesis 1 not only teaches *about* creation; it also brings its reader and hearer into conformity with order: "The man who observes the law is at once a citizen of the cosmos, directing his actions in relation to the rational purpose of nature, in accordance with which the entire cosmos also is administered."[15] With this conformity in mind, Philo compared the conformity of the reader, the law, and the cosmos to a seal and the impression it leaves.[16] Theological and moral inquiry, which include reflection and commentary on Genesis 1, is both discursive and formative; it informs and conforms, it teaches and shapes *simultaneously*.

There is, in Philo's exposition of Genesis 1, a sense of expectation or anticipation that grows as the days of creation progress. The structure inherent to the cosmos is gradually revealed, and finally consummated in the human being. Humans have the honor of being created last, as if "guests" invited to a "banquet," after "all the

---

14. *Opif.* §2.
15. *Opif.* §3.
16. *Opif.* §6.

preparations for the feast have been completed."[17] By creating man in his image last, God instilled a circular, or dialogical movement in the cosmos as "the beginning and the end [are] harmonized together in a necessary and loving relationship."[18] The consummation of the cosmos is not properly located in the human as such, but in a partnership with God, the momentum of which is toward love.

Philo developed the shape of that relationship with his reflection on the seventh day. While the sixth day (Gen. 2:3) reflects the cosmos's conformity with the perfect order of the Logos, the seventh day symbolizes the sacred. Its sacrality is reflected in the observation and holiness of the seventh day of the week.[19] Philo instructs his reader to keep this day holy by contemplating the law in order to purify oneself, examine one's conscience, and improve one's character.

Thus, contemplating the cosmos participates in ethical and spiritual formation. As David Runia observes, the narrative of the hexaemeron was important to Philo because it connected creation to the Law, and Law is the singular propaedeutic or *paideia* for the ailment of the passions to which the first humans succumbed.[20] While the six days symbolize the perfect order of creation, humans must work to regain this order through the rigorous moral purity called for by the Law.

Origen: Christ Is the Beginning of All Things

Origen's writings on Genesis are among the earliest Christian reflections on creation.[21] Together with Philo's commentary,

---

17. *Opif.* §78.
18. *Opif.* §82.
19. The seventh day was to be a day for Jews to rest from work in order "to concentrate on one thing only ... the improvement of their character ... sand the examination of their conscience." *Opif.* §128.
20. See Runia, *On the Creation of the Cosmos*, 18; and David Dawson, *Allegorical Readers and Cultural Revision in Ancient Alexandria* (Berkeley: University of California Press, 2001), 75.
21. Peter Bouteneff, *Beginnings: Ancient Christian Readings of the Biblical Creation Narratives* (Grand Rapids: Baker Academic, 2008), 89.

Origen's treatment of Genesis helped define the agenda for subsequent Christian speculation about creation. Genesis was a key locus of his thought, and treatments of it can be found across his vast body of exegetical and philosophical works.[22] Yet, whereas Philo saw an almost mathematical consistency between the cosmos and the law, Origen saw in Genesis 1 a revelation that the metaphysical order and the material world are but shadows of a deeper spiritual reality originating in the *Logos*, Jesus Christ. It is about this latter reality that Origen was most concerned. Conformity to and development in this spiritual reality require the Christian to transcend the obstacles and cares of the material world. Origen's chief interest in Genesis 1 therefore lay in its spiritual value. Homily 1 of his sixteen *Homilies on Genesis* is perhaps one of the best surviving examples of his engagement with Genesis itself.[23]

Origen was a careful interpreter, attentive to the literal sense of the text. In this homily, Origen's figural interpretation is regulated by something like Augustine's own approach to figural language in scripture; when the literal aspect of the text produces an impossible meaning, the exegete ought to employ a figural interpretation that respects the bounds of the text. Thus, a text does not contain either an historical or a figurative sense. Rather, the scriptural text harbors within itself, within its historical aspect, deeper truths that the Spirit has hidden.

At times, Origen referred to this hidden meaning as a law. So, for instance, "[W]e are to realize that with this external story are interwoven certain other matters which, when considered and

---

22. See Bouteneff, *Beginnings*, esp. 89-119; and Ronald Heine, "The Testimonia and Fragments Related to Origen's Commentary on Genesis," *Zeitschrift für Antikes Christentum* 9 (2005): 122-42.

23. Homily 1 in Origen, "In Genesim homilae," in *Origenes Werke VI: Homilien zum Hexateuch*, ed. W. A. Baehrens (Leipzig: J. C. Hinrichs, 1920), 1-21. English translation from *Homilies on Genesis and Exodus*, trans. Ronald Heine (Washington, DC: Catholic University Press, 1982), 47-71.

comprehended in their inward meaning, provide with *a law* which is useful to men and worthy of God."[24] The simultaneity of historical and figural, or "inward" meanings leads the reader into and through the text to moral and anagogical truths. While on the surface this appears to be a more complicated and speculative approach, in reality it is highly practical insofar as its aim is to lead one's audience to moral wisdom and, ultimately, to transformation.

Origen's figural interpretation is explicitly christological and soteriological: "In the beginning God made heaven and earth. What is the beginning of all things except our Lord and 'Savior of all,' Jesus Christ . . . ?"[25] Whereas Philo had included a panegyric to Moses, and a lengthy reflection on order at the beginning of his commentary, Origen's homily jumps right into the figurative, moral significance of the narrative. The events of the narrative, like the division of light from dark, or of water and dry land, signify stages of development in the spiritual life. But, above all, these events signify Christ. Indeed, Christ is the Logos, the firstborn of all creation: "In this beginning, therefore, that is, in his Word, 'God made heaven and earth.' . . ."[26] Genesis 1:1, therefore, is about the *who,* by whom all things were made, rather than *what* was made. The creation story in Origen's interpretation establishes an important foundation for spiritual and moral development.

While moral and spiritual development is evident in the above exegesis, it is not immediately clear how Origen's homily is a political

---

24. Origen, *De principiis,* ed. Paul Koetschau, Origenes Werke V (Leipzig: J. C. Hinrichs, 1913), IV.3.4 (328). English translation from *On First Principles,* trans. George Butterworth (Gloucester, MA: Peter Smith, 1973).
25. "In. Gen. Hom.," 1.1. See J. C. M. Van Winden, OFM, "In the Beginning: Early Christian Exegesis of the Term *archè* in Genesis 1:1, inaugural address, Leiden 1967," in *Arche: A Collection of Patristic Studies,* ed. J. Den Boeft and David T. Runia (Leiden: Brill, 1997), 89: "First there is Paul's statement that Christ is 'the first-born of all creation.' . . . Origen . . . was not the first to connect Christ with the creation."
26. "In. Gen. Hom.," 1.1, citing 1 Tim. 4.10, Col 1.15, and John 1.1-3.

reading of Genesis. His creation-Christology, however, has very practical benefits for the reader, especially readers of a particular community. Origen saw in Genesis 1 a political topography: Christ is the beginning of a new kingdom. In order to progress therein, one must learn to divide matter and spirit. Diligent citizens of heaven are "zealous . . . divider[s] of that water which is above and that which is below [the firmament]."[27] The heavenly citizen rigorously separates himself from anything (the waters of the abyss) that might keep him from his heavenly abode.[28] Note that Origen's dualism has a strong teleological orientation: it was meant to prompt the audience to fulfill their duties in the heavenly city.

So, too, his cosmological speculation was marked by these pastoral and political aims. The ones who walk in the light are those who are illuminated by Christ, "just as the day is illuminated by the sun."[29] Just as the sun, moon and stars are set in the sky to not only distinguish the night from the day but also to illuminate the earth, so too Christ, the Church, and the saints illuminate the mind and manner of life of man. The Church, learning the moral lessons contained in scripture ("the signs by [Christ's] precepts"), gives the light of Christ to the darkened world.[30] And "drawing near" to Christ illuminates one more.[31] Christ enables man to progress by discerning between good and evil thoughts as they arise in the heart. Progress is a matter of upward movement as humans allow their good thoughts to ascend like a bird into the firmament. The analogy is clear: humans rise by freeing themselves from the mundane, terrestrial world, thereby rising to the divine.

---

27. "In. Gen. Hom.," 1.2.
28. See "In. Gen. Hom.," 1.2. Furthermore, as the dry land brings forth fruit bearing plants and trees, anyone who does not bear fruit, "becomes 'fuel for fire.'"
29. "In. Gen. Hom.," 1.2.
30. See "In. Gen. Hom.," 1.5: "*Christus illuminans ecclesiam suam signa dat per praecepta sua.*"
31. "In. Gen. Hom.," 1.6.

This is, however, no mere spirit/matter dualism, but continues to serve Origen's theo-political purposes. The declaration that creatures of the water and air are good, in Gen. 1:21-23, presents a problem for Origen's typology, that sea creatures represent evil thoughts while birds represent good thoughts.[32] The homily attempts to avoid this problem by explaining that glory is only won through struggle, that by overcoming the adversity of these evil thoughts the saints win merit in heaven. This is the goodness that God sees; there is a utility even in the struggle with evil thoughts: "Those things which are opposed to the saints are good for them because they can overcome them and when they have overcome them they become more glorious with God."[33] This is the same struggle to which Paul refers in his advice to put to death fleshly desires.[34] These affections are symbolized by the terrestrial beasts, which are "clearly said to be have been created by God. . . . But it is not unprofitable to relate these words to those which we explained above in a spiritual sense."[35] That is, these beasts signify "the impulses of our outer man . . . our carnal and earthly man."[36]

Thus, Origen imbued his spiritual anthropology with significant moral value. For Origen, the essence of humanity is in the spiritual experience, the inner man. Success, ascension, liberation, life: these are all spiritual states. For instance, humans have dominion to the extent that they overcome and avoid spiritual pitfalls. Humans rule by distinguishing that which is from God and that which is from the world.[37] And human rule and distinction are made possible by

---

32. "In. Gen. Hom.," 1.8: How can "the great whales and creeping creatures [be] interpreted as evil and the birds as good when scripture said about all together, 'And God saw that they were good'?"
33. "In. Gen. Hom.," 1.10.
34. Col. 3:5.
35. "In. Gen. Hom.," 1.10.
36. "In. Gen. Hom.," 1.11.
37. See Ibid.

the image of God in man, which is also a matter of spirit not flesh.[38] Origen knew this, of course, because God is not corporeal.[39] However, the spiritual image is made in the likeness of Christ.[40] Taking on the image of man, Christ makes it possible for humans to progress by participating in the spiritual image of God. This participation constitutes a distinctly Christian, spiritual way of life.[41] Origen's singular interest, in this homily, was this spiritual life. He employed tropological and allegorical interpretation in order to move his audience above material realities into a process of "slow transformation through discipline and instruction . . . on [the] journey toward God."[42] The journey through the symbols provided by the material world is one of spiritual achievement by the inner man toward the end of the Kingdom of Heaven, wherein the Son makes "his dwelling with us in the Holy Spirit."[43]

Basil the Great and the Ascetical Politics of Creation

Basil of Caesarea was arguably one of the greatest heirs to Origen's legacy, especially in Origen's ascetic interpretation of the world. His *Homilies in Hexaemeron* (ca. 378 C.E.) show significant reliance on Origen's homily on Genesis 1, as well as Philo's *De opificio*. For our purposes, this reliance is most apparent in Basil's emphasis on transformation through the contemplation of the creation event. Basil saw an anagogical order inherent to the cosmos, a movement toward the ancient homeland in the structure of creation itself.[44]

---

38. See "In. Gen. Hom.," 1.13.
39. See Ibid.
40. See Ibid. Christ, "our Savior who is 'the first born of every creature.'"
41. See J. Rebecca Lyman, *Christology and Cosmology: Models of Divine Activity in Origen, Eusebius, and Anthanasius* (Oxford: Clarendon Press, 1993), 80.
42. Van Winden, "In the Beginning: Some Observations on the Patristic Interpretation of Genesis 1:1," 105.
43. "In. Gen. Hom.," 1.17.
44. See Basil, *Hexaemeron*, 6.1: "ἡ ἀρχαία πατρὶς ἡμῶν."

If Origen's theo-political reading of Genesis presented the world in largely negative terms in contrast to the spiritual homeland (the heavenly city), Basil's homilies on Genesis 1 were far more optimistic about heavenly citizenship even here in the material world.

The world for Basil was a school for souls, a classroom for an education in divine politics.[45] For Basil, it is the whole work of creation, the unfolding of the divine order, which makes the cosmos both beautiful and highly useful in the process and pedagogy of return.[46] Whereas for Origen's homily on Genesis, conformity with and return to the Word was accomplished by dividing oneself and one's spirit from the material world, Basil's *Hexaemeron* trains the reader in conformity with and return to the Word by going deeper into and through the world.

Creation is instructive, therefore, in a positive and generous sense; the world is a divine schoolhouse in which humanity learns to recover an ancient beauty.[47] Reading the world pedagogically, therefore, requires an ascetic training, for humans need to learn how to contemplate. But obstacles to contemplation originate first and foremost in the self. By contrast, the created world is a vestige of its creator; contemplation of that vestige leads to wonder and praise.

---

45. On Basil's relationship to Philo, see "'Where, Tell Me, is the Jew . . . ?' Basil, Philo, and Isidore of Pelusium," *Vigilae Christianae* 46 (1992): 172; Runia believes that Basil's in the earliest Christian commentary on the hexaemeron to survive, and that Philo's *Opif.* is a major source for the text. See also Richard Lim, "The Politics of Interpretation in Basil of Caesarea's 'Hexaemeron,'" *Vigiliae Christianae* 44 (1990): 351-70.
46. See Basil, *Hexaemeron*, 1.7. See Frances M. Young, "Creation and Human Being: The Forging of a Distinct Christian Discourse," in *Studia Patristica XLIV*, ed. J. Baum et al. (Lueven: Peeters, 2010), 344: "[T]he really striking thing about the *Hexaemeron* is its general tone of sheer wonder at creation, its affirmation that nothing is superfluous or wrong or out of place, everything contributes to the rich tapestry of the created order and its beauty."
47. On Origen's influence on Basil, see Charlotte Köckert, *Christliche Kosmologie under kaiserzeitliche Philosophie. Die Auslegung des Schöpfungsberichtes bei Origenes, Basilius und Gregor von Nyssa vor dem Hintergrund kaiserzeitlicher Timaeus-Interpretationen*, Studien und Texte zu Antike und Christentum (Tübingen: Mohr Siebeck, 2009).

Thus, developing a contemplative gaze, and then contemplating creation, entails a simultaneous education in the self.

Basil held that self-knowledge entails a liturgical response to the creator, namely, praise. Note the use of the first person plural pronoun in the following: "If we are penetrated by these truths, we shall know ourselves, we shall know God, we shall adore our Creator, we shall serve our Master, we shall glorify our Father. . . ."[48] Key moments in his homilies, like the preceding, show that Basil counted on communal, daily contemplation of creation in order to actualize the harmony between the cosmos and humanity that would facilitate the return to God.[49] Returning to God is far from a solipsistic affair. Rather, the Son draws people to himself and the *patria* through the Church.

Although the *Hexaemeron* begins with the order of the cosmos that originates in God, it quickly moves to a consideration of the role that scripture plays after the Fall in purifying the soul for contemplation.[50] Moses exemplifies this purified soul.[51] Basil commended not only attending to Moses' life, but also his inspired teaching (the Torah) as the beginning of purifying ourselves. Here, Basil had in mind something like theology as inquiring after God through scripture, and this inquiry is part of ascetic purification: "Moses has anticipated enquiry by engraving in our hearts, as a seal and a safeguard, the awful name of God. . . ."[52] God is the source of existence as well as the foundation of right knowledge and action: "It is He, beneficent Nature, Goodness without measure . . . [who is] the origin of all that exists, the source of life, intellectual light. . . ." The only adequate

---

48. Basil, *Hexaemeron*, 4.6.
49. As in when Basil described conformity or contrast of human behavior to characteristics of lesser parts of creation (e.g. *Hexaemeron* 7.4, 7.6; 8.5, 8.8).
50. See *Hexaemeron*, 6.1.
51. See *Hexaemeron*, 1.1.
52. *Hexaemeron*, 1.1.

response to the source of all is adoration, for God is "a worthy object of love for beings endowed with reason, the beauty the most to be desired."[53]

But love and praise are not only reasonable responses. They are constitutive of the development and growth into the harmony with ourselves, others, and God. As Basil introduced the communal worship and life of the Church, he employed the words of Genesis to do so. The unity of creation and ecclesia in Basil's homily signaled the importance of creation for the contemplation of God. It is necessary to see creation as a sign of God. An extended engagement with God's creative activity, Basil argued, should to shape the reader's habits of action and contemplation.[54]

Creation entails not a simultaneous event, but rather a gradual communication and unfolding of divine order. Basil's reflections on creation extended beyond the primordial creation itself to the activity of the Holy Spirit in the Church. Divine order, he argued, is not exhausted by the finite creation, but continues to unfold in the world, especially through the Church. Thus, Genesis gives the careful reader tools by which she can connect creation and salvation, the world and the Church in a seamless tapestry.[55] Advancing beyond the tropological reading of the hexaemeron advanced by his predecessors, Basil's *Hexaemeron* argues that the cosmology of Genesis is both analeptic and proleptic. It calls us forward as it simultaneously calls us back. It is Προαναφώνησις[56] As Genesis narrates something that is so archaic and, indeed, esoteric, it also communicates an essential, soteriological, and anagogical truth. It pinpoints and describes the

---

53. *Hexaemeron*, 1.2.
54. See *Hexaemeron*, 1.2.
55. Philip Rousseau, *Basil of Caesarea*, Transformation of the Classical Heritage (Berkeley: University of California Press, 1998), 321: "The work was . . . a study of salvation—the salvation of the individual, but also of the whole human community."
56. In *Hexaemeron* 1.3, Basil used the term Προαναφώνησις to describe the dual aspect of Genesis: it looks back (*ana-*) while simultaneously looking forward (*pro-*).

origin in order to foretell the goal. But of course, for Basil, the origin is the goal. However, this origin has been revealed and transformed by Christ.

Just as the transformation of the cosmos is a progressive, unfinished work, so too, the Church is a work in progress. More precisely, the Church is the sign of the transformation of the cosmos. And for those in the Church, the biggest obstacle to progress is the self. Or more precisely, it is the self that refuses to accept personal responsibility for evil that obstructs unity with others and God. Basil stressed, "You are the master of your actions. Do not look for the guiding cause beyond yourself, but recognize that evil, rightly so called, has no other origin than our deliberate choices. . . ."[57] However, the "most difficult science is to know one's self."[58] The reader must turn to divine revelation to break through the barriers to self-knowledge. Holy teaching reveals the true origin of human life, which is God: "It is then to his living image, to Him who has said 'I and my Father are one,' 'He that hath seen me hath seen the Father,' that God says 'Let us make man in our image.'"[59]

Through this turn to revelation, Basil taught that any proper anthropology and cosmology has God in Christ as its source and object. And the same would be true for politics if the politics of the Church were defined first and foremost as communal worship. Basil stressed that right cosmology leads to doxology: communal reflection, repentance, and adoration. Scripture forms its reader by directing her to true praise.[60] By walking the reader through the structured ascent of the days of Genesis 1, the reader mimics through *ascesis* the progressive structure of creation in her own life. Indeed,

---

57. *Hexaemeron*, 2.5.
58. *Hexaemeron*, 9.6.
59. Ibid.
60. *Hexaemeron*, 9.6. For Basil, true worship of the creator demands the Church. See Rousseau, *Basil*, 329-31.

just as God finishes creation through a series of structured steps, so too humanity becomes complete through rigorous education and training in scripture and praise.[61] Education, praise, and transformation are, therefore, Basil's primary tropes for cosmology. Membership in the new community of the Church made the assimilation of the divine order possible. In and with this community one learned to return to the ancient fatherland.

Ambrose of Milan and the Christological Politics of the Created Body

In the decade after Basil delivered his hexaemeral sermons, Ambrose wrote his own commentary on Genesis 1.[62] It is not uncommon to dismiss the originality and power of Ambrose's *Exameron*, especially when compared to Basil's *Hexaemeron*. The shared traits between the two series are unmistakable. The two works' cultural proximity and structural similarity are, as Quasten surmises, the likely reasons behind many modern scholars' failure to recognize the "originality" of Ambrose's text.[63]

However, Ambrose's mastery of Roman sources (Virgil, Cicero, and Lucretius), his use of poetic verse,[64] and his synthesis of the natural and socials sciences in service of scriptural commentary mark the *Exameron* as a work deserving its own analysis. Combining sociological and natural observation, and steeped in a tradition of commentary and preaching, Ambrose gave his audience and readers a

---

61. See Rousseau, *Basil*, 319.
62. *Exameron*, in CSEL 32.1 (Vienna: F. Tempsky, 1897), 3-261. All references to Ambrose's *Exameron* according to day and chapter.
63. Johannes Quasten, *Patrology*, trans. Placid Solari (Westminster, MD: Christian Classics, 1986), IV:153; Boniface Ramsey, *Ambrose*, The Early Church Fathers (London: Routledge, 1997), 56.
64. See Savage's Introduction in *Saint Ambrose: Creation, Paradise, and Cain and Abel*, trans. John Savage, Fathers of the Church (New York: Fathers of the Church Inc., 1961), viii-ix. Ambrose's theological aims, including his interventions in the Arian controversies in Milan, should also be considered when assessing the *Exameron's* value. See, Quasten, *Patrology*, IV:154.

sophisticated and meaty treatment of Genesis 1.[65] The sophistication and complexity of Ambrose's homilies on Genesis 1 reside in the Incarnational insights that he teases out of the days of creation.

One aspect of Ambrose's interpretation of Genesis 1 deserves special attention, given the political and moral nature of our investigation. The sermons on creation culminate not in the creation of humanity, but in the Sabbath, God's rest. Ambrose highlighted the fact that the Sabbath happens immediately after the creation of humanity. This coincidence of stages in creation is seen as a proleptic sign of the redemptive work of the Incarnation. Indeed, for Ambrose, God's rest on the seventh day prefigures the incarnate Christ's paschal rest.

For Ambrose, the beginning of creation is not day 1, but God. The word 'beginning' (*principium*) is polyvalent, for it can reasonably signify time, number, foundation, conversion, art, intention, and power.[66] But theologically, beginning and end are united, the alpha and omega. As Origen had already insisted, the divine beginning is Christ. Ambrose was, however, more incarnational than Origen; the *Exameron* invokes not merely the eternal Word, but, more precisely, the Word made flesh. Paradoxically, "the Lord is holy above all creatures for the very reason that He assumed a body."[67] Ambrose explicitly united the activities of creation and salvation by showing that Christ's salvific, incarnate mission is not merely a demonstration of his holiness; his mission is the source of his holiness.

This is not to say that God's holiness is absent before the incarnation. Rather, Ambrose located the *ratio* of the incarnation already in the creation account. Specifically, that holiness is on display already in humanity insofar as humanity reflects the incarnation,

---

65. See Ramsey, *Ambrose*, 20-28.
66. *Exameron*, I.4.
67. Ibid.

albeit proleptically. Made last of all creatures, humanity gathers together and recapitulates the creation in the combination of body and intelligence. The human is also the image of God. Ambrose saw a triune source of this image. For, who else is the Lord addressing other than the members of the trinity? Like Basil, Ambrose affirmed the creative cooperation of Father and Son, citing John 10:30: "I and the Father are one."[68] Moreover, Basil and Ambrose both placed a premium on the Trinitarian origin of the image; having seen the Son, man has seen the Father. Indwelt by the Spirit and having seen the Son, man has likewise seen the source of the image. Ambrose argued that this image is the self that humans are to know and keep: "Attend to thyself alone . . . to your soul and mind, whence all our deliberations emanate and to which the profit of your works is referred. Here only is the fullness of wisdom, the plenitude of piety and justice of which God speaks—for all the virtues come from God . . . that soul of yours is painted by God, who holds in Himself the flashing beauty of virtue and the splendor of piety."[69]

While it was a common trope in hexaemeral literature to proscribe self-knowledge through the contemplation of creation, the *Exameron* added a Solomonic and pastoral note: "Keep thyself."[70] Education in the self is not simply a matter of didactic knowledge, but rather an imperative to steward and care for the gift given in creation. For Ambrose, the goal of expositing Genesis 1 is found in both knowing and caring for the image of God.

Knowing and caring for the image as found in humanity require, however, not more ascetic discipline, but the grace of God, without which *ascesis* is impossible. Ambrose sharpened the christological focus by wedding the process of formation and education to a

68. *Exameron*, 6.7.
69. Ibid.
70. *Exameron*, 6.6.

christological impulse at the heart of creation itself. Yes, "thyself" refers to the soul, which is the image of God in humanity. But, he adds, "The soul . . . is made to the image of God, *in form like the Lord Jesus.*"[71] Formation and care of the soul are christological mandates, for care of the soul is fundamentally a matter of being conformed to Christ. Hence, Christology is the axis upon which turn anthropology and creation. And, in terms of caring for the soul, Christology grounds the moral formation of Christians.

As the part of the human being that can reflect God, the soul is that which requires transformation "into his very image from glory to glory."[72] Man has lost that splendor and radiance, that "celestial image," of his soul, exchanging it for a "terrestrial one." But the image is not totally lost, nor is humanity left adrift. Rather, the unfallen image already prefigures Christ in three ways: the use of the body to worship Christ; the incarnation of the Son in human form; and God's sabbath rest which anticipates the Christ's rest in the tomb.

Ambrose observed that God rests only after he imparting his image:[73] "He found rest after he had made man in his own image. . . . He found repose in the deep recesses of man, in man's mind and purpose, for He had made man with the power of reasoning, an imitator of himself, a striver after virtue, and one eager for heavenly grace."[74] God's repose is not a matter of delight in his creature. Rather, his repose is in his Son, and, moreover, a prolepsis of the rest of Christ in the tomb: "It may well be that He had given a symbolic picture . . . of the future Passion of the Lord, thus revealing that in man one day Christ would find repose. He anticipated for Himself repose in the body for the redemption of mankind, as He declares

---

71. *Exameron*, 6.8.
72. Ibid.
73. See *Exameron*, 6.8 & 6.10.
74. *Exameron*, 6.10.

in His own words. . . ."[75] Christ's mission, as we saw above, is the definitive image of his holiness. Thus, we see a "symbol" of that holiness already in the creation account.

The human person, therefore, is made in anticipation of and for the purpose of honoring the Son. Alluding to Philippians 2, Ambrose interpreted the human body christologically: "The knee is the gift of the most high Father to His Son: 'that in the name of the Lord every knee. . . .'"[76] Kneeling is an interesting action for Ambrose to note here; kneeling is not a solitary, abstract act. Rather, it locates the person kneeling. It signifies and reinforces a particular relationship with the one to whom reverence is shown. And it publically demonstrates that reverence. Ambrose here referred to Philippians 2 to evoke the political significance of kneeling. He may have also thought of Daniel 3, at least as a negative example of the political significance of the gesture.

The human knee not only praises the Son; it prefigures the worship of the Son in its creation. God loves "humility and faith. The leg expresses the emotion of humility" while the mind ascends to the faith of the coequality of the Father and the Son.[77] The Father instills this in creation, anticipating the incarnation of the Son. Reflection on this, even in the action and life of the soul's body, the soul is educated in this humility. This ascetical and political education is bolstered by contemplation of Christ's exemplary bodily and spiritual obedience, all of which is prefigured and contained in the Sabbath rest.

Contemplation of creation and worship of Christ, therefore, are fundamentally formative practices. They conform the person to Christ, in whose image the person is already made. Thus, Ambrose did not distinguish between Christ the Logos, who is the exemplar of

---

75. Ibid.
76. *Exameron*, 6.9.
77. Ibid.

humanity in creation, and the Incarnate Christ who is the exemplar and source of our salvation. Rather, Ambrose saw in the very creation of Adam the seeds of salvation, such that when the Father looks upon the divine image in the first man he sees the worship, image, *and rest* of the perfect man, his Son.

Going one step further, Ambrose argued that creation and, more precisely, humanity could only be understood properly in light of God's saving activity in the Son's exemplarity, life, death, and resurrection. The *Exameron's* emphasis on the incarnational source, form, and end of creation demonstrates a uniquely Ambrosian contribution to the tradition of contemplation on creation. The work of the six days culminates to the last day, the seventh day, on which humanity is shown to be the epitome of creation. However, the significance of humanity rests squarely on the incarnational holiness that humanity symbolizes. We participate in that holiness only insofar as we employ our members for worship of the Son.

Here is where Ambrose's incarnational insight shows its full moral and political value. Creation, for Ambrose, instructs the reader not only in right understanding of the process by which God brings his creation to perfection but also rest through instruments prefigured even in the creation before the fall. Proper response to this realization is the worship of Christ. To that end, Ambrose saw in Genesis 1 that creation instructs the reader in a distinctly christological way of action and being. If the Incarnate Christ is also the creator God, then how much more should we look to find the signs of our salvation already at work in contemplating the creation? And in turn, how much more should we look to creation to ground our action, our worship?

Ambrose, like Philo, Origen, and Basil before him, thought that creation was a fecund ground for working out his salvation. As he looked at creation, he saw that the human body is illuminated by the divine radiance shining through, "the splendor of grace and the reflection of its paternal nature . . . its brilliance is in accord with that divine reflection."[78] But that reflection is marred. In spite of humanity's self-disfigurement, scripture reveals that God responds by planting the seeds of salvation already in creation. A humble and truly human response to this God is the bent knee. But as we have seen, worship is not merely an ecclesial action for Ambrose. Rather, it is the foundation of right human action. Ambrose saw Christ as the source of human existence as well as the exemplar of a new way of life, a way of life that drew humans together toward their fulfillment and perfection. And, as we have seen above, worship as a way of life is neither solipsistic nor therapeutic, but the beginning of a new politics, a kneeling politics, the politics of Kingdom.

Conclusion

Despite their differing emphases, for both Ambrose and Basil, as well as Origen and Philo, the creation story was above all an opportunity and invitation to contemplate and to worship. Creation calls upon the rational creature to see the Creator in the effects of his creation. And this contemplation leads, in an almost formulaic fashion, to certain patterns of living that are consonant with the order that God instills in his good earth. For Philo, this order was almost mathematical, whereas for Origen, the physical order of the world was full of obstacles to mystagogical ascent.

Building on the gains of Philo and Origen, Basil and Ambrose maintained this contemplative, ascetic tradition. They both deepened the christological reflection imparted by Origen. For Basil, Genesis 1 is analeptic and anagogical. It is a story about the unfolding of God's order in the world, an order to which we progressively learn

---

78. *Exameron*, 6.7.

to conform, an order that God calls beautiful and to which we are called to return. For Ambrose, it is a proleptic allegory, a story about God's providential and archetypal patterns laid in the foundation creation. Redemption and perfection are prefigured even before the fall. Creation is the backdrop, the setting in Christ's portrait, which is a portrait of the perfect man in whom God rests, a man who himself is the image of God restored to creation.

While the cosmology of a reader today will almost certainly be radically different, the need for ascetic discipline and formation remains. Ambrose's call to know and care for oneself as the image of God eclipses worldly politics. It places a claim on the reader to come to terms with not only one's origin as a creature, but also with the form and *telos* of one's life. And if we agree with Basil and Ambrose, that the key to the good life rests in Christ, then Christ's presence today in his ecclesial body politic will necessarily play a part in our contemplation of creation, and vice versa. For caring for oneself, as a Christian, is never a solipsistic enterprise. Rather, it automatically opens to the neighbor, the one to whom in Christ, as source and savior, we are being drawn ever nearer.

6

The Apocalyptic Figure of Francis's Stigmatized Body

The Politics of Scripture in Bonaventure's Meditative Treatises

Travis E. Ables

In keeping with the broader purposes of this book, which link the theological interpretation of Scripture to the political constitution of the communities of its interpretation, I want to examine an episode in the historical reception of Francis of Assisi. The polemical dispute over the figure of Francis in the latter part of the thirteenth century highlights dynamics of the accessibility of scripture, participation in Christ, and clerical-lay tensions that shoot throughout late medieval theology. Luther was not the first to raise questions about lay interpretation of scripture. In what follows, I hope to show that the political implications of lay access to scripturally informed *imitatio*

READING SCRIPTURE AS A POLITICAL ACT

christi were central to the authorship of Bonaventure, the thirteenth-century mystic, theologian, and minister general of the Franciscan Order from 1257 to 1274, who inherited the leadership of the order at a time when fierce debate was erupting over the rule of life mandated by Francis. Central to this debate were concerns about lay participation in the order, the interpretation of scripture, and the wider political implications of Francis's apocalyptic role in salvation history. In this chapter, I show how Bonaventure understood Francis as an apocalyptic figure whose life was ordered around the imaginative reinhabitation of scripture through contemporaneity with Christ, and that this apocalyptic reopening of scripture created a new politic for the body of Christ.

Bonaventure is so often described as a master of theological synthesis that the political context of his authorship tends to be overlooked.[1] His great mystical treatises, including the renowned *The Journey of the Soul into God* (*Itinerarium Mentis in Deum*), were written in the late 1250s and early 1260s, around or shortly after the time of his election as minister general of the Franciscan order. The treatises recontextualize for the needs of the wider order the theological themes of the academic works produced when he was *magister* in the Franciscan school at Paris, but they also reflect and speak to the state of the Franciscan order at a particularly tumultuous point in its early history. Bonaventure's central aim in these works is to consolidate a distinctively Franciscan hermeneutic of scripture, while at the same time delineating a political boundary against the nascent party of the radicals who would later become known as the Spirituals.[2]

---

1. A textbook example is Gilson's often-quoted statement about Bonaventure that "the totality of the system means so much that the mere notion of fragments has no meaning at all. You can either see the general economy of his doctrine in its totality, or see none of it." Cited in Kevin Hughes, "St. Bonaventure's Collationes in Hexaëmeron: Fractured Sermons and Protreptic Discourse," *Franciscan Studies* 63 (2005): 107 n. 2.

Everyone agreed that the ministry of Francis was of epochal importance. The question was how Francis and his order fit into the broader trajectory of salvation history. By the time of Bonaventure's accession, that debate had become centered in a scandal over the twelfth-century apocalyptic visions and biblical commentaries of Joachim of Fiore. Gerard of Borgo San Donnino had produced a book of Joachim's writings and a sensationalistic gloss, the Eternal Evangel (*Liber introductorius in evangelium eternum*), that interpreted Joachim's prophecies literally, announcing the imminent advent of the third age,[3] the supersession of the two Testaments and the Roman church, and the rise of the antichrist pope to persecute the mendicant orders.[4] A growing faction of Protospirituals, discontent with what they perceived as the increasing laxity of the Franciscans' stance on Francis's vow of poverty, used Gerard's scandalous treatise to galvanize "their own struggle to preserve the Rule and Testament of St. Francis in every syllable" as "part of a cosmic conflict."[5] John of Parma, Bonaventure's predecessor as minister general, had resigned in disgrace due to his associations with these radicals.[6]

2. This is the conventional terminology, although following David Burr, *The Spiritual Franciscans: From Protest to Persecution in the Century after Saint Francis* (University Park, PA: Pennsylvania State University Press, 2001), I will use the term *Protospiritual*, as Burr argues that radical reactions to the mainstream order were too nascent and inchoate prior to 1274 to be fully identified with the later Spiritual party.
3. For a short introduction to Joachim, see Bernard McGinn, ed., *Apocalyptic Spirituality: Treatises and Letters of Lactantius, Adso of Montier-en-Der, Joachim of Fiore, The Spiritual Franciscans, Savonarola* (New York: Paulist, 1979), 97–112; and E. Randolph Daniel, "Joachim of Fiore: Patterns of History in the Apocalypse," in *The Apocalypse in the Middle Ages*, ed. Richard K. Emmerson and Bernard McGinn (Ithaca, NY: Cornell University Press, 1992), 72–88. As Marjorie Reeves documents, Joachim had used the language of *status*, not *etas* or *tempus*. The third "age" for Joachim is a "new quality of life rather than a third set of institutions," a contemplative era of liberty and fraternity. See *Joachim of Fiore and the Prophetic Future* (New York: Harper Torchbooks, 1976), 6–7. Gerard, who had predicted the 1260 date for the apocalypse, literalized the *status*, and his insertion of the Franciscans as the *novi viri* prophesied by Joachim is the vector through which Joachim becomes the progenitor of the Spirituals.
4. On Gerard, see Reeves, *Joachim of Fiore*, 33; Burr, *The Spiritual Franciscans*, 38.
5. Reeves, *Joachim of Fiore*, 38.
6. Although Bonaventure may have shared a real degree of sympathy with Joachim himself.

Bonaventure was forced to deal with the Protospirituals' expectation that the apocalypse would take place in 1260, along with their demands for literal adherence to Francis's deathbed *Testament*.[7] At stake in the debate between Bonaventure and the Protospirituals was thus not only the significance of Francis for the order and the wider church, but the way scripture was to be read in the context of apocalyptic expectations regarding the role of Francis and his order.

So it is into this heated context that we must insert Bonaventure's meditative treatises, and understand their political resonances. It has been remarked, for example, that Bonaventure's *Life of St. Francis*, the *Legenda maior*, which has traditionally been denigrated by historians as a derivative work, should instead be interpreted as a polemical treatise with a high degree of originality;[8] a similar contextualization would also remove the meditative treatises from their old idealization as spiritual masterpieces and theological syntheses. While the meditative treatises are, arguably, in fact both of these things, such dehistoricization runs the risk of obscuring some of the more radical theological adaptations and transformations Bonaventure performs within them, which in turn renders their enduring theological relevance somewhat anodyne.

In *The Triple Way* (*De triplici via*), which was written some time

---

See Burr, *The Spiritual Franciscans*, 29–31. On Joachim's reception by the Franciscans in Bonaventure's time, see Marjorie Reeves, *The Influence of Prophecy in the Later Middle Ages* (New York: Oxford University Press, 1969), 175–81; Reeves particularly points to the convergences of Bonaventure's *Collationes in Hexaemeron* with Joachim's writings; ibid., 179–81. She calls Bonaventure a Joachite *malgré lui*.

7. The *Testament* was decreed nonbinding by Gregory IX in *Quo elongati* in 1230. On the reception of Francis's *Testament*, see André Vauchez, *Francis of Assisi: The Life and Afterlife of a Medieval Saint*, trans. Michael F. Cusato (New Haven: Yale University Press, 2009), 200–205.

8. Susan J. Hubert, "Theological and Polemical Uses of Hagiography: A Consideration of Bonaventure's *Legenda Major* of St. Francis," *Comitatus* 29, no. 1 (1998): 49–55. The traditional reading is represented by John R. H. Moorman, who states that the *Legenda maior* "supplies us with practically no new information"; *The Sources for the Life of S. Francis of Assisi* (Manchester: Manchester University Press, 1940), 142, cited in Hubert, "Theological and Polemical Uses," 53.

after Bonaventure's epiphany on La Verna,[9] the figure of the stigmatic Francis is offered in such a way as to relocate the apocalyptic expectations of the Protospirituals, while at the same time rhetorically organizing, cohering, and popularizing a series of theological adaptations Bonaventure had adumbrated in his lectures as *magister* in Paris. Important to this theological vision is the synthesis of Augustinian and Pseudo-Dionysian versions of Neoplatonist metaphysics, although unlike the similar synthesis effected by Aquinas, Bonaventure's highly specific and strategic set of theological adaptations are filtered through his reception and reinterpretation of the twelfth-century mystical traditions. This series of combinations, which have both epistemological and eschatological dimensions, is regulated by his attention to Francis's apocalyptic figure. Finally, I will conclude by taking a look at the wider political significance of the Franciscan hermeneutic, particularly among the para-Franciscan movements.

The Triple Way and the Franciscan Transformation of Mystical Theology

The overriding factor driving Bonaventure's midcentury writing is the need to provide a Franciscan hermeneutic that does justice to the tradition of affective (imaginative, emotive) devotion that characterized the order, while avoiding the excesses of Joachim and Gerard's apocalyptic typology. To this end, Bonaventure employs a strategic recontextualization of Dionysian apophatic theology in terms of the Augustinian-Gregorian tradition of the spiritual reading

---

9. The epiphany is recorded in the *Itinerarium*, prologue 2–3; Bonaventure comes to understand Francis's vision of the crucified seraph as signifying "the uplifting of our father himself in contemplation but also the road by which one might arrive at this experience" in "six levels of uplifting illuminations." Translation from *Works of St. Bonaventure*, vol. 2, *Itinerarium Mentis in Deum*, ed. Philotheus Boehner, OFM, and Zachary Hayes, OFM, rev. ed. (St. Bonaventure, NY: Franciscan Institute, 2002).

of scripture. There are several texts we could look at here, but I will choose an often-overlooked treatise, *The Triple Way*. It is chronologically sandwiched between the magisterial *The Journey of the Soul into God* and the influential piece of imaginative meditation, *The Tree of Life* (*Lignum vitae*); but as much as the justly famed *Journey*, it betrays Bonaventure's creative reappropriation of his sources and his application of them to novel ends.

The Triple Way is an examination of the threefold mystical hierarchy of purgation, illumination, and perfective union, taken from Dionysius's *Celestial Hierarchy*, and how that hierarchy is present in the three "ways" of meditation, prayer, and contemplation (*meditatio, oratio, contemplatio*).[10] Unlike the *Journey*, though, the text is not a neat progressive contemplative ascent following the Neoplatonic pattern of "outward, inward, and upward."[11] Instead, the three parallel practices of meditation, prayer, and contemplation are each internally structured according to the purgation-illumination-union progression. I will take each "way" or *via* in turn.

The way of meditation, *via meditatio*, in the first chapter sets out the program for the treatise. It summarizes the logic of the spiritual interpretation of scripture. The synthesis is readily evident: Bonaventure correlates the purgation, illumination, and union of meditation with the traditional three senses of scripture, moral,

---

10. Bonaventure takes pains to explicate his Dionysian-Augustinian hybridization in an appendix. For the treatise, I will use the translation of F. Edward Coughlin in *The Works of St. Bonaventure*, vol. 10, *Writings on the Spiritual Life* (St. Bonaventure, NY: Franciscan Institute, 2006), 81–133. The appendix is found at 3:11–14.
11. This idea derives originally from Plotinus, and is expressed most memorably by Augustine's phrase *ab exterioribus ad interiora, ab inferioribus ad superiora* ("From exterior to interior, from lower things to higher," as translated in *Expositions of the Psalms 121–150*, trans. Maria Boulding, OSB [Hyde Park, NY: New City, 2004], 145.5, p. 404). The essential idea is that the ascent to God progresses from sensory apprehension of external, material things, to the intellect that perceives them, to the divine ideas in which the intellect participates and thus to the momentary, fleeting vision of the divine essence itself. See *Confessions* 7.17.23 for a classic description of the Augustinian Neoplatonic ascent.

allegorical, and anagogical (or mystical). He does not discuss the content of scripture as such, and does not offer the intense imagery of the passion of Christ found in the *Tree of Life*; instead, the chapter should be read as an outline of the "grammar" of the spiritual senses of scripture in terms of the monastic practice of the meditation on the Bible, or *lectio divina*, as it is commonly known. The first Dionysian stage, purgation (*De triplici via* 1:3–9), corresponds to the moral sense, which Bonaventure describes in the traditional tones of Gregorian compunction that dwells on the remembrance of sin in preparation for the elevation of the soul. The discussion of illumination (1:10–14) then outlines an allegorical grammar for reading scripture by focusing on the doctrinal themes of the Bible, rendered clear to a suitably purified intellect. Finally, once the intellect is illuminated for the reading of scripture, the flame of wisdom in perfective union (1:15–17) turns toward the anagogical sense that elevates the heart to mystical vision. In a classically Neoplatonic pattern, instantly recognizable from the *Journey*, the reader turns their heart away from the love of creatures, toward the divine Spouse, and raises it aloft in an apophatic movement of unknowing: union with the spouse is an elevation into the ineffable Beloved.

In this brief overview of the first chapter on *meditatio*, we can detect the distinctively Augustinian flesh Bonaventure puts on Dionysian bones when we tease out the way apophatic negation is achieved in *meditatio*—it is through affection, the loving faculty of the will: "Through love the soul is in the presence of [the Spouse] who is most highly desirable."[12] This is new, because in Dionysius, the movement from illumination to union is through the intellect, and takes place in the "mysterious darkness of unknowing."[13] However,

---

12. 1:16, translation slightly modified.
13. Pseudo-Dionysius, *The Mystical Theology*, in *The Complete Works*, trans. Colm Luibheid and Paul Rorem (New York: Paulist, 1987), 1.3 (1001A). Unlike the angelic beings, who know the

as Paul Rorem has documented, Bonaventure's interpretive tradition reads Dionysius's "unknowing" through the love mysticism of Hugh of St. Victor, who, roughly a century before Bonaventure, explained Dionysius's supraintellectual movement into divine darkness as occurring through a love that goes beyond intellect: "Love surpasses knowledge, and is greater than intelligence."[14] Thus, Hugh takes up the Gregorian idea that "love itself is a kind of knowledge" (*amor ipse intellectus est*)[15] for interpreting Dionysius, and in turn Hugh's reading is employed by Bonaventure to correlate Dionysian negation with affection throughout *The Triple Way*.

In unpacking this affective twist on negative theology, Bonaventure's mystical reading strategy creatively combines a series of tropes current in the twelfth through the thirteenth centuries. He imports Victorine bridal mysticism to articulate the volitional, affective union with God characteristic of the Franciscan movement, but in so doing, transforms the former. First, he uses imagery of passionate eroticism, drawn from a series of allusions to the Song of Songs, to dramatize the theme of loving desire. Indeed, at times, *The Triple Way* seems to be a series of glosses on the Canticles.[16] An

---

One through unmediated participation in the One's self-knowledge, discursive human beings experience union with God only in unknowing. Dionysius describes one of these angelic beings, the seraphim, as "penetrating warmth, the overflowing heat of a movement which never falters and never fails," a flame that illuminates and purifies the intellect but is by nature unapproachable. See the *Celestial Hierarchy*, in Luibheid and Rorem, *The Complete Works*, 7.1 (205B–C); 15.2 (329A–B).

14. Key is the cosmological function of the cherubin and seraphim, who "surround by desire what they do not penetrate by intellect," and whose love must "go through as far as the bridal chamber." See Rorem, "The Early Latin Dionysius: Eriugena and Hugh of St. Victor," in *Modern Theology* 24, no. 4 (Oct. 2008): 610. The translations are Rorem's.

15. See especially Bernard McGinn, "Love, Knowledge, and *Union Mystica* in the Western Christian Tradition," in *Mystical Union in Judaism, Christianity, and Islam: An Ecumenical Dialogue*, ed. Moshe Idel and Bernard McGinn (New York: Continuum, 1996), 59–86.

16. For the extensive tradition of monastic and mystical commentary on the Canticles, see esp. Denys Turner, *Eros and Allegory: Medieval Exegesis of the Song of Songs* (Kalamazoo, MI: Cistercian Publications, 1995); E. Ann Matter, *The Voice of My Beloved: The Song of Songs in Western Mediaeval Christianity* (Philadelphia: University of Pennsylvania Press, 1990).

illustration of this transformation occurs in the chapter on prayer, the *via oratio*, which is also the briefest. In the final stage of the progression of the chapter, corresponding to perfective union, the heart "must rise up to a pleasing sense of harmony and mutual conversation as between the Spouse and the bride, as we are taught by the Holy Spirit in the Song of Songs" (2.4). But Bonaventure then combines this bridal mysticism with devotion to the cross: as one's delight in God is reformed and made communicable with others, "the world is crucified to you . . . *you* [are crucified] to the world . . . [you are] crucified *for* the world, such that you wish to die for all so that all might please God. This, then, is the stage and level of the perfection of charity" (2.8).[17] The pleasures of the bridal chamber are enacted through identification with the cross.

Identification with the executed Christ is a distinctively (though not completely unique) Franciscan theme, inspired by Francis's reception of the wounds of stigmata, and it is at this point that the figure of Francis becomes important as a hermeneutical norm for Bonaventure. As Zachary Hayes notes, one key difference between *The Triple Way* and the contemporaneous *Journey* is the absence of the person of Francis from the former.[18] But the echo of Francis *is* present in the rather sudden, and otherwise inexplicable, introduction of a brief discussion of martyrdom in *The Triple Way's* chapter on contemplation, which turns out to be a thematic crux (3:2).[19] The seventh and final step of purgation, "repose," cannot be attained, states Bonaventure, "unless martyrdom is desired." This idea of a

---

17. [Emphasis added].
18. *The Hidden Center: Spirituality and Speculative Christology in St. Bonaventure* (St. Bonaventure, NY: The Franciscan Institute, 2000), 46.
19. At first, the discussion of martyrdom seems like an odd move, given that "the wish for martyrdom is absurd in time of peace," as one of Bonaventure's great modern commentators scoffs (J. Guy Bougerol, *Introduction to the Works of Bonaventure*, trans. José de Vinck [Paterson, NJ: St. Anthony Guild, 1964], 158). But of course Bonaventure is talking about extreme self-denial.

death that identifies with Christ, cocrucifixion, sets the stage for the last chapter, and is key to setting out the distinctive Franciscan reading of scripture.

The *Triple Way*'s final chapter follows the pattern we have already seen, correlating the purgation-illumination-union progression with volitional union, explicitly couched in terms of affection through nuptial and crucifixion imagery (3.7). The illuminative way that leads to union focuses on the incarnation in terms of the suffering of Christ: the reader is to "cling to the Son with affectionate compassion and suffer along with the Son of God who is totally innocent, meek, noble, and lovable" (3.3). What follows reads like a précis of the *Tree of Life*, the graphic treatise on the incarnation and passion, as Bonaventure's prose vividly focuses on the paradox of the "origin of all things, the Savior of all humankind" who is tortured and suffers for human redemption. This contemplation of the passion is instrumental to enacting the affective union we have already seen: contemplation begins with intellect, which in this case is the assent of reason with the dogma of the incarnation and hypostatic union, an assent that opens up into the operation of the will in affection. Reason leads to the movement of compassion for the suffering Christ, to admiration, and so on to the desire to "embrace the cross" ourselves "with a desire for suffering."

To fully understand why Bonaventure discusses martyrdom, we need to cast an eye toward the *Life of St. Francis*, Bonaventure's commissioned biography of Francis. This will help us understand the way Francis, whose life is a performance of cocrucifixion, functions as an apocalyptic key to the reading of scripture. The *Life* is structured around six visions of the cross that occur in key moments of Francis's life, culminating with his reception of the stigmata.[20] The ninth

---

20. *The Life of St. Francis*, 13.10, in Cousins, *Bonaventure*.

chapter concerns Francis's desire for martyrdom, which Bonaventure ties to the same themes of affective union, bridal mysticism, and crucifying identification we have just seen: "Jesus Christ crucified always rested like a bundle of myrrh in the bosom of Francis's soul, and he longed to be totally transformed into him by the fire of ecstatic love."[21] This burning love makes Francis long to "emulate the glorious triumph of the holy martyrs in whom the flame of love could not be extinguished nor courage be weakened."[22] Francis even went to Egypt to try to realize this desire, but the Sultan Malik-al Kamil did not oblige;[23] Francis's martyrdom with Christ on the cross would come, rather, in the form of the stigmata.

The famous vision of the crucified seraphim on La Verna in the *Life* (13.3), as reported by Bonaventure, represents the culmination of Francis's perfecting union with Christ, a union accomplished through the "Seraphic ardor of his desires," which enables Francis to so identify with Jesus through compassion that he is transformed into the likeness of Christ "not by the martyrdom of his flesh, but by the fire of his love consuming his soul."[24] It is not accidental that the phrase for "consuming his soul," *incendium mentis*, is the subtitle of *The Triple Way*: the conflagration of the soul by the ardor of charity stems from compassionate identification with the crucified Christ and culminates in perfecting union with him. Thus we see a thematic correspondence between *The Triple Way* and the *Life* that places the *imitatio christi* in a key place that organizes Dionysian, Augustinian, and Victorine mystical traditions through the unifying figure of Francis (thus, we are perhaps talking about an *imitatio francisci*), all

---

21. Ibid., 9.2.
22. Ibid., 9.5.
23. On the rather mixed results of his visit to Egypt in 1219, see Augustine Thompson, *Francis of Assisi: A New Biography* (Ithaca, NY: Cornell University Press, 2012), 66–71.
24. *Life of St. Francis*, 13.3.

in the service of crafting a meditative reading of scripture (*meditatio*) enacted through prayer (*oratio*) and contemplation (*contemplatio*).²⁵

Like Francis, the reader of Bonaventure's meditative treatises is called to enact—to perform—the life of Christ read in the Gospels through sympathetic, compassionate identification. Like Francis, the reader is to embody martyrdom through their burning desire for union with the crucified one. And as we will now see, like Francis, the reader thereby inhabits the apocalyptic inbreaking of God's work in rebuilding the church.²⁶ But that is ultimately a political question, and in the following section, I will return to the polemical undercurrent of Bonaventure's work to highlight the political and eschatological thrust that the meditative, affective Franciscan reading of scripture carried in his meditative treatises.

The Apocalyptic Politics of Francis's Stigmatized Body

It is time to make connections between the confluences of mystical traditions in Bonaventure's writing and the political concerns I pointed to in the introduction. The issue is apocalyptic politics, signified by the figure of Francis. In short, the question of the day was this: Who is Francis in salvation history, and where does the order he founded sit within the turning of the ages that his appearance presages? Putting it this way already highlights the parallel with Christ, and as I have noted earlier, the Protospirituals' view of Francis's eschatological significance would lead them to ascribe to him the status of *alter christus*, another Christ, who would usher in the eschaton. Bonaventure shares their conviction that Francis

---

25. On the later history of Francis's significance as an imitator of Christ, see Lester K. Little, "*Imitatio Christi*: The Influence of Francis of Assisi on Late Medieval Religious Life," in *Defenders and Critics of Franciscan Life: Essays in Honor of John V. Fleming*, ed. Michael F. Cusato and G. Geltner (Boston: Brill, 2009), 195–218.
26. I am thinking here of Francis's calling in 1205 at San Damiano, where he heard the voice of God telling him to rebuild the church.

is the paradigmatic exemplar of identification with Jesus for the order, but he does not follow them in this radical exaltation of Francis's significance.[27] For both, Francis's pattern of *imitatio christi* had apocalyptic significance; the question was whether that signified the end of the age, or some other, less literal-minded, valence.

Bonaventure's understanding of Francis's apocalyptic importance is found in the way he draws a parallel between Francis and the angel of Rev. 5:2-5, whose function is to announce the coming of God in glory to vindicate God's people. Right at the heart of *The Triple Way* (the middle section of the middle chapter), the seventh step of illumination identifies Dionysius's light of truth with the opening of the seven seals of the scroll by the angel in Revelation; each scroll, Bonaventure says, is a revelation of the suffering of the Lamb that discloses various dimensions of the divine, creation, and the soul. The revelatory function of the suffering of Christ is the heart of the *Life* as well; in that treatise, as I mentioned above, Bonaventure uses a cruciform narrative structure to associate Francis with the apocalyptic angel via his compassionate cosuffering with Christ;[28] moreover, in the prologue Bonaventure characterizes Francis as an angelic and hierarchic man who manifested the grace of God in the last days by his example of apostolic perfection.[29]

The identification of Francis with an apocalyptic irruption in history, marking an eschatological transition of some kind, is one Bonaventure shared with Joachim of Fiore and the Protospirituals, as well as later Spirituals like Peter Olivi.[30] But the rhetorical program of

---

27. The *alter christus* term first occurs in the fourteenth century; for sources of the term, see Little, "*Imitatio Christi*," 195 n. 3.
28. *Life of St. Francis*, 13.10. Regis Armstrong had argued that the *Legenda* is structured according to the Dionysian purgation-illumination-union pattern in "The Spiritual Theology of the *Legenda Major* of Saint Bonaventure" (PhD dissertation, Fordham University, 1978).
29. *The Life of St. Francis*, prologue 1.
30. See Reeves, *The Influence of Prophecy*, 175–81; David Burr, "Bonaventure, Olivi and Franciscan Eschatology," *Collectanea Franciscana* 53 (1983): 23–40.

the *Life* and *The Triple Way* places this convergence of Francis and the eschaton within an implicit polemical context against the Joachites and Protospirituals. Whereas the latter held to a cataclysmic view of history, Bonaventure's eschatological periodization is subordinated to a much more christologically driven dynamic. Francis's stigmata is not so much a sign of the last stage of the imminent end times as it is a recapitulation of the center point of history;[31] Francis is not an *alter christus*, but rather a sign that the life of Christ was returning to the church in the apostolic life of the Lesser Brothers. Apocalypticism for Bonaventure is a way of thinking about contemporaneity with Christ, rather than the oncoming storm of the end times, more a typological performance of the Gospel narrative than charts of the tribulation. The apocalyptic significance of Francis, therefore, was not that of an epochal shift into the third age of the church; his stigmata signified the eschatological coincidence of the life of evangelical poverty with the ministry of Jesus, as guided by the imaginative reading of scripture.

I have remarked already that Bonaventure's reconfiguration of intellect and illumination as *imitatio christi* recasts Dionysian intellectualism in terms of the fire of love of affectivity. Victorine bridal mysticism is reappropriated in terms of cruciform identification: the wound of love is not just the desire for the absent spouse, but reliving the nails of Christ's passion. In reading *The Triple Way* in light of its more sustained development in the *Tree of Life*, we have to recall how Franciscan reading was, as Sarah McNamer has observed, a rhetoric of "intimate scripts."[32] Bonaventure's baroque

---

31. We should think here of Bonaventure's decidedly non-Joachite trinitarian theology, wherein Christ is the center of the Trinity; cf. *Collationes in Hexaemeron* 1.10–14; 8.12; 11.6. Cf. Hayes, *The Hidden Center*, 194–98.

32. "These writings . . . were not crafted primarily to be admired—even by God—as aesthetic artifacts. They had serious, practical work to do: to teach their readers, through iterative affective performance, how to feel"; *Affective Meditation and the Invention of Medieval Compassion* (Philadelphia: University of Pennsylvania Press, 2010), 2.

treatises of interlocking threes and sevens reflect a trinitarian metaphysics of exemplarity and hierarchy made accessible in texts designed for memorization, meditation, and visualization, "a useful device for comprehension and a tool of further meditation."[33] The emphasis upon the affective dimension of the knowledge of God served the popular purposes of an order oriented to preaching by example and service, whose spirituality was deeply imbued with Francis's appreciation of the divine revealed in nature.[34] In this sense, Bonaventure's texts are performative as much as they are didactic. The understanding of illumination as *imitatio* is a way of developing the legacy of an order, which, after all, began as a band of unlearned lay preachers, by synthesizing ancient mystical traditions around the beauty of cross as the tree of life, the glory of the life of Jesus that the Franciscans sought to inhabit. We should think, for example, of Francis's reenactment of the nativity at Greccio that Bonaventure records in the *Life* (10.7; see figure 1 and discussion in the conclusion below): Francis's purpose was didactic, true, but it was at least as much driven by the desire to embrace the bridegroom by becoming so intimate with him as to enter his history and bear his wounds within Francis's own body. Francis's stigmata signify the literal interpenetration of his life by the life of Christ.

I have called this an apocalyptic politics because at stake in the dispute with the Joachites and the Protospirituals was a very complex set of questions about the integrity and mission of the Franciscan tradition following the eruption of the controversy over Joachim and the Eternal Evangel. It is tempting to cast the debate in absolutist

---

33. Mary Carruthers, "Moving Images in the Mind's Eye," in *The Mind's Eye: Art and Theological Argument in the Middle Ages*, ed. Jeffrey F. Hamburger and Anne-Marie Bouché (Princeton, NJ: Princeton University Press, 2006), 289.
34. See Scott Matthews, *Reason, Community, and Religious Tradition: Anselm's Argument and the Friars* (Burlington, VT: Ashgate, 2001), who makes this a point of comparison against the Dominicans' emphasis upon intellect, fitting for those who focused upon the preaching of doctrine.

(and anachronistic) terms, as if Bonaventure's moderating position on education and the ownership of property spelled the end of the Franciscan ideal; or, on the other hand, as if Bonaventure's opposition to the Joachites represents a refusal of the unsettling tradition of revolutionary millenarian utopianism that has followed from Joachim's writings. And indeed there are important points to be made from both of those perspectives. But what often gets missed in such debates is another issue that connects directly to the themes of *The Triple Way* and the *Tree of Life*: the status of the Franciscan order as a popular movement.

I have argued above that *The Triple Way* presents a kind of theological grid for the reading of scripture, grounding the classic Augustinian-Gregorian tradition of spiritual reading in a Dionysian metaphysical framework, organized by the passion of Christ as re-presented in Francis's stigmata. Although *The Triple Way* is a text oriented toward clergy (internal evidence suggests that the treatise was addressed to a clerical, and therefore male, audience),[35] it nonetheless should be seen as a sketch of the theological logic that is embodied in *The Tree of Life*, an enormously influential and popular text that helped birth an entire tradition of visual meditation on scripture, which reached its pinnacle in the Pseudo-Bonaventurian *Meditationes vitae christi*.[36]

Thus one dimension of the politics involved in Bonaventure's typological eschatology is a rebuke to the increasing elitism of the Protospirituals, who were coming to embody something like a politics of purity. The issue with the Protospirituals was not

---

35. Bonaventure warns against the "desire for women" in 1:5, and 1:12 speaks of "sacerdotal grace" that the reader possesses.
36. The *Meditationes* are usually attributed to Johannes de Caulibus, and dated to the mid-fourteenth century. See *Meditations on the Life of Christ: An Illustrated Manuscript of the Fourteenth Century*, trans. Isa Ragusa and Rosalie B. Green (Princeton, NJ: Princeton University Press).

clericalization; the momentum of the Spiritual movement would become, in part, deeply anticlerical, seeking to preserve the purity of the *imitatio francisci*, which certainly was deeply inspiring to laity—at least those few who could aspire to a vow of apostolic poverty. Instead, the issue is a debate about the apocalyptic significance of Francis's stigmata. For Bonaventure, the stigmata signified a profound way of taking up the life of Jesus into one's own body—in Francis's case, through literally reenacting the narrative of Christ's nativity, life, and passion; and in the case of his followers, in reinhabiting Christ's history imaginatively and affectively through scripture. For the Protospirituals, though, the coming age of new "spiritual men," *viri spirituales*,[37] was entered through a narrow gate accessible to few, to those marked by unusual piety, contemplative and visionary tendencies, zeal about the Rule, and capable of withstanding persecution from the hierarchy.[38] Against such apocalyptic politics, Bonaventure's theology is a moderating influence, to be sure—even a compromise position. But one can very well argue that Bonaventure's generalate represents an attempt to preserve the Franciscan order's popular status so as to allow it to carry on its mission of reform and renewal—a mission virtually impossible to fulfill on the model of Francis's little band of followers living in absolute poverty. If the order were to continue to attract lay followers, the tertiaries, a moderating position on poverty was necessary, for whom fulfillment of the Rule lay in penance and inner conversion rather than literal observance.[39] Francis found martyrdom in the ardor of desire, not literal death; his followers embodied the intent of his Rule in like manner, by desire and love, not literal reenactment.

37. See Daniel, "Joachim of Fiore," 73.
38. Burr, *The Spiritual Franciscans*, 40–41.
39. Jennifer Kolpacoff Deane, *A History of Medieval Heresy and Inquisition* (New York: Rowman & Littlefield, 2011), 129. Deane's discussion of the Spiritual controversy is helpful and balanced.

What I am suggesting, on the one hand, is that a popular theological politics is receiving support, structure, and guidance in Bonaventure's mystical treatises. They are an attempt to codify a Franciscan reading of scripture that idealizes Francis and offers a kind of *imitatio francisci*, but does so for the purpose of maintaining Francis's popular appeal and accessibility.[40] This is not to go so far as to say that Bonaventure wanted to (re)democratize and laicize the order; but it is to argue that the reading of scripture in *The Triple Way* and the *Tree of Life* draws on a welter of mystical traditions, held together with affective glue, in order to preserve the popular political bent of Francis's performance of the life of Christ. On the other hand, in these treatises we see an apocalyptic tradition up for debate. If John of Parma and Gerard of Borgo San Donnino expected a new age of *viri spirituales*, a kind of mendicant millennium, as it were, Bonaventure locates the significance of Francis's apocalyptic irruption in a pattern of life and *imitatio*; the apocalypse less as the doom of the age and the vindication of the few and brave spiritual men, and more the interpenetration of the ages that Francis bore in his stigmatic wounds,[41] accessible by the side of the crib of Christ. Identification with Christ, whether it was Francis taking on the Marian role in the *crèche* (see below), or being united with the crucifixion on La Verna, was one of longing and the training of holy desire in inhabiting scripture imaginatively and affectively. Francis may have become an unattainable exemplar by Bonaventure's time, in the sense that he had been idealized, and that the simplicity of his

---

40. For an excellent discussion of the revolution in piety that the Franciscans helped mediate, see Miri Rubin, *Mother of God: A History of the Virgin Mary* (New Haven: Yale University Press, 2010), 197–216.
41. For a similar account of Bonaventure's portrait of Francis, see John V. Apczynski, "What Has Paris to Do with Assisi? The Theological Creation of a Saint," in *Finding Francis in Literature and Art*, ed. Cynthia Ho, Beth A. Mulvaney, and John K. Downey (New York: Palgrave Macmillan, 2009), 79–93.

life had been lost in the tumultuous politics of Franciscan history; but *The Triple Way* and Bonaventure's mystical treatises still present him as an eschatological signifier whose effects on the reader were as much somatic as hermeneutic.

Conclusion: Francis and Contemporaneity with Christ

The underlying thrust I have been lifting out of Bonaventure's treatises is illustrated in Giotto's *Crib at Greccio*, in the St. Francis cycle of the upper church of San Francesco, Assisi (figure 1). The painting is a marvel of performative, participatory meditation, inviting the viewer into Francis's enactment of scripture, in what I have described as an apocalyptic contemporaneity with Christ. At the same time, the painting illustrates many of the tensions we have been tracing in this chapter. The painting shows Francis, a layman, nevertheless dressed as a deacon, in a Marian posture and embracing the infant Jesus in the crib in the bottom right quarter of the painting. Franciscan friars, who are dressed in clerical robes, inhabit the roles of the shepherd and magi. The viewer, though, is drawn to the woman who stands at the threshold of the *tramezzo*, or choir screen, at the focal point of the image. She occupies a liminal, or perhaps transgressive, space in the painting: excluded from the altar, but apparently just about to step over the threshold, while gently avoiding the gaze of the viewer who is already in that privileged space. As Beth Mulvaney describes it, the *Crib* offers "a particularly Franciscan approach to the abstract and divine by appealing to the beholder's imagination in invoking the concrete and material as well as the more human realm of feelings and experiences."[42] It invites imaginative, affective viewer

---

42. "Standing on the Threshold: Beholder and Vision in the St. Francis Cycle in the Upper Church of San Francesco, Assisi," in *Beyond the Text: Franciscan Art and the Construction of Religion*, ed. Xavier Seubert and Oleg Bychkov (Saint Bonaventure, NY: Franciscan Institute Publications, 2013), 96.

participation, even as it clericalizes Francis and his brothers (apart from the diaconal robes, note that Bonaventure had set Francis's nativity performance in a forest, while Giotto has moved it inside a church) and replicates the hierarchy of access, with laywomen, the lowest tier, standing outside of the *tramezzo*.[43] Still, the viewer occupies a place within—identifying with the woman on the threshold, but standing beyond her alongside Francis himself, drawn into the unflinching gaze he exchanges with the infant Jesus, a gaze that effortlessly and imaginatively spans the twelve centuries between Christ and Francis. The painting exhibits the (gendered) tension of clericalization and lay access in the late-thirteenth century, but at the same time, one sees the impulse of an order seeking to fulfill Francis's embodiment of an apocalyptic spirituality performed in the simple enactment of the Gospel narrative. It invites the viewer in, encouraging accessibility and iterability, even as it places the viewer in a place—behind the altar—where the lay tertiaries, and indeed Francis himself, could never go. It is the perfect encapsulation of the tensions of the Franciscan order in the late-thirteenth century, even as it shows how the *imitatio francisci*, for all that, could not be lost.

---

43. Ibid., 96–97.

Figure 1: *The Celebration of Christmas at Greccio*, by Giotto, ca. 1300. Fresco, San Francesco, Upper Church, Assisi.

7

"For He is Our Peace"

Thomas Aquinas on Christ as Cause of Peace in the City of Saints

Matthew A. Tapie

Most scholars who have commented upon Aquinas's view of peace have done so in the context of discussing his teaching that peace, defined as the "tranquility of order" (*tranquillitas ordinis*), is the aim of a just war.[1] Although "civic peace" falls short of the perfect peace that

---

1. In Thomas Aquinas, *Summa theologiae* 2a-2ae q. 29.2. All English translations, unless otherwise noted, are taken from Thomas Aquinas, *Summa Theologica*, trans. Fathers of the English Dominican Province, 5 vols. (New York: Benziger, 1948). Aquinas adopts Augustine's definition of peace as *tranquillitas ordinis*. Avery Cardinal Dulles observes that, "political theorists have frequently dealt with . . . civic peace . . . according to Saint Thomas" (Avery Cardinal Dulles, *A Church to Believe In: Discipleship and the Dynamics of Freedom* [New York, NY: Crossroads Publishing, 1983], 149). Most scholarly comment upon Aquinas's view of peace treats the concept in the context of his teaching on war (2a-2ae q. 40). John Finnis's treatment of peace is representative since he emphasizes Aquinas's teaching that genuine peace is not the absence of war but the maintenance of the common good. Finnis, "The Ethics of War and Peace in the Catholic Natural Law Tradition," in *Christian Political Ethics*, The Ethikon Series in Comparative Ethics (Princeton, NJ: Princeton University Press, 2008), 191-216 (193).

the saints will possess in heaven, such peace is a positive state of civil well being, and not merely the absence of war.[2] Scholarly focus on this good-but-imperfect peace in the secondary literature creates the impression that peace in Aquinas mostly concerns the peace of the city of man, and has little to do with the church.

However, as Gregory M. Reichberg has shown, Aquinas's commentary on the Gospel of Matthew, especially his comment upon Matt. 5:39 ("Do not resist evil"), indicates a more complex picture, which Reichberg refers to as a "two stage theory."[3] Although the use of force is licit for the civil power (*respublica*), Reichberg shows that, for Aquinas, peacemaking is the appropriate response to evil for the "agency" of the church whose members' actions proceed directly from charity, and therefore "steadfastly . . . [avoid] any

---

See also Heinz-Gerhard Justenhoven and William Barbieri, eds. *From Just War to Modern Peace Ethics* (Berlin: De Gruyter, 2012); Gregory M Reichberg, Henrik Syse, and Endre Begby, "Thomas Aquinas: Just War and Sins Against Peace," in *The Ethics of War: Classic and Contemporary Readings* (Oxford: Wiley-Blackwell, 2006), 169–98; Richard Miller, "Aquinas and the Presumption against Killing and War," *Journal of Religion* 82, no. 2 (April 1, 2002): 173–204; James Turner Johnson, "Aquinas and Luther on War and Peace," *Journal of Religious Ethics* 31, no. 1 (Spring 2003): 3–20. Aside from Matthew Levering's helpful but indirect comment on peace in the *Commentary on John* in John Yocum, *Aquinas On Scripture: An Introduction To His Biblical Commentaries* (London, UK : T&T Clark, 2005), the only scholars that directly address the subject are Francis McMahon, "A Thomistic Analysis of Peace," *Thomist* 1, no. 3 (July 1939): 169–92; and Edwin J. Buers, "Saint Thomas Aquinas and Peace," Catholic University of America, M. A. Thesis 1934. R. A. Johnson advances the position that Aquinas's theological method represents a "nonviolent" theological confrontation of the Cathars. Johnson, *Peacemaking and Religious Violence: From Thomas Aquinas to Thomas Jefferson* (Eugene, OR: Pickwick Publications, 2009).
2. Peace as "tranquility of order" is to be distinguished from evil peace (*Summa theologiae* 2a-2ae q. 40.1 ad. 3). The idea that peace is not the absence of war is not an original concept and can be traced to the Stoics, Neo-Platonists, Aristotle, and Plato. James Turner Johnson, *The Quest for Peace: Three Moral Traditions in Western Cultural History* (Princeton, NJ: Princeton University Press, 1987), 68.
3. Gregory Reichberg, "Thomas Aquinas between Just War and Pacifism," *Journal of Religious Ethics* 38, no. 2 (June 1, 2010): 219–41. The idea of a dual agency in regard to evil should *not* be misunderstood as two separate spheres of activity, one secular and the other sacred. As Elizabeth Phillips points out, premodern authors "used the term 'secular' not to mean that which is not 'sacred,' but to mean that which is temporal and not eternal." See her discussion of the relation of Aquinas's political theology to Augustine's in *Political Theology: A Guide for the Perplexed* (New York: T&T Clark, 2012), 26; 32–36.

responsibility whatsoever for the shedding of blood."[4] Based on a thorough examination of relevant texts in the *Summa theologiae* and commentary on Matthew, Reichberg argues that, for Aquinas, the church "has a natural affinity, with respect to its own proper order of activity, with a nonviolent, 'redemptive' response to evil."[5]

This essay takes Reichberg's treatment of war and peace in Aquinas as a point of departure and explores the concept of an ecclesial "affinity" for peace in two of Aquinas's commentaries that contain teaching on peace as it relates to the church: the commentary on the Gospel of John, and the commentary on Paul's letter to the Ephesians.[6] When one attends to Aquinas's comments on peace in

---

4. Reichberg, "Thomas Aquinas," 219. One of the merits of Reichberg's essay is that he demonstrates that Aquinas's comments concerning the permissibility of armed violence are scattered throughout the *Summa theologiae* and biblical commentaries. After a thorough analysis of the texts he concludes that the most focused attention to the "dual exigencies" of church (*ecclesia*) and state (*respublica*) appears in Aquinas's commentary on Matthew. Just war and nonviolence "represent ways of dealing with evil, the first by active resistance especially on behalf of the innocent under attack, the second by the voluntary acceptance of harm, assumed out of love for the spiritual good of the attacker. The first pertains first and foremost to the kingdoms (*respublicae*) of this world . . . [and] the second pertains to a kingdom that transcends this world, the Church (*ecclesia*), led by Christ, who directs actions of all its members to the goal of eternal life . . . the unity of the Church is constituted by the bond of charity; hence, only what proceeds directly from charity, as poured into human hearts by the Holy Spirit, is properly speaking 'of the Church.' Acts of violence, even licit violence, as with just war, cannot be attributed to the Church as such" (ibid., 238–39). Reichberg admits that Aquinas's approval of knightly religious orders (made up of lay brothers) sits in tension with this interpretation, but argues Aquinas viewed such measures as a provisional exception to the general rule that warfare pertains to the civil power whereas the church avoids shedding of blood (ibid., 235).
5. Reichberg does not think this affinity for nonviolence can be limited to priests and bishops: "Aquinas typically frames this response by reference to the expectations incumbent upon ordained priests, since, on the sacramental rationale . . . they especially represent Christ within the Church. Yet, this call to nonviolence, as embodied in the 'counsels of perfection,' was *not* understood by him to be a prerogative of priests alone, for he was well aware of the numerous female and lay martyrs. As a consequence, the distinction between nonviolence and just war does not neatly parallel the related distinction between clergy and laity" (ibid., 238-39 [*emphasis added*]).
6. I am indebted to Kevin Hughes, Gregory Reichberg, and William Mattison for their comments on earlier drafts of this essay. All citations of Aquinas's commentaries are from the Latin/English Aquinas Institute edition, which is based on Fabian Larcher's translation of the Marietti edition of the commentaries: Thomas Aquinas, *Commentary on the letters of Saint Paul to the Galatians and Ephesians*, vol. 39 (Lander, Wyoming: Aquinas Institute for the Study of Sacred Doctrine,

these commentaries with attention to what Stephen E. Fowl has called the "multivoiced literal sense" of Aquinas's interpretation of scripture[7] it becomes clear that Aquinas employs the same literal meaning of "peace" from the commentary on John to explain the meaning of Paul's phrase, "For he is our peace," in the Ephesians commentary. I argue that Aquinas understands Paul's words about Christ in Eph. 2:14, "For he is our peace," to refer not to perfect peace in heaven but to an ecclesial peace established by Christ among the city of the saints here on earth. Indeed, for Aquinas, the church is Christ's gift of peace. I show that this concept of ecclesial peace in Aquinas possesses a political character since he says that the church "is a city" in that its citizens share in common with one another the "particular acts" of faith, hope, and charity.[8]

Below, I present this political and ecclesiological dimension of peace in Aquinas in two steps. First, I show how Aquinas's interpretation of the literal meaning of Christ's gift of peace in the commentary on John ("My peace I give you") is deployed to interpret Paul's words about Christ ("For he is our peace") in Eph. 2:14. Second, I explain what Aquinas refers to as the cause, purpose, and bond of peace in the Ephesians commentary: Christ himself caused

---

2012); and *Commentary on the Gospel of John, Chapters 9–21*, vol. 36 (Lander, Wyoming: Aquinas Institute for the Study of Sacred Doctrine, 2013).

7. The idea that the literal sense can refer to a number of realities. Stephen E. Fowl, "Thomas Aquinas and the Multifaceted Literal Sense of Scripture," Paper presented at the SBL Annual Meeting, Christian Theology and the Bible Section: The Literal Sense of Scripture According to Various Interpreters, Chicago, November 17, 2012. Fowl goes into greater detail concerning the multivoiced or multifaceted literal sense of scripture in his essay, "The Importance of a Multivoiced Literal Sense of Scripture: The Example of Thomas Aquinas," in *Reading Scripture with the Church: Toward a Hermeneutic for Theological Interpretation*, ed. A. K. M. Adam et al. (Baker Academic, 2006), 35–50.

8. The overlooked ecclesiological dimension of true-but-imperfect ecclesial peace in Aquinas's thought might serve as a resource for contemporary calls for a Catholic peace theology and ethics of peacemaking. See Scott Appleby, Robert J. Schreiter, and Gerard Powers, eds. *Peacebuilding: Catholic Theology, Ethics, and Praxis* (Maryknoll, NY: Orbis Books, 2010); and Robert John Araujo's discussion of contemporary Catholic thought on these themes in *Religion, War, and Ethics: A Sourcebook of Textual Traditions*, ed. Gregory M. Reichberg and Henrik Syse (Cambridge: Cambridge University Press, 2014).

peace when he reconciled Gentiles and Jews into one body for the purpose of "making peace" (Eph. 2:15), and "fellow citizens" of this body are called by God to preserve unity through the cultivation of four virtues that Aquinas says prevent peace from disappearing among members.

A brief comment on Aquinas's approach to scripture might help the reader to appreciate Aquinas's interpretation of peace in the biblical commentaries. That Aquinas was a theologian deeply shaped by reading scripture is evidenced in his upbringing in liturgical and biblical-patristic culture[9]; his training in the monastic tradition of *lectio divina*; his attraction to the Order of Preachers; and his discussion of scripture in the "inaugural sermons" (presented at the ceremony for his installment as *magister in sacra pagina* or master of the sacred page) at the university of Paris, not to mention the requirements of the office of *magister* itself.[10] Perhaps the clearest indication that Aquinas was a theologian of scripture is the frequent use of the Word of God in the *Summa theologiae*[11] as highest authority (a commonplace practice in the scholastic hierarchy of sources),[12] and the fact that Aquinas wrote commentaries on five Old Testament books (Psalms, Job, Isaiah, Jeremiah, and Lamentations); commentaries on two of the Gospels (Matthew and John); and on all of the Pauline letters.[13]

---

9. Fergus Kerr, "Thomas Aquinas," in *The Medieval Theologians: An Introduction to Theology in the Medieval Period*, ed. G. R. Evans, 1st ed. (Wiley-Blackwell, 2001), 201–20.
10. The office of the *magister in sacra pagina* in the twelfth century consisted of a threefold function: *legere* (to read scripture and comment verse by verse); *disputare* (to teach through objections and responses on a given theme); and *praedicare* (to preach). See Jean-Pierre Torrell, *Saint Thomas Aquinas*, vol. 1: *The Person and His Work*, revised (Washington, DC: Catholic University of America Press, 2005), 54. The inaugural sermons can be found in *Thomas Aquinas: Selected Writings*, ed. and trans. Ralph McInerny (London: Penguin Classics, 1999), 3–17.
11. See Pim Valkenberg, *Words of the Living God: Place and Function of Holy Scripture in the Theology of St. Thomas Aquinas*, Publications of the Thomas Instituut te Utrecht, vol. 6 (Leuven: Peeters, 2000), 207.
12. See Servais-Théodore Pinckaers, "The Sources of the Ethics of St. Thomas Aquinas," in Stephen J. Pope, ed., *The Ethics of Aquinas* (Washington, DC: Georgetown University Press, 2002), 19.

For Aquinas, the literal sense (*sensus litteralis*) of the biblical text was the basis for all theology.[14] The literal sense (to be distinguished from the *sensus spiritualis* or spiritual sense) refers to concepts in scripture that have some referent in reality: "To know the literal sense is to know the reality intended by the author and signified by those words."[15] The literal sense is "the first important level of signification" since it is the basis for any spiritual interpretation of the text.[16]

What is important for my purpose here is to point out that Aquinas thought the literal sense of scripture could refer to a number of realities. As Fowl observes, "any particular passage of scripture may legitimately support a diversity of interpretations, each of which counts as the literal sense of that passage."[17] What Fowl calls the "multivoiced literal sense" of scripture is evident in how Aquinas

13. See Eleonore Stump, "Biblical Commentary and Philosophy," in *The Cambridge Companion to Aquinas*, ed. Norman Kretzmann and Eleonore Stump (Cambridge: Cambridge University Press, 1993), 252–68 (252–53). Aquinas's "biblical commentaries" are actually lectures designed for the medieval classroom. The lectures would be taken down by a cleric who Aquinas thought would be capable of the work. Aquinas is thought to have lectured on Paul's letters twice, 1265–1268 and 1272/3. The lecture on John is dated around 1270–1272. Christopher T. Baglow, *"Modus Et Forma": A New Approach to the Exegesis of Saint Thomas Aquinas with an Application to the Lectura Super Epistolam Ad Ephesios*, Analecta Biblica 149 (Roma: Pontificio Istituto biblico, 2002), (120; 165); See Thomas Weinandy et. al., Preface, in *Aquinas on Doctrine* (London, UK: T&T Clark, 2004), xiii–xv (x).
14. Fowl points out that although this was not unique, Aquinas was "in a decided minority in his day" (Fowl, "Thomas Aquinas and the Multifaceted Literal Sense of Scripture,"). See also Mark Johnson, "Another Look at St. Thomas and the Plurality of the Literal Sense of Scripture," *Medieval Philosophy and Theology* 2 (1992): 118–42. For Aquinas's comments on hermeneutics see 1a q 1 a. 10 ad. 2; *Quaestiones de quodlibet*, 7.6.1–3, 145–48; *Super epistolam ad Galatas lectura*, 4.7; *Quaestiones disputatae de potentia*, 4.1. Busa, *Sancti Thomae Aquinatis Opera Omnia*.
15. John Boyle,"St. Thomas Aquinas and Sacred Scripture," Aquinas Lecture, presented at the Notre Dame Seminary, New Orleans, April 8, 2011. This "reality" could include history, etiology, and analogy. When this first level of reference is employed to point to another level of meaning it pertains to the spiritual.
16. Ibid. The spiritual sense is organized into three variations informed by three periods of salvation history: Old Testament figures of Christ; moral action of Christians (based on action of Christ); and the anagogic meaning as foreshadowing future glory: "All three spiritual meanings interpret the objects of a certain status in salvation history as a sign of a subsequent status. . . ." (ibid.). It should be noted that Thomas does not always provide a spiritual interpretation of a verse of scripture. See Thomas Rik Van Nieuwenhove and Joseph Wawrykow, *The Theology Of Thomas Aquinas* (Notre Dame, IN: University of Notre Dame Press, 2005), 393–94.
17. Fowl, "Thomas Aquinas and the Multifaceted Literal Sense of Scripture," 2.

interprets Christ's words, "My peace I give you," since this verse becomes the interpretive key for his reading of Paul's words about Christ as peace of the church in Eph. 2:14: "For he is our peace."

Christ's Peace in Aquinas's *Commentary on John*

Before examining Aquinas's interpretation of peace in the commentary on John it is helpful to observe that in the *Summa theologiae* 2a-2ae q. 29, Aquinas teaches that there exist four types of peace: 1) concord; 2) apparent or false peace; 3) true but imperfect peace; and 4) perfect peace. "Concord" is simple agreement among the wills of various persons concerning one thing. However, when concord is focused on evil as its object, such concord is only apparent peace or what Aquinas calls the "peace of the wicked."[18] For Aquinas, there is a difference between true and false peace: "There can be no true peace except where the appetite is directed to what is truly good. . . . Hence true peace is only in good men and about good things. The peace of the wicked is not a true peace but a semblance thereof. . . ."[19] Aquinas explains that truly good peace is when the "chief movement of the soul finds rest in God."[20] True peace can be had in two ways. In the vulnerable condition of faith, peace in this life is always possessed imperfectly since there are certain things within and without which disturb peace. In the invulnerable condition of the beatific vision (seeing God face to face), truly good peace is possessed perfectly.[21]

In the commentary on John, Aquinas follows Augustine's

---

18. An example of apparent peace might be concord among thieves concerning a plan to rob a particular house or the tranquility that falls upon a city due to the curfew imposed by a tyrant.
19. In *Summa theologiae* 2a-2ae q. 29.2.
20. *Summa theologiae* 2a-2ae q. 29.2 ad. 4. Aquinas states that without sanctifying grace, peace is not real but merely apparent (2a-2ae q. 29.3 ad 1).
21. See *Summa theologiae* 2a-2ae q. 29.2 ad. 4. I am indebted to Gregory Reichberg for pointing out the helpful language of "vulnerable and invulnerable condition" as it relates to peace.

interpretation of John 14:27, "Peace I leave with you; my peace I give you," when he explains that the two references to the term peace may communicate a twofold meaning. In this verse, "peace" can mean true-but-imperfect peace as well as perfect peace. This twofold meaning of peace mirrors Aquinas's treatment of the term in *Summa theologiae* 2a-2ae q. 29. In the commentary on John, Aquinas says Christ's words, "Peace I leave with you," which refer to true-but-imperfect peace, whereas, Christ's words, "My peace I give you," refer to perfect peace.

"Peace I Leave with You": Our Present and Imperfect Peace in this Life

Aquinas explains that the first form of peace—the peace Christ *leaves* with the disciples—brings order to "three things," which he says must "be put in order within us" (the intellect, will, and sensitive appetite).[22] The peace that Christ leaves with the disciples effects a "calmness of mind." This calmness of mind consists of the following: 1) a reason liberated from disordered affections; 2) a tranquility of soul, which is defined as not being harassed by emotional states; 3) a simplicity of heart, which refers to the will entirely set toward God and neighbor. It is important to recognize that this first form of peace ("peace I leave with you"), which orders the interior disposition of the person, can be a peace that is had now, in this present life.[23]

However, there is a downside to this peace. Because it is a peace that is had in this world it is also subject to disturbance. Therefore, following Augustine, Aquinas reasons that since this peace—although it is true peace had now—is an imperfect peace, and therefore *cannot* be described as the peace that belongs to Christ. This first description

---

22. *In Ioan.* 14.7.1962.
23. It is this form of peace as ordering of intellect and will that McMahon identified as "from Christ" in his discussion of peace in charity in "A Thomistic Analysis of Peace," 186–87.

of the peace Christ left us in this world emphasizes that true-but-imperfect peace is *not* Christ's but ours. The peace that belongs *to* Christ (perfect peace) is not yet a peace that the saints share.

"My Peace I Give You": Our Future, Perfect Peace in the Heavenly Jerusalem

Next, Aquinas comments upon Christ's words, "My peace I give you," and explains that this phrase refers to the perfect peace possessed by Christ. Nevertheless, Christ's own peace is, again, not ours in this world because Christ's peace is undisturbed and "has always been perfect." Indeed, how could any peace that *belongs to Christ* be imperfect? Christ always had this second kind of peace because he was "always without conflict." Therefore, when Christ says "*my peace* I give you," he refers to the perfect peace to be obtained in our "native land," the heavenly Jerusalem.

"My Peace I Give You": Christ as Author of the Present Peace of the Saints in this Life

However, Aquinas seems to think this interpretation of "My peace I give you" is lacking an important distinction.[24] Aquinas writes, "Since whether in this world or in our native land, all the peace possessed by the saints comes to them through Christ . . . why does our Lord, when speaking of the peace of the saints in this life not say, my peace I give to you, instead of reserving this for the peace of our native land?"[25] Here, Aquinas is concerned to articulate how the peace of the "church militant" or saints *in this life (pace sanctorum*

---

24. Aquinas seems to be taking up Augustine's speculations about the "My" of Christ's "My peace I give You." He cites Augustine's comment on John 14:27, which he includes in the *Catena Aurea*. Aquinas, *Catena Aurea: Commentary on the Four Gospels Collected Out of the Works of the Fathers* (Southampton, UK: Saint Augustine Press, 1997).
25. *In Ioan.* 14.7.1963.

in via) can be described as a peace that is *also of Christ* despite our imperfect condition. How can a disturbed peace, which the church clearly experiences in schism and conflict, also be described as Christ's peace? Is there any sense in which the peace of the saints is a sharing in the peace that belongs to Christ? Matthew Levering summarizes the problem as follows: "[I]s it not theologically erroneous to suggest that 'my peace [I give you]' refers solely to perfect peace of heaven, since any peace that followers of Jesus enjoy on earth also comes from Jesus and is a real sharing in his peace?"[26]

Aquinas does not reject the first interpretation of "My peace I give you" (perfect peace enjoyed by the saints) but he does add a distinction which provides an important shade of meaning to the literal sense of Christ's words since the distinction makes theological room for speaking about how the pilgrim church truly shares in Christ's peace in the present. Aquinas explains that the *present peace* of the saints can indeed be described as "of Christ" in the sense that Christ is the author (*auctoris*) or originator of this peace: "We should say that each peace, of the present and of the future, is that of Christ. But our present peace is Christ's because he is only its author."[27]

Although we do not hold Christ's peace in the same way Christ himself possesses peace, the peace that the church has now is still a peace that is of Christ.[28] The present peace of the saints—despite its imperfect condition—is also Christ's peace because, it is a peace authored by Christ. It is in this sense that the peace of Christ can also be described as belonging to the church now. Here, Aquinas's

---

26. Matthew Levering, "Reading John with St. Thomas Aquinas," 116.
27. *In Ioan.* 14.7.1963. Aquinas actually explains that there are *two* ways in which Christ's own peace is present in the lives of the saints here and now. First, there is peace that is authored by Christ and had now by Christians; second, there is peace that is authored by Christ and had now by Christians as well as peace of Christ in future glory. The second is essentially a restatement of his first interpretation of "My Peace I Give you" as the future peace of the saints. I list only the first to simplify the presentation.
28. *In Ioan.* 14.7.1963.

move deepens the notion that the church, although it exists under the two conditions of faith (now) and beatific vision (future) is one church. The church that hopes to share Christ's perfect peace is also the church established by Christ's gift of peace.

In the commentary on Ephesians, Aquinas deploys this second interpretation of "My peace I give you" (as present peace which Christ causes among the saints) in order to articulate a rich ecclesial vision of Paul's phrase in Eph. 2:14, "For he is our peace. . . ." It should become clear that a communal or ecclesial concept of true-but-imperfect peace emerges in these two commentaries and compliments Aquinas's concise categories of peace in the *Summa theologiae*.

The Cause, Purpose, and Bond of the Present Peace of the City of the Saints in the Commentary on Ephesians

In the second chapter of his commentary on Ephesians, Aquinas comments upon the blessings of Christ. Included among the blessings is the truth that the Gentiles have been "converged with the Jewish people" and were reconciled to God.[29] It is in this context of his discussion of Christ's reconciliation of Gentiles and Jews that Aquinas draws upon his second interpretation of "My peace I give you," which emphasizes Christ as author or cause of peace. Indeed, when Aquinas interprets Paul's words in Eph. 2:14, "For he is our peace, who has made both one," his commentary includes what Aquinas refers to as the cause, purpose, and bond of the saints, and consists of the following: 1) Christ as cause of the true-but-imperfect peace of the saints; 2) the purpose of the true-but-imperfect peace of the saints as the unification of two peoples into "one body," which he says,

---

29. *Ad Eph.* 2.5.110. As Christopher Baglow has observed, for Aquinas, the relationship between Jewish and Gentile Christians becomes the major theme of chapter two and serves as a concrete pole that bounds his exposition of the entire epistle. Baglow, "Modus et Forma," 165.

is peace; 3) how this true-but-imperfect ecclesial peace is preserved among the faithful.

Christ as Cause of the Ecclesial Peace of the Saints

Aquinas identifies Christ as cause of the convergence between Gentiles and Jews. He states that this convergence is precisely what Paul refers to when he says, in 2:14, "For he is our peace, who has made both one." Aquinas explains Paul's reason for saying this: "Christ is the cause of this drawing together, [and] for [this] reason he affirms *for he is our peace, who has made both one.* This is an emphatic way of speaking to better express the reality, as though he said: rightly do I say that you are drawn near each other, but this occurs through Christ since *he is himself our peace,* that is, he is the cause of our peace."[30] Immediately after his explanation of "For he is our peace," Aquinas cites John 14:27, "My peace I give you." He explains further that, "It is useful to adopt this way of speaking, when the totality of the effect depends on its cause."[31] As he did in the commentary on John, Aquinas identifies Christ as cause of the peace that belongs to the church now, in the era of grace. Drawing together Jews and Gentiles in one body is an effect caused solely by Christ.

Reconciliation of Jews and Gentiles in One Body as the Purpose of the Ecclesial Peace of the Saints

The material in Ephesians concerning how the blessing of Christ affects the church (Eph. 1–2) then allows Aquinas to elaborate upon

---

30. *Ad Eph.* 2.5.111
31. *Ad Eph.* 2.5.111. The manner of the convergence includes both Christ's fulfillment and destruction of the ceremonial law, a source of enmity between the two peoples. I have discussed this aspect of his thought at length in *Aquinas on Israel and the Church: A Study of the Question of Supersessionism in the Theology of Thomas Aquinas* (Eugene, OR: Pickwick, 2014).

how and why Christ has caused peace for the church. Aquinas comments that Paul makes the purpose of this convergence between Jews and Gentiles clear when he says, "that he might make the two in himself into one new man, making peace."[32] The end (*finis*) of the convergence effected by Christ is that the "two peoples would be formed into one people."[33] Commenting upon Paul's metaphor for the convergence of Jews and Gentiles as a structure being built into a holy temple (Eph. 2:21) with Christ as the cornerstone, Aquinas says Christ is called a cornerstone on account of the convergence of both Jews and Gentiles, whom he refers to as "two walls" joined to a corner.[34] "As two walls are joined at the corner," he writes, "so in Christ the Jewish and pagan peoples are united."[35] Aquinas, therefore, understands the present peace of the saints as Christ's creation of a new social situation of Jews and Gentiles united into the temple of his body.

The ecclesial unity of these two peoples united in one body is peace because Christ "killed hostility" between them and between these people and God: first, "[Christ] killed the hostility that had arisen through the law between the Jews and the gentiles" by fulfilling the Old Testament symbols, and, second, he "killed in himself" the hostility that existed between God and men through sin. The purpose of the convergence is Christ's reconciliation of humankind and God. It is for this reason that Paul states, "that he might reconcile us both . . . in one body of the Church."[36] Christ made both peoples into one body by "joining into unity both the Jews who worshiped the true God and the gentiles who were alienated from God's cult."[37]

32. *Ad Eph.* 2.5.111.
33. *Ad Eph.* 2.5.116.
34. *Ad Eph.* 2.6.131. That Aquinas assumes Paul's building metaphor as contained within the literal sense of scripture is clear when he pauses to explain that the building metaphor can also be understood allegorically.
35. *Ad Eph.* 2.6.129.
36. *Ad Eph.* 2.5.118.

That Aquinas thinks the unity of this body also requires the activity of peacemaking is evident when he explains Paul's use of the phrase "one body." By this phrase, Paul means, "be united in the bond of peace that you may be one body."

The Virtues that Preserve the Ecclesial Peace of the City of Saints

When Aquinas moves on to comment upon what is often referred to as the "ethical material" in Ephesians (chs. 4–6), and especially Paul's words that the Ephesians ought to "walk worthy of the vocation to which [they] were called" (Eph. 4:1–2), he describes their vocation, and he does so using the political terms borrowed from Ephesians chapter 2: "[Y]ou should be attentive to the dignity to which you were are summoned, and you ought to behave in a way conformable to it . . . *you are called to be fellow citizens with the saints* (Eph. 2:19)."[38] This civic language is prompted by Paul's words that Gentiles are no longer "aliens" to the "commonwealth of Israel" (Eph. 2:12) and are now "citizens with the saints" (Eph. 2:19). Aquinas explains that here, the Apostle draws a conclusion concerning the present state of the church. In Aquinas's view, Paul's description of the community of the faithful as fellow citizens is described by Augustine in the *City of God*: "two loves have formed two cities. For the love of God, even to the contempt of self, namely, of the man loving builds the heavenly city of Jerusalem. But the love of self, even to the contempt of God, builds the city of Babylon." After citing these famous words from Augustine, Aquinas writes, "Everyone, then, either is a citizen with

---

37. *Ad Eph.* 2.5.111. In addition to Aquinas citing John 14:27 "My peace I give you" to explicate 2:14, there is a second key intertextual connection in Aquinas where Christ as literal cause of peace of the church is referenced. Immediately after commenting on "he hath made both one." Aquinas cites John 10:16. "And other sheep I have, that are not of this fold; them also I must bring. And they shall hear my voice; and there shall be one fold and one shepherd." This connection runs both ways between the commentaries since the commentary on John also contains a citation of Eph. 2:14.
38. *Ad Eph.* 4.1.190. [*emphasis added*].

the saints if he loves God to the contempt of self . . . or, if he loves himself even to the contempt of God, he is a citizen of Babylon."[39]

Aquinas remarks on the political character of the church again when he comments on how the theological virtues provide an identity that is both ecclesial and political. He says that the community of the faithful *is* a city (*civitas*) because its members possess the infused virtues: "If the [community of the faithful is] considered in themselves, it is a city since they have in common with one another the particular acts of faith, hope and charity. In this way, the community is a civil one. . . ."[40]

Since the faithful are also citizens, they are expected to behave in a manner worthy of God's calling to maintain "unity of the Spirit in the bond of peace" (*unitatem Spiritus in vinculo pacis*).[41] Seeking to explicate Paul's words in Eph. 4: 2 ("With all humility, mildness, with patience, supporting one another in charity . . ."), Aquinas explains that, "Four virtues must be cultivated" in order to preserve the peace of the city: humility, meekness, patience, and charity.[42] Cultivation of these four virtues preserves the present peace of the city of the saints against four vices that cause "dissension," "disturbances," and "turmoil." Without the cultivation of these virtues, peace "disappears" from the society. Aquinas then comments on each of the four virtues that must be cultivated as well as the corresponding vices to be shunned.[43]

First, the city of the saints must guard against pride, the queen of all vices, because it "causes dissension among members of the body."[44]

---

39. *Ad Eph.* 2.6.125.
40. *Ad Eph.* 2.6.126.
41. There is also a thematic correlation in the commentary between 2.5.121, which discusses the cause and form of peace, and the explication of "careful to keep the unity of the Spirit in the bond of peace," in 4.1.187.
42. *Ad Eph.* 4.1.191.
43. *Ad Eph.* 4.1.191.
44. *Summa theologiae* 2a-2ae q. 162.8.

Aquinas understands pride as "the disordered desire for exaltation."[45] "When one arrogant person decides to rule others, while the other proud individuals do not want to submit, dissension arises in the society and peace disappears."[46] In order to eliminate this obstacle to ecclesial peace, the city of the saints must cultivate the virtue of humility, which Aquinas identifies elsewhere as mutual submission to one another out of reverence for God.[47]

In addition to pride, anger (defined as the desire to punish or to have revenge) is a threat to maintaining the peace of the church:[48] "An angry person is inclined to inflict injury, whether verbal or physical, from which disturbances occur."[49] Anger, explains Aquinas, is the result of sorrow, which scripture also refers to as bitterness. At the root of this bitterness is memory of wrongs. Aquinas says that all bitterness arises from "the memory of past injuries"[50] and produces "a craving for revenge." However, Aquinas interprets Paul's words, "Be angry: and do not sin. Do not let the sun go down upon your anger." as indicating a good and bad form of anger.[51] For Aquinas, Paul's statement, "Be angry," indicates the good form of anger: one should be angry at their own sin as well as the sin of others.[52] Anger is evil when, contrary to justice, it strives for revenge. Regarding the bad form of anger, it may arise in a person but it should not be acted upon: "should it happen that anger wells up within you—which is human—do not sin. You must not be led on to act upon it." Aquinas

---

45. *Summa theologiae* 2a-2ae q. 162.1 ad. 2.
46. *Ad Eph.* 4.1.193.
47. *Summa theologiae* 2a-2ae q.161.1; 3 ad. 1; q. 162.6. Aquinas considers humility as one of the potential parts of the virtue of temperance.
48. Anger is not evil when it promotes justice. Anger can be evil in excess or deficiency (see *Summa theologiae* 2a-2ae q. 158.2).
49. *Summa theologiae* 2a-2ae q. 158.2.
50. *Ad Eph.* 4.10264.
51. *Ad Eph.* 4.8.250. The good form of anger seeks a just vindication.
52. "A man can be mad at himself for his own sins, and at his fellow man because of his sins" (*Ad Eph.* 4.8.250).

says "do not persist in anger, but cast it off before sunset; for although the first impulses of temper are excusable, due to human frailty, it is illicit to dwell on them."[53] In order for the church to "discard" this bad form of anger, the cultivation of the virtue of meekness is required.[54] Meekness suppresses the passion for revenge.[55] Meekness helps remove anger in two ways: it enables the person to retain control over rational powers and therefore assists in the capacity to speak the truth to others.[56] Aquinas says that cultivating the virtue of meekness among the faithful "softens arguments and preserves peace."[57]

Impatience is the third obstacle to preserving the peace of the church. Occasionally, explains Aquinas, some who possesses the first two virtues (humility and meekness) and "refrain from causing trouble nevertheless will not endure patiently the real or attempted wrongs done to himself."[58] Aquinas is aware that pride or anger in some can cause hardship for others—even those who possess humility and meekness. Such hardship can give rise to sorrow, anger, and hatred, among the members of the church.[59] For this reason, Aquinas says the body must guard against these potential disturbances by cultivating the virtue of patience.[60] Patience is not simply endurance of hardship but is, on Aquinas's account, caused by charity, which proceeds from the love of God above all things:[61] "Now the fact that a man prefers the good of grace to all natural goods, the loss of which may cause sorrow, is to be referred to charity, which loves God above

---

53. *Ad Eph.* 4.8.250.
54. Aquinas considers meekness as a potential part of the virtue of temperance.
55. See *Summa theologiae* 2a-2ae q. 157.1, 3, 4 ad. 3.
56. *Summa theologiae* a. 4 ad. 3.
57. *Ad Eph.* 4.1.191.
58. *Ad Eph.* 4.1.191.
59. *Ad Eph.* q. 136.2 ad. 1.
60. *Ad Eph.* q. 136. Aquinas considers impatience as a part of the virtue of fortitude.
61. *Ad Eph.* q. 136.3 ad. 3.

all things."⁶² The virtue that the citizens of the faithful must possess in order to endure the hardship of their fellow citizen's real or attempted wrongs is possible only if the faithful cultivate patience by cherishing the good of grace over natural goods. Aquinas will say further on that the inordinate desire for material goods is a sin that causes corruption in the members of the body. The degree to which the members of the faithful desire material goods in an inordinate way will directly impugn their capacity to patiently endure the hardship of living together as a community because they have learned to desire not God above all things and the grace that God gives but other things. Therefore, Aquinas thinks the peace of the church can be preserved only when its citizens love God above material things.⁶³

"Inordinate zeal" is the fourth vice that threatens peace. Such zeal causes members to pass judgment on "the faults of others" or "whatever they see, not waiting for the proper time and place."⁶⁴ Zealous judgment of others' failures is the opposite of "bearing with one another in charity" (Eph. 4:2). Aquinas is not discouraging judgment of others' faults along the lines of the contemporary idea that one ought not judge another person's deeds. Rather, charity requires judgment but with the aim of correction. The proper way to bear the failures of others is by means of "fraternal correction," which is chiefly an act of the virtue of charity⁶⁵ aimed at the correction of the wrongdoer.⁶⁶ Correction of others is part of what it means to "bear with the weak."⁶⁷ However, to discern whether and how correction

---

62. *Summa theologiae* 1a-2ae q. 136.3.
63. See Stephen Fowl's discussion of similar themes in chapter six of *Engaging Scripture: A Model for Theological Interpretation* (Eugene, OR: Wipf & Stock, 2008).
64. *Ad Eph.* 4.1.193. Emended.
65. See *Summa theologiae* 2a-2ae q. 33.1. It is secondarily an act of prudence, which executes and directs the action (*Summa theologiae* 2a-2ae q. 33.2 ad. 3).
66. *Summa theologiae* 2a-2ae q. 133. Eleonore Stump points out that, on Aquinas's terms, "there is no obligation to seek out wrongdoers in order to reprove them, or to spy on people in order to know what their wrong actions are." Eleonore Stump, *Aquinas* (New York: Routledge, 2005), 328.

takes place requires prudence: "When someone falls," writes Aquinas, "he should not be immediately corrected—unless it is the time and the place for it."[68] Indeed, Aquinas says that if there is no concern for the circumstances surrounding another person's moral failure, judging leads to turmoil. Moreover, Aquinas thinks the act of fraternal correction requires the virtue of mercy: "With mercy these should be waited for since 'charity bears all things' (1 Cor. 13:7)."[69] Therefore, patient endurance of the faults of others in the community is not enough to preserve peace. Aquinas thinks the virtue of mercy is necessary to properly address those failures.[70]

In addition to the four virtues that preserve peace, Aquinas also addresses forms of spiritual corruption that can harm the peace of the church, including lying,[71] anger (mentioned two more times), and stealing.[72] Aquinas thinks that Paul's words "steal no more" are not simply about theft but about the "contaminating desire for transitory goods. . . ." which he also refers to as the "inordinate desire for temporal goods."[73] He frequently turns to the theme of harmful language among Christians, which he calls, "wicked and injurious words."[74] Evil speech consists of false words by which a person means one thing and says another; futile and vain talk; perjury and

---

67. *Summa theologiae* 2a-2ae q. 33 ad. 3.
68. Stump, *Aquinas*, 328. Aquinas's discussion of this act of charity includes important distinctions I lack the space to treat here. See Eleonore Stump's helpful treatment of fraternal correction.
69. *Summa theologiae* 2a-2ae q. 30. Aquinas thinks fraternal correction is one of the spiritual works of mercy. See *Summa theologiae* 2a-2ae q. 33.4.
70. See *Ad Eph.* 4.1.191.
71. See *Ad Eph.* 4.8.248. Aquinas says that lying corrupts a person's rational powers. This is why Paul says "putting away lying, speak the truth" (Eph. 4:25). Paul "bans lying because through this sin of the tongue (*peccatum oris*) the truth of reason is corrupted."
72. He refers to these as personal "sins of disorder" and sins that consist in the "disorder of others" (*Ad Eph.* 4.8.247).
73. *Ad Eph.* 4.9.253.
74. Aquinas's comments are based on several texts, including the following: "Let no evil speech proceed from your mouth . . ." (Eph. 4:29); "Let all bitterness and anger and indignation and clamor and blasphemy be put away from you, with all malice. And be kind to one another; merciful, forgiving one another. . . ." (Eph. 4:31–30).

blasphemy.[75] Such words or actions "upset or sadden other men" and weaken the peace of the society of saints.

Conclusion

In this brief sketch of the peace of the saints in the Ephesians commentary, I have shown that Aquinas's multivoiced literal sense of scripture allows him to overcome a difficulty concerning the concept of peace as it pertains to the pilgrim church, which he detects in Christ's words, "My peace I give you." How can a peace that belongs to Christ also be described as a peace of the church if it is subject to disturbance? Aquinas overcomes this difficulty by articulating the way in which the saints have received the gift of Christ's peace now, since Christ is the cause of their present peace.

In the Ephesians commentary, Aquinas adds a significant communal dimension this notion of true-but-imperfect peace. He draws upon the idea that Christ is author of present peace in order to describe the cause of peace in the church, its purpose, and how it is persevered among the saints. Christ's gift of peace ("My peace I give you") is the same reality that Paul refers to when he says, "For he is our peace." Indeed, Christ's gift of peace is the church—the eschatological union of Jews and Gentiles, the two walls of the temple of his body. Aquinas thinks the church is a city with a distinctive vocation to preserve unity "in the bond of peace" by cultivating the virtues of humility, meekness, patience, and mercy. Despite disturbances and failures, the church is a city of peace. Indeed, since the church *is a city*, its ecclesial peace can be described as "civic" peace, though it is a civic peace sustained by the love of God above material things.

---

75. See *Ad Eph.* 4.9.259. Perjury is addressed in *Summa theologiae* 2a-2ae q. 98.1–4; blasphemy in 2a-2ae q. 14.

8

War and the Ethics of Evangelization

The Great Commission in Sixteenth-Century Spanish Political Thought

David M. Lantigua

At first look, the early modern political culture of the Iberian kingdom of Castile under the Catholic Monarchs Ferdinand and Isabel, and later the Spanish King and Holy Roman Emperor Charles (1516-1556), clearly illustrates what John Howard Yoder called "Constantinianism." The Spanish attempt to reclaim and expand the borders of Latin Christendom through the *reconquista* of the Moors, the inquisitions of *conversos*, and the conquests of Amerindian "infidels" in the New World, were all violent assertions of God's rule through the coercive power of empire. These Constantinian practices typified "what Jesus had rejected" by "seizing godlikeness" and "moving *in hoc signo* from Golgotha to the battlefield."[1]

Yoder was especially attentive to the "fundamental wrongness" inherent to Christendom, that is, "its illegitimate takeover of the world: its ascription of a Christian loyalty or duty to those who have made no confession and, thereby, its denying to the non-confessing creation the freedom of unbelief that the nonresistance of God in creation gave to a rebellious humanity."[2] The denial of freedom to unbelievers through civil religious establishment appears as the original sin of Christendom.[3] The conversion-or-exile mandate of the 1492 Alhambra decree directed against Iberian Jews and the conversion-or-enslavement policy toward Amerindians codified in the 1513 *Requerimiento* represent notorious examples of the Castilian denial of freedom in a Constantinian mode.

Despite the rhetorical and normative strength of Yoder's notion of Constantinianism, his description paints Latin Christendom in monolithic, and predominantly negative, terms.[4] With Christendom's fusion of throne and altar, it appears as a static-like entity evangelically inert and impotent in confessing Christ as victor to the established powers.[5] This hermeneutic tends to obstruct the recognition and appreciation of significant theological developments for Gospel social ethics embodied in the Latin church of the Spanish Renaissance. For this reason, the work of Oliver O'Donovan is more amenable for our inquiry. O'Donovan provides richer analytic resources than Yoder in order to recognize the legacy, rather than just the shadow, of Christendom in the West.

O'Donovan's interpretation of Christendom in *The Desire of the*

---

1. John Howard Yoder, *The Priestly Kingdom: Social Ethics as Gospel* (Notre Dame, IN: University of Notre Press, 2001), 145.
2. Yoder, *The Royal Priesthood: Essays Ecclesiastical and Ecumenical* (Scottdale, PA: Herald Press, 1998), 109.
3. Ibid., 245–46.
4. Yoder, *The Priestly Kingdom*, 144.
5. Yoder, *The Royal Priesthood*, 246–47. Yoder does give very brief attention to radical Franciscans and the Waldensians as positive proto-Protestant expressions within Christendom of Gospel-inspired "free church" movements though he does not develop this line of inquiry.

Nations supplies a more fruitful descriptive starting point: "The Christendom idea has to be located correctly as an aspect of the church's understanding of *mission*. . . . It was the missionary imperative that compelled the church to take the conversion of the empire seriously and to seize the opportunities it offered. These were not merely opportunities for 'power.' They were opportunities for preaching the Gospel, baptizing believers, curbing the violence and cruelty of empire and, perhaps most important of all, forgiving their former persecutors."[6] Significantly, O'Donovan abandons Yoder's radical suspicion of Christendom by indicating that the church in the Latin West existed for a missionary purpose committed to proclaiming the truth and love of Christ in order to convert and constrain the political powers of the world. As William Cavanaugh rightly observes, O'Donovan's work "is helpful not merely because it makes a positive account of Christendom possible, but because it makes the Constantinian shift *explicable*."[7] Christendom appears then as "a very complex series of attempts to take seriously the inherently political nature of the church and its instrumental role in the integral salvation of the world in Jesus Christ."[8]

O'Donovan also adds an important normative dimension to his descriptive analysis of Christendom: "Mission is not merely an urge to expand the scope and sway of the church's influence. It is to be at the disposal of the Holy Spirit in making Christ's victory known. It requires, therefore, a discernment of the working of the Spirit and Antichrist. These two discernments must accompany each other: to trace the outline of Christ's dawning reign on earth requires that one trace the false pretension too."[9] The Antichrist idea yields self-

---

6. Oliver O'Donovan, *The Desire of the Nations: Rediscovering the Roots of Political Theology* (New York: Cambridge University Press, 1996), 212.
7. William T. Cavanaugh, *Migrations of the Holy: God, State, and the Political Meaning of the Church* (Grand Rapids: Eerdmans, 2011), 128.
8. Ibid., 129.

critical resources within Christendom's historical expression of faith. O'Donovan's account brings into relief a Christendom tradition of social ethics in early modern Spain committed to announcing the Gospel's transformative and liberating power for all peoples under God's rule against Satan's violent oppression through idolatry and the overreaching worldly assertions of church and empire.

The Social Ethics of the Great Commission in the New World

The Lord's Great Commission of the apostles provided the scriptural locus for Spanish political thought during the Renaissance. All the major political actors of Spain between 1492 and 1493 shared a common vision that Providence had elevated Ferdinand and Isabel to bring the Good News of salvation to the ends of the earth. The Admiral Christopher Columbus understood himself as the one chosen to 'take possession' of the people of the Indies to better serve the Catholic monarchs. And Pope Alexander VI gave the ecclesiastical seal of approval in his letter *Inter caetera* (1493) by affirming the praiseworthy intention of Columbus and the Spanish crown "to take control of these mainlands and aforesaid islands, their natives and inhabitants, and to bring them to the Catholic faith."[10]

Of this Gospel imperative to preach everywhere, no early modern Spaniard denied in the least. However, within this colonial matrix of Spain during the first half of the sixteenth century two distinctive Christian social imaginaries clashed with unprecedented vigor in the political history of Christendom.[11] Each of which regarded the task of the Great Commission, or the method of evangelization, in

---

9. O'Donovan, *The Desire of the Nations*, 214.
10. Pope Alexander IV, *Inter caetera* (1493). Cited in W. Eugene Shiels, *King and Church: The Rise and Fall of the Patronato Real* (Chicago: Loyola University Press, 1961), 79.
11. Charles Taylor has used the concept of "social imaginary" as an explanatory device for the legitimization of social practices distinct from Hegelian idealism and Marxist materialism. See *Modern Social Imaginaries* (Durham: Duke University Press, 2004), chap. 2.

radically opposed ways. Luis Rivera Pagán has identified these two social imaginaries in the following sense: "The first could be called *evangelizing conquest*, and it proposes to achieve, by force if necessary, dominion over the aborigines as a necessary condition to facilitate their evangelization. The second can be called *missionary action*, and it consists of reasonable persuasion through convincing arguments and adherence of the will through attraction."[12] The clarity of these two social imaginaries was evident in the strategic use of scripture, chronicles, symbols, exemplars, and ecclesiastical practice to carry out sharply divergent ethics or norms of evangelization. *Evangelization by conquest* represented an extension of the medieval-crusader social ethic across the Atlantic. From this perspective, the Spanish *conquistas* were a continuation of the *reconquista*, whose origins were synonymous with the crusades. The primary aim of Spanish conquest was to advance imperial Catholic sovereignty through the mutually reinforcing social practices of war and enslavement. In direct contrast, the method of *peaceful missionary action* generated an apostolic social ethic capable of providing a reflexive critical voice towards the crown and the church. Vocal proponents of this view in the first half of the sixteenth century (mostly Dominicans) considered it a categorical mistake to identify Amerindians residing in their own native lands with Muslims who had taken over formerly Christian lands like Moorish Spain, the Holy Land, and, most recently, Constantinople in 1453.[13]

When the sixteenth-century Spanish chronicler Francisco López de Gómara wrote his *General History of the Indies*, which he dedicated

---

12. Luis N. Rivera Pagán, *A Violent Evangelism: The Political and Religious Conquest of the Americas* (Louisville: Westminster/John Knox, 1992), 226.
13. This categorical distinction came from the Master General of the Order of Preachers Tomasso de (Vio) Cajetan's Commentary on the *Summa theologiae*. See Charles Cardinal Journet, *The Church of the Word Incarnate: An Essay in Speculative Theology*, trans. A. H. C. Downes, vol. 1 (New York: Sheed and Ward, 1955), 226–27.

to Emperor Charles V, he began with a telling claim: "The conquest of the Indies began once the conquests of the Moors ended, and that is because the Spaniards should always wage war with infidels."[14] The conceptual link between *reconquista* and *conquista* was not merely rhetorical, but an intractable ideological rationale for holy war. The *reconquista* impressed itself as a "fundamental memory of every Spaniard."[15] Consider, for example, the Spanish conquistador of Mexico and the Aztec empire, Hernán Cortés, who reportedly had the Constantinian inscription "By this sign we shall conquer" (*in hoc signo vincemus*) on the cross of his banner. Cortés's devotion to holy war and its worldly and eternal benefits emerge from his diary: "[A]s Christians we were obliged to fight against the enemies of our faith, and that we would as a result earn glory in the next life, and in this one such great honor and fame as no other generation has merited until now."[16]

The legal justification for Spanish conquest was outlined in the *Requerimiento*, which stipulated that the Catholic monarchs had been entrusted by Pope Alexander VI to convert and control the newly discovered territory across the Atlantic. The *Requerimiento* was used both by Cortés in Mexico and Francisco Pizarro in Peru. Read aloud in an incomprehensible language, the legal document gave native listeners a "choice" of either recognizing Spanish sovereignty or denying it with disastrous consequences. A key biblical narrative to justify the conquests was Joshua's seizing of Canaan, beginning with

---

14. Francisco López de Gómara, *Historia General de las Indias* (Barcelona: Linkgua Ediciones, 2008), 19: "*Comenzaron las conquistas acabadas la de moros, porque siempre guerreasen españoles contra infieles*" (All translations of Spanish and Latin texts are author's own unless indicated otherwise).
15. Shiels, *King and Church*, 30.
16. Cited in Rivera Pagán, *A Violent Evangelism*, 56.

Jericho, by force of arms.[17] The Indies were the new Promised Land (*la tierra de Promisión*) overflowing with silver and gold.

The lawyer and purported author of the *Requerimiento*, Juan López de Palacios Rubios (1450-1524), had also composed a treatise establishing the papal and imperial foundations for Spanish conquest of the Indies called *De las Islas del Mar Océano* (Libellus de insulis oceanis). *De las Islas* provided the biblical, philosophical, and canon legal support for the *Requerimiento*. Palacios Rubios appealed to Deut. 20:10-12, which allegedly presented the divine sanction for conquest according to the Mosaic law: "When you draw near to a town, before anything offer it peace. If they accept it and open their doors to you, everyone in the town shall be spared as your subjects and forced laborers. But if they do not surrender but resist you with force, then you shall conquer them."[18] For Palacios Rubios, scripture justified the forced labor system (or the *encomienda*) in the New World, which exacted tributes to the crown through Amerindian services in mining and agriculture in exchange for protection and instruction in the faith. As the Book of Joshua 16:10 indicated, certain Canaanites lived as tributaries, or forced laborers, within Israelite lands.[19] The Amerindians, just like the Canaanites of old, would be spared from war and death if they submitted to Spanish rule as its subjects and laborers.

Palacios Rubios even employed Aristotle's *Politics* to explain why some of the native peoples were "so inept and incapable of governing themselves." He stated that "they could be considered slaves, born to serve rather than command (according to the Philosopher in Book 1 of the *Politics*); therefore, as a result of their ignorance, they should

---

17. Rolena Adorno, *The Polemics of Possession in Spanish American Narrative* (New Haven: Yale University Press, 2007), 265–66.
18. Juan López de Palacios Rubios, *De las Islas del Mar Océano* (Libellus de insulis oceanis), trans. Paulino Castañeda Delgado et. al. (Navarra: EUNSA, 2013), 116–18.
19. Ibid., 384.

submit to the wiser, as servants to their lords."[20] Despite the usefulness of Aristotle's doctrine of natural slavery to justify Spanish colonial interests, Palacios Rubios was thoroughly papal monarchical, as were many of the Spanish royalists during the fifteenth and sixteenth centuries. The pope's fullness of power, founded on Christ's supreme lordship, justified a worldwide sovereignty (*dominium totius orbis*) extending to the temporal affairs of non-Christians. This hierocratic-papalist view was the *sine qua non* for the logic of the *Requerimiento*. Conversely, the appeal to ecclesiastical power as superior to secular authority—a legacy of the medieval church reforms beginning with Pope Gregory VII—also proved to be the fissure point by which the social ethics of the Gospel could work reflexively to unmask and critique the anti-Christian elements of the imperial crusader ethic of evangelization by conquest.

The general position toward the relationship between spiritual and temporal powers could be summarized in the moderate Dominican political view presented by Juan de Torquemada (d. 1468) and Cardinal Cajetan (d. 1534) that the church has temporal power only regarding spiritual things (*in ordine ad spiritualia*).[21] This moderate view was neither an endorsement of worldwide papal sovereignty seen among Spanish papalist-royalists, nor a radical subordination of church politics to secular power as seen in Marsilius of Padua and Niccolò Machiavelli. Rather, it upheld the belief that in certain egregious cases where secular law or authority has drastically failed to protect what is necessary for salvation, then it belongs to the church

---

20. Ibid., 118: "*aliqui eorum ita sunt inepti et imbecilles, quod se nullo modo gubernare sciunt, quapropter, largo modo, possunt dici servi, quasi nati ad serviendum non autem ad imperandum, ut tradit Philosophus, Politicorum, lib. 1, et hoc modo, insipientes, servire debent prudentibus, vel subditi dominis.*"
21. For an overview of the influence of the Spanish Dominican Juan de Torquemada on the moderate view relevant to the affair of the Indies, especially in the arguments of Vitoria, see Thomas M. Izbicki, "An Argument from Authority in the Indies Debate," *The Americas* (Jan. 1978): 400–406.

to intervene in temporal matters. Francisco de Vitoria (1492-1546), the theologian and pioneer of what was later known as the School of Salamanca, imparted the moderate Dominican position to a vibrant generation of scholastic thinkers including his student Domingo de Soto, and the renowned "Protector of the Indians," Bartolomé de las Casas (1484-1566).

It is precisely among these Dominicans during the rule of Emperor Charles that we find a clear, principled theopolitical opposition and resistance to the crusader ethic of evangelization by conquest. Their explicit appeals to scripture for promoting the salvation of both Spaniards and Amerindians by condemning the political and economic excesses of the former in order to promote greater justice and freedom for the latter will occupy the remainder of our analysis. In Las Casas's classic and definitive defense of the Amerindians (the *Apologia*) presented before the Council of the Indies in 1550 for five days in Valladolid, Spain, he contrasted the pagan and even satanic elements of Spanish conquest with the apostolic ethic of evangelization:

> Christ seeks souls, not property. He who alone is the immortal king of kings thirsts not for riches, not for ease and pleasures, but for the salvation of mankind, for which, fastened to the wood of the cross, he offered his life. He who wants a large part of mankind to be such that, following Aristotle's teachings, he may act like a ferocious executioner toward them, press them into slavery, and through them grow rich, is a despotic master, not a Christian; a son of Satan, not of God; a plunderer, not a shepherd; a person who is led by the spirit of the devil, not heaven. If you seek Indians so that gently, mildly, quietly, humanely, and in a Christian manner you may instruct them in the word of God and by your labor bring them to Christ's flock, imprinting the gentle Christ on their minds, you perform the work of an apostle and will receive an imperishable crown of glory from our sacrificed lamb. But if it be in in order that by sword, fire, massacre, trickery, violence, tyranny, cruelty, and an inhumanity that is worse than barbaric you may destroy and plunder utterly harmless peoples who are ready to renounce evil and

receive the word of God, you are children of the devil and the most horrible plunderers of all.[22]

Let us now turn to the topic of war in the New World, which demonstrated how the power of God's word entrusted to the church could intervene in political debate to expel falsehood and idolatry, promote Amerindian natural rights, and liberate souls from injustice. Scripture supplied these Dominican thinkers with religious moral norms for carrying out distinct political acts related to constraining war and identifying the Christian parameters of intervention in Amerindian affairs in accordance with a Gospel social ethic.

"Why Should I Judge Outsiders?" The Pauline Constraint on Holy War

The fissure point of Spanish political thought concerning the affair of the Indies broke open through the preaching of the first Dominicans on the island of Hispaniola in 1511. These friars from Salamanca were the first to condemn the abuses of the Amerindians under the forced labor system and wars of conquest by affirming their humanity and rationality. As the conquests, slaving expeditions, and forced labor continued in the New World, the critical moral voice of resistance to evil on behalf of Amerindian claims of justice and freedom was carried on by the intellectual and political efforts of Spanish Dominican theologians such as Vitoria, Soto, and Las Casas during the reign of Charles.

Although there were certain differences in how these thinkers reflected on the affair of the Indies, and what actions should be taken by the crown, it is important to highlight their shared theological commitment to scripture as a critical resource for curbing Spanish

---

22. Bartolomé de las Casas, *In Defense of the Indians*, trans. Stafford Poole (DeKalb, IL: Northern Illinois University Press, 1992), 40.

abuses against Amerindian peoples with respect to war, intervention, and evangelization. As friars of the Order of Preachers they firmly believed that the primary purpose of Spanish presence in the New World was to carry out the Great Commission assigned by Christ. Therefore, Spanish activity in the Indies must avoid making the Gospel scandalous to its hearers. Their moderate Dominican position rejected the dominant papalist-royalist view on the grounds of both scripture and their scholastic theological convictions.

The Dominicans denied the common legal opinion stemming from Pope Innocent IV, and later the canonist Hostiensis, that the pope and Christian rulers under papal guidance could directly intervene in pagan temporal affairs to judge and punish sinful acts considered contrary to natural law when respective rulers failed to do so.[23] With Genesis 19 providing the biblical warrant, Palacios Rubios supported the view of the medieval canonists: "The pope is able to punish gentiles—who have nothing except the natural law—if they do what is contrary to the precepts of nature, just like the Lord punished the Sodomites who sinned against the natural law."[24] Among the sins most opposed to natural law is the practice of idolatry, because "it is naturally self-evident to worship the one creator God, and not the creature."[25]

It is revealing that Innocent IV's commentary on a crusade letter served as the basis for this canonistic teaching on Christian-infidel relations justifying nothing short of a holy war to abolish idolatry. From the papalist-royalist Palacios Rubios to the imperial-humanist Juan Ginés de Sepúlveda (d. 1573), the common rationale for Spanish

---

23. For an in-depth treatment of this common opinion among the canonists tracing its influence to the early modern period, see the unparalleled study in English by James Muldoon, *Popes, Lawyers, and Infidels: The Church and the Non-Christian World, 1250–1550* (Philadelphia: University of Pennsylvania Press, 1979).
24. Palacios Rubios, *De las islas*, 276: "*poterit papa punire gentilem qui non habet nisi legem naturae, si contra naturae praecepta fecerit, sicut Dominus punivit Sodomitas qui contra legem naturae peccabant.*"
25. Ibid., 278.

Christian intervention in the political life of unbelievers during the first half of the sixteenth century rested on the legal title of removing idolatry to allow for effective evangelization. In the famous debate at Valladolid, Spain (1550-1551) between Sepúlveda and Las Casas, the former argued that the Amerindians "can be conquered and punished by this cause alone of not abiding by the natural law or for being idolaters."[26] This common justification of holy war first supplied by Innocent IV provided the ideological armature for early modern imperialism.[27]

The Spanish Dominicans resisted this opinion principally on two grounds: one canonistic-legal and the other scholastic-theological. The speculative theological views of St. Thomas Aquinas as appropriated by Cajetan were of monumental importance to the Spanish Dominican defense of Amerindian political authority independent of imperial claims to the contrary. In particular, the most relevant teaching of Aquinas from the *Summa theologiae* was that "divine law, which is from grace, does not abolish human law, which is from natural reason."[28] Commenting on this Thomistic dictum, Thomas O'Meara notes: "Indian political structures emerged out of natural law and not from a humanity corrupted by the fall. . . . Neither the fact that the Indians were not Christians nor their involvement in questionable forms of cult or immorality argued for the employment of violence against them."[29] A discourse of Amerindian natural rights emerged out of this scholastic-theological context.[30]

---

26. Juan Ginés de Sepúlveda, *Aqui se contiene una disputa o contoversia*, in *Tratados de Fray Bartolomé de las Casas* I (Mexico: Fondo de Cultura Económica, 1965), Objeción séptima, 310–11.
27. Jonathan Boyarin, *The Unconverted Self: Jews, Indians, and the Identity of Christian Europe* (Chicago: University of Chicago Press, 2009), 46.
28. *Summa theologiae* 2a-2ae q. 10 ad. 10: "*Ius autem divinum, quod est ex gratia, non tollit ius humanum, quod est ex naturali ratione.*"
29. Thomas F. O'Meara, OP, "The Dominican School of Salamanca and the Spanish Conquest of America: Some Bibliographic Notes," *The Thomist* 56, no. 4 (Oct 1992): 555-82, (571–72).

The Spanish Dominicans were also quite conversant in the canon legal tradition, by which they retrieved important and neglected juridical principles for critiquing violent colonial practices, especially holy wars of conquest. The scriptural teaching that provided the legal and political constraint on wars of idolatry came from St. Paul's First Letter to the Corinthians. Paul taught Christians that they should avoid associating with other brothers and sisters who exhibit sexual misconduct, robbery, and idolatry. Believers can make a judgment of those who are within the Christian community, but not those outside. As the Apostle indicated, "For what have I to do with judging those outside? Is it not those who are inside that you are to judge? God will judge those outside."[31]

Medieval scholar of Judaism Solomon Grayzel referred to this Pauline teaching concerning the scope of judgment as the *foris* principle.[32] Gratian, the pioneer of medieval canon law, incorporated the principle into the medieval *Decretum* to refer specifically to those unbelievers outside the Church, who belong to divine judgment rather than human judgment. Grayzel noted that the *foris* principle established boundaries in medieval society so that Christians could not interfere with Jews in their spiritual matters.[33] In the context of the New World, the *foris* principle provided a traditional juridical constraint protecting Amerindian unbelievers in their spiritual and political affairs from overreaching ecclesiastical power and Christian political authority.

Although the Spanish lawyers employed other biblical examples

---

30. For a longer treatment of the political significance of St. Thomas's teaching in the context of New World debates over Amerindians, see the author's "The Freedom of the Gospel: Aquinas, Subversive Natural Law, and the Spanish Wars of Religion," *Modern Theology* 31, no 2 (April 2015): 312-37.
31. 1 Cor. 5:12–13.
32. Solomon Grayzel, "Introduction" to *The Church and the Jews in the XIIIth Century* (Detroit: Wayne State University, 1989), 3-45, (12).
33. Ibid., 12.

such as Genesis 19 and the Israelite conquest of Canaan to justify the punishment of Amerindians, the Dominican theologians relied on the *foris* principle to prohibit holy wars of conquests. The well-known *Relectio de Indis* of Francisco de Vitoria delivered at the University of Salamanca in January of 1539, which began with the Lord's Great Commission in Matt. 28:19 as its hermeneutical starting point, was significant in this regard. Vitoria explicitly identified the Pauline *foris* teaching in order to reject two common justifications for the Spanish conquests on the basis of papal power and punishing sins against the natural law.

With respect to the first justification, which was utilized in the *Requerimiento*, Vitoria's first *relectio* on ecclesiastical power delivered in 1532 had already ruled out such a title:

> [T]he pope has no dominium in the lands of the infidel, since he has power only within the Church; as the Apostle said, what has he to do to judge them also that are without? (1 Cor. 5:12). Unbelievers possess true dominion, since the Apostle teaches that even the faithful must pay them tribute (Rom. 13:6), and says that their power is ordained of God and that their laws must be obeyed. But they do not have their dominion from the pope, since it is clear he would rather they not have it – and indeed make efforts to overthrow pagan empires. Therefore the pope is not lord of the whole world.[34]

In one full sweep against the "obsequious flattery" of the papacy by Roman sycophants, Vitoria employed St. Paul to deny Christian jurisdiction over infidels (1 Cor. 5:12) and affirm infidel political rule (Rom. 13:6). When Vitoria returned to the question in *De Indis*, he restated his argument that because Jesus Christ had no temporal rule, much less does the pope as the Vicar of Christ.[35] Vitoria's moderate Dominican position held that the papacy only has temporal

---

34. Francisco de Vitoria, "On the Power of the Church," in *Political Writings*, ed. Anthony Pagden and Jeremy Lawrance (Cambridge: Cambridge University Press, 1991), 47-108, (84).
35. Ibid., "On the American Indians," 260.

power in so much as it is necessary for the administration of spiritual matters. However, since "1 Cor. 5:12 shows that he has no spiritual power over the barbarians, it follows that he can have no temporal power over them either."[36]

The *Requerimiento* supplied no legitimate basis for war against infidels or the confiscation of their goods since it was founded on a contrived title. In contrast to the *Requerimiento*, Vitoria absolutely prohibited infidel refusal to convert to the Christian faith as a title for war. As he tersely put it, "war is no argument for the truth of the Christian faith." The theologian had heard "only of provocations, savage crimes, and multitudes of unholy acts." But even if the Spaniards were performing miracles and exemplary acts as signs of the true religion and the Indians still refused to convert, "this was still no reason to declare war on them and despoil them of their goods."[37] That is because religious belief, which is a matter of free will, is greatly diminished by the use of fear and threats and would only lead to a servile faith that is nothing less than sacrilege.

Relatedly, the title for war on the basis of punishing unbelievers for their sins against natural law was also precluded under the *foris* principle. Without proper jurisdiction there is no ground for punishing unbelievers either. For Vitoria, the view of Innocent IV and Palacios Rubios supporting intervention and war to punish pagan sins ignores St. Paul's point "that the judgment of unbelievers, whether they be fornicators or idolaters, is none of his business."[38] Vitoria refused to read the Old Testament narrative of the Israelite taking of Canaan in Spanish colonial terms. Instead, he explicitly stated that "the people of Israel never occupied lands of the unbelievers either on the grounds that they were infidels or idolaters

36. Ibid., 263.
37. Ibid., 271–72.
38. Ibid., 274.

or because they were sinners against nature. . . ." Echoing Cajetan, Vitoria concluded that God allowed conquest in this biblical instance as a singular "special gift," or, perhaps according to traditional just war criteria.[39]

The *foris* principle was arguably the central point of contention at the Valladolid junta between Las Casas and Sepúlveda in their debate over the religious coercion of Amerindians. Las Casas's *Apologia* relied extensively on the principle to reject both the immodest claims of papal jurisdiction and, following the newer imperial-humanist arguments of Sepúlveda, the universal claims of punishing violations of natural law upon which the royal title allegedly rested independent of papal authorization. Las Casas, a bishop of Chiapas trained in canon law, applied the teachings of Augustine, Gratian, and Aquinas on the Pauline principle to the Amerindian case.[40] He presented his argument supporting the immunity of infidel outsiders on the basis of their free will and the apostolic ethic of evangelization. Las Casas saw it as a rule and principle that the church has no jurisdiction over unbelievers and that "it has no power at all to uproot idolatry against the will of idolaters."[41]

The general rule that Las Casas derived from the *foris* principle was stated summarily in the *Apologia*, which illustrated the Christian faith's commitment to a people's natural immunity from coercion in religious matters: "[I]f against their wills we should completely abolish their ceremonies, they would have, in addition to the great number of other resulting abuses, only an apparent adherence to the Christian faith and the Christian religion, and we would appear to be openly compelling them to embrace the faith—and this is forbidden."[42] The use of force and violent coercion to punish

39. Ibid., 275.
40. Las Casas, *In Defense of the Indians*, chaps. 7–10.
41. Ibid., 66.

idolaters, who have not freely embraced the faith—so contrary to Christ's example—presented a most serious obstacle to the genuine reception of the Gospel.

Defending and Liberating the Innocent from Death

Although the *foris* principle prohibited the crusader ethic of war to abolish idolatry, the Spanish Dominicans were not pacifists and still had to address the legitimacy of war in the context of the Indies. But they did so under the shared belief that all human beings, as rational creatures made in God's image, possess moral freedom and, by extension, control (or *dominium*) over their possessions and political affairs. A whole ensemble of legal rights was applicable universally to both Christians and infidels on the basis of natural law, which prioritized the right to life (or self-preservation) and the right of defending oneself or others (*ius defendendi*).

Before his death in 1546, Vitoria taught in *De Indis* that there might be possible or arguable titles for just war in the Americas on the basis of a "law of nations" (*ius gentium*), having the sanction of popular support from the whole world and natural law. For this reason, "No kingdom may choose to ignore this law of nations."[43] Vitoria, as a matter of debate rather than certainty, considered possible titles for Spanish rule overseas involving armed conflict with the Amerindians. He did so on the basis of protecting and defending Spanish ambassadors and missionaries whose rights to travel and preach were violated (just titles one and two). He also believed that if Amerindians were violently hindered from converting (just title three); or held in tyranny and bondage as either Christians or unbelievers (just titles four and five); or if they required necessary assistance from a foreign

---

42. Ibid., 70.
43. Vitoria, "On Civil Power," in *Political Writings*, 3–44, (40).

ally (seventh title), then it might be legitimate to exercise the rights of war.[44]

With respect to the possible title of defending allies against unjust aggressors, Vitoria proposed that this was the legal justification for the expansion of the Roman Empire.[45] On this point, Soto and Las Casas diverged from Vitoria's uncritical portrayal of Roman imperialism.[46] Soto's *Relectio de dominio* delivered in 1535 claimed that the Roman imperial title for war was "their right in force of arms" by which "they subjugated many unwilling nations through no other title than that they were more powerful."[47] In the defense at Valladolid, Las Casas declared "the Roman Empire did not arise through justice but was acquired by tyranny and violence."[48]

Vitoria's turn to the law of nations for thinking about just war should not detract from recognizing the theological and biblical foundations of his Christian worldview. His argument for a right of traveling (*ius peregrinandi*) served as the cosmopolitan basis for social communication, hospitality, trade, and even preaching the faith to non-Christians. And although he found congruity here with the Roman legal concept of the *ius gentium*, he established this right more securely in nature and scripture: "'I was a stranger and ye took me not in' (Matt. 25:43), from which it is clear that, since it is a law of nature to welcome strangers, this judgment of Christ is to be decreed amongst all men."[49] The Samaritan story (Luke 10:29-37) enabled

---

44. Perhaps most controversially, Vitoria even considered "for the sake of argument" the hypothetical case of barbarian peoples unsuited to govern themselves due to their mental deficiency. Despite the strange fact that Vitoria already excluded the Amerindians from this category in the first part of the *relectio*, Vitoria makes it clear that this benevolent paternalism must be done in conformity with the precepts of Christian charity and love of neighbor.
45. Vitoria, "On the American Indians," 289.
46. David A. Lupher, *Romans in a New World: Classical Models in Sixteenth-Century Spanish America* (Ann Arbor: University of Michigan Press, 2003), chap. 2.
47. Cited in ibid., 65.
48. Las Casas, *In Defense of the Indians*, 321.
49. Vitoria, "On the American Indians," 279.

him to argue that foreigners must treat Spaniards as their neighbors and are obliged to love and welcome them so long as the Spaniards do no wrong or harm.

De Indis should be understood alongside Vitoria's follow-up lecture on the right of war (*Relectio de iure belli*) offered in the summer of 1539. In that posterior lecture, Vitoria dismissed "difference of religion" and "enlargement of empire" as legitimate causes for war and reduced his argument to a single cause: war can only follow from a serious injury.[50] It can be said then that "the only such right that Vitoria recognized unreservedly was a right to protect innocent human life."[51] The category of innocence was precisely what gave Vitoria's arguments such moral force. When the theologian wrote to the Spanish provincial of the Dominicans concerning Pizarro's conquest of Peru, he was adamant that the natives had not committed the slightest injury nor was there any ground for war resulting in the capture and execution of the Inca Atahualpa. Since these Amerindian peoples were fellow humans and neighbors, the conquerors were guilty of "utter impiety and tyranny" as seen in the pillaging of Cuzco and the sacred burial sites (or *guacas*) of the Incas.[52]

However, Vitoria's analysis cut both ways. Though well aware of the Spanish atrocities and acts of avarice under the cloak of religion, he was also eminently concerned with addressing the problem of innocent Amerindians who were oppressed by their own rulers and laws. In this context, the notorious practice of human sacrifice attracted his attention. Again, scripture informed his moral judgment. The biblical ethic of neighbor-love as seen in the Prov. 24:11 mandate to "Rescue those who are being dragged to death" was

---

50. Ibid., "On the Law of War," 302–4.
51. Brian Tierney, "Vitoria and Suarez on *ius gentium*, natural law, and custom," in *The Nature of Customary Law*, ed. Amanda Perreau-Saussine and James Bernard Murphy (Cambridge: Cambridge University Press, 2007), 108.
52. Vitoria, "Letter to Miguel de Arcos, OP," 333.

paramount to this discussion in Spanish political thought. Vitoria was careful to point out—consistent with the *foris* principle—that forceful intervention and even war in such cases was not in order to punish sins against natural law, but to protect the innocent from suffering injury.[53] Yet, in presenting this scenario as a possible title to war in *De Indis*, he made the significant point "that in lawful defense of the innocent from unjust death, even without the pope's authority, the Spaniards may prohibit the barbarians from practicing any nefarious custom or rite.... The barbarians are all our neighbors, and therefore anyone, and especially princes, may defend them from such tyranny and oppression."[54] Vitoria intimated a rather modern-sounding rational justification here to restrict violent religious practices without the need to resort to papal authority.

After citing the Proverbs mandate, he further remarked: "this applies not only to the actual moment when they are being dragged to death; they may also force the barbarians to give up their rites altogether. If they refuse to do so, war may be declared upon them, and the laws of war enforced upon them; and if there is no other means of putting an end to these sacrilegious rites, their masters may be changed and new princes set up."[55] Under this arguable just title to defend the innocent from gravely immoral religious practices, Vitoria left open the possibility of complete regime change through war. This claim demonstrates an important tension in Vitoria's analysis whereby his prohibition of waging war against those who refuse to convert (and by extension their idolatrous practices) runs up against the duty to protect innocent unbelievers, which may include abolishing any pagan religious practices that might harm them.

When Las Casas turned to the issue of human sacrifice, he was

---

53. Ibid., "On Self-Restraint," 225.
54. Ibid., "On the American Indians," 288.
55. Ibid.

confronted with the same moral claims from scripture as Vitoria. In this "new case" involving Indian cases of human sacrifice Las Casas had to address Sepúlveda's imperial-humanist argument justifying war and conquest to prevent the alleged thousands of deaths annually.[56] In opposition, he aptly stated in the *Apologia* that "war against the Indians, which we call in Spanish *conquistas*, is evil and essentially anti-Christian," not to mention unlawful.[57] This point had already been made in his earliest treatise on the peaceful method of evangelization, which was the "only way" that Christ taught to the apostles when he sent them out as sheep among wolves.[58] The Indians were the only ones who had a lawful right of self-defense against the Spaniards, as evident in the native rebellion led by Enriquillo.[59]

Notwithstanding the moral and rhetorical strength of Las Casas's critique of the *conquistas*, he could not simply turn a blind eye to the death of innocent Amerindians even if their oppressors were not Spaniards. After all, "the Indians are our brothers, and Christ has given his life for them."[60] Stopping human sacrifice to protect the innocent was gaining support from imperial humanists like Sepúlveda bent on subjugating and civilizing Amerindians. It demanded a Christian response grounded in the Gospel ethic. On this point, Las Casas agreed with and diverged from Vitoria. Like Vitoria, Las Casas allowed for the possibility of intervening in a foreign society in order to liberate innocent persons from oppression. Furthermore, both of them agreed, contrary to Sepúlveda, that this intervention was not for punishing sins against natural law, but *strictly* for the protection of the innocent from death.

---

56. Las Casas, *In Defense of the Indians*, 185.
57. Ibid., 355.
58. *Bartolomé de las Casas: The Only Way*, ed. Helen Rand Parish (Mahwah: Paulist Press, 1992).
59. Francis Patrick Sullivan, *Indian Freedom: The Cause of Bartolomé de las Casas, 1484–1566* (Kansas City: Sheed and Ward, 1995), 191–92.
60. Las Casas, *In Defense of the Indians*, 362.

Unlike Vitoria's appeal to the universal law of nations, Las Casas viewed the protection innocent persons as an ecclesial activity inseparable from the ethic of evangelization. He increased the ecclesial and papal role while limiting its abuse under the *foris* principle, as seen in the following passage:

> It is the concern of the Church and the Pope, to whom the pastoral care of the whole world has been entrusted by Christ, to prevent the slaughter of such innocent persons lest their souls, whose salvation should be of special concern, should perish forever. It is the business, then, of the Church and the Vicar of Christ, as the universal pastor and curate of the whole world, to exercise jurisdiction authoritatively and in Christ's name in this case, not in order to punish or subjugate unbelievers by reason of their crime, since it is not the business of the Church "to pass judgment on those outside . . . but of those who are outside, God is the judge". . . but in order to take the steps necessary to prevent slaughter of such innocent persons.[61]

Las Casas, in contrast to Vitoria's proto-modern international thinking, identified "the rulers of the world" as private persons in the juridical sense meaning that "they cannot pronounce judgment outside the boundaries of each individual kingdom." However, this did not rule out the possibility that the church might appoint some Christian ruler or private person to liberate the oppressed.[62] Las Casas thereby strengthened, rather than attenuated, the inherently political nature of the church by viewing innocent persons outside the visible body of Christ as potential adopted members of the church, following their free consent. Although this expanded the range of papal power beyond Vitoria's view, it did so only to the extent that the Vicar of Christ as the leader of the universal church can intervene to protect the defenseless innocent among outsiders who may ultimately lose

---

61. Ibid., 186.
62. Ibid., 186–87.

the gift of hearing the Good News of salvation because of the great injustice of state-sanctioned murder.

More than aware of the conceits of illegitimate claims of papal power to justify violence against unbelievers, Las Casas did not refer to the Pope as "lord of the world," but as a "steward" or servant of the Supreme Prince and Universal Lord of all—Jesus Christ.[63] Though this interpretation of church politics (or coercive jurisdiction) seems less than appealing to modern minds, we must highlight what was at stake here for Las Casas. In his view, the defense of the innocent abroad under the express approval of the church and the papacy afforded the best chance of allowing the word of God to exercise a reflexive disciplinary power on political activity without licensing Christian political powers to use force in foreign intervention (or conquest) on the basis of an independent imperial-humanist civilizing agenda as proposed by Sepúlveda.

The purpose of Las Casas's ecclesial turn regarding intervention was not to turn the church into a war-mongering band of robbers as the conquistadors had done; rather, it was to identify the limits of using force in necessary situations and to increase commitment to people most in need. After evil has been effectively stopped, the church "must go further" by caring "unceasingly for the salvation of souls, so that all peoples in the world may attain salvation." Even though it is the church's concern to prevent the murder of innocent persons, "it nevertheless must do this with such discretion as not to give rise to some greater evil to the other peoples that would be a hindrance to their salvation and would thereby frustrate the fruit and purpose of Christ's passion."[64] In other words, if intervention becomes a scandal to the Gospel and an obstacle to evangelization, then it must be abandoned.

63. Ibid., 260.
64. Ibid., 187.

War, according to Las Casas, was simply not an acceptable Christian response to human sacrifice in the Indies. It had led to immeasurable innocent deaths and instilled hatred of the faith. Furthermore, the direct attack against pagan religious customs by means of war—no matter how shockingly violent and objectively evil such customs were—would be seen by unbelievers as a *Christian* attack on their society's sacred way of life. Citing Pope Gregory the Great's policy toward Jews in late antiquity, Las Casas concluded: "Of what use is it when and if their practices of long standing are forbidden to them? It contributes not at all to their conversion to the faith."[65]

From Las Casas's perspective, a prince's war against a pagan religion outside of his political jurisdiction would appear as nothing less than forced conversion to another religion or civilization. Instead of war, Las Casas proposed a gradual approach patiently committed to long-term preaching of the Gospel supported by virtuous conduct and teaching about grave evils as the best antidote to human sacrifice. If that were achievable but did not yield the desired results, then some restrained force could be used only to stop the killing of innocent people.[66] What that intervention with moderate force short of warfare finally looks like and entails, Las Casas never says. However, it was for him a necessary alternative to violent conquest within the social ethics of Christendom.

Conclusion

Yoder portrayed the social ethics of Christendom as the "illegitimate takeover of the world," a denial of freedom to unbelievers. Though this was evident in the crusader ethic of evangelization by conquest,

---

65. Ibid., 188.
66. Bartolomé de las Casas, *De thesauris*, in *Obras completas* 11.1, ed. Paulino Castañeda Delgado and Antonio García de Moral (Madrid: Alianza Editorial, 1988–1990), 434–35.

there is a far more interesting story in Christendom about the Gospel's ability to speak truth to imperial and ecclesiastical power and defend the immunity and natural rights of unbelievers. The critical voice of Gospel social ethics as seen among the Spanish Dominicans was reflected in Pope Paul III's famous letter *Sublimis Deus* (1537), which condemned missionary wars as satanic and defended the liberty and possessions of Amerindians. Relatedly, the 1542 "New Laws" of Emperor Charles eliminating wars of conquest and abolishing the forced labor institution was the most powerful expression, albeit short-lived, of the influence of Gospel social ethics on royal policy.

"The last and greatest of the legal accomplishments of Christendom," O'Donovan writes, "was the conception that there exists, not merely as an ideal but in fact, an international law, dependent on no regime and no statute, but on the Natural Law implanted in human minds by God, and given effect by international custom and convention."[67] Vitoria's turn to the *ius gentium* as a strategy for expanding the rule of law between "nations," which contributed to the development of universal natural rights in the Christian tradition, highlights a remarkable legacy of Christendom on the church's social ethics. But so too does Las Casas's ecclesial turn to the papal guardianship of freedom and the natural rights of the whole world under Christ's rule. Both strategies of carrying out the ethic of evangelization and love of one's neighbor remained viable Christian alternatives to the demonic crusader ethic of evangelization by conquest in the early modern colonial world.

---

67. O'Donovan, *The Desire of the Nations*, 236.

9

The Unexceptional King

Political Theology in Shakespeare's Richard II

Anthony D. Baker

In what turns out to be the last moments of his life, the title character of Shakespeare's *Richard II* mashes up two separate scenes from the Synoptic Gospels. In his defense, he is in solitary confinement in a castle dungeon, with apparently no copies of Jerome's Bible at hand.

His mind is, he says, mixed with several sorts of thoughts, and even the highest of thoughts that "people" his newly confined world are complex ones:

> ... The better sort
> As thoughts of things divine, are intermixed
> With scruples, and do set the faith itself
> Against the faith, as thus: 'Come, little ones,'
> And then again,
> 'It is as hard to come as for a camel
> To thread the postern of a small needle's eye.' (5.5.11–17)[1]

If Richard is recalling the eighteenth chapter of Luke's gospel, where Jesus is displeased on seeing his disciples rebuke a collection of children, and so says, "Suffer the babes to come unto me, and forbid them not" (Luke 5:16),[2] he ignores a contextual shift two verses later that paves the way for the verse that sets "the faith itself against the faith." Here it is not children brought to him, but a rich ruler who runs to him and asks what he must do to possess eternal life. The children go away blessed, the ruler sad, prompting Jesus' quip to his disciples: "Surely it is easier for a camel to go through a needle's eye, than for a rich man to enter into the kingdom of God" (18.25).

Richard is, to use a tired but quite apt *cliché*, in a crisis of faith. Earlier, when he sits atop the throne and commands the nobles and the soldiers, there is no separation at all between himself and God. "In God's name and the King's," the Lord Marshal heralds all supplicants to the throne, "say who thou art" (1.3.11). Here, the king's name is almost a pleonastic addendum to the divine, and addendum installs an array of questions: Do they always speak in the same voice? Could the king speak in his own name? Indeed, could God's name bring judgment on the name of king?

The many theological questions buried within Lord Marshal's "and" are the very ones, in fact, that surface as the play develops. Richard deals irresponsibly with his nobles, and in particular the family of John of Gaunt, exiling Gaunt's son and looting the family's wealth. When he runs off to make expensive war in Ireland, Gaunt's son Bolingbroke returns from exile and gathers a force of peasants and soldiers. It would seem a bloody conflict is brewing, as in the

---

1. All quotations from *Richard II* are taken from Stephen Greenblatt, ed., *The Norton Shakespeare, Based on the Oxford Edition* (New York: W. W. Norton & Co., 1997).
2. Scriptural citations are from the Geneva Bible, https://archive.org/details/TheGenevaBible1560, accessed June 5, 2015. This is the version of the Bible that is generally agreed to be the one Shakespeare most often quotes. I have modernized the spelling, but otherwise left the text intact.

plays that tell the consequent history that culminates in the War of the Roses. In *Richard II*, though, the battle is one of "gentle words" (3.3.130), and rarely even words between the two opposing sides: most often it is Richard, as in the prison scene, who is set against himself, championing his irrevocable claim in one breath, despairing over his Icarus-like plunge in the next. By the time Bolingbroke is crowned Henry IV, Richard has become almost a holy fool, equivocating circles around the new king's court. Theological questions are central to his equivocations: Does God speak through him? Is God now even inviting him to come near, or rather pressing him away like the poor camel? Is he Christ, and his former subjects so many Judases? Or is he a Judas to himself, alongside them? In other words, Richard responds to the threat of deposition not by rallying the faithful masses, but by prying apart the immediacy of the divine-human identification into a series of introspective theological mediations.

Alongside this theological inquiry into divine presence, the bloodless insurrection opens a set of political questions that readers and audiences generally take to be the primary thematic turf of the play:[3] Is Bolingbroke right to rebel? In what sense might he claim such a right? Moreover, does Richard ever, in fact, cease to be king? He is, as John of Gaunt insists, God's "deputy anointed in his sight" (1.3.38), and the play repeatedly asks whether it is even possible to undo what God has done. The deposition scene is a bizarre "Black Mass" event,[4] made all the more bizarre by Richard's earlier assertion that "The breath of worldly men cannot depose / The deputy elected

---

3. Jean-Christophe Mayer, "Shakespeare's Religious Background Revisited: *Richard II* in a New Context," in Dennis Taylor and David Beauregard, eds., *Shakespeare and the Culture of Christianity in Early Modern England* (New York: Fordham University Press, 2003), 103–4, shows that the chronicled narrative of Richard had already become a lodestone for questions about "legal" revolt prior to Shakespeare's play. Part of my argument here is that Shakespeare complicates these matters with more penetrating theological questions.
4. Marjorie Garber, *Shakespeare After All* (New York: Anchor Books, 2004), 262.

by the Lord," nor can "all the water in the rough rude sea . . . wash the balm" from his head (3.2.50-53). Now this has changed: "Mark me how I will undo myself," he says to Bolingbroke, and hands over crown and scepter, washing away the sacramental balm with his own tears, and unsaying his oaths with his own tongue (4.1.193).

Has he in fact unkinged himself? Can he? Immediately upon handing over the crown he accuses himself of treason, thus suggesting the he is still the true king. This is the dialectic still playing itself out in prison, when thoughts of one sort persuade him he is king, and then thoughts of another sort tell him the opposite:

> . . . Sometimes am I king;
> Then treason makes me wish myself a beggar,
> And so I am. Then crushing penury
> Persuades me I was better when a king.
> Then am I kinged again, and by and by
> Think that I am unkinged by Bolingbroke,
> And straight am nothing. (5.5.33-38)

If he is king, then he is not king, since his own act of treason unkings him; if he is not king, he can only know this by imagining himself to be the king again, and then immediately recollecting how it is that he was deposed. Even as he is struck down at the scene's end, he seems to be undecided: "Thy fierce hand," he says to his killer, "Hath with the King's blood stained the King's own land" (5.5.110). The doubling of the term here might suggest that he is still at the end waffling between two allegiances, just as he is waffling between the two gospel figures: King Henry's realm is now stained by King Richard's blood.

My proposal here is to read both of Richard's confusions together, the more obvious political one—*Is he king or not?*—layered atop the more subtle theological one—*Is God for or against Richard?* Though they may seem to be at heart the same question, I suggest they are not, and moreover that separating them yields a suggestive image of a kind of Godward sovereignty. Layering these questions, I shall argue, allows a nuanced reading of the play, but also a nuanced account of the relation of divine and human sovereignties. While wondering whether he is Judas or Christ, a little one or a camel, Richard begins to construct a political theology that is richer and suppler than much of what currently goes by that name.

Richard's Other Body

If Shakespeare is entangling politics with theology, to what extent does his play offer a political theology? The question is obviously anachronistic, since the discipline that goes by that name is a twentieth-century phenomenon that originated in Carl Schmitt's controversial conclusion that "all significant concepts of the modern theory of the state are secularized theological concepts."[5]

Shakespeare, though, has been from the discipline's founding heavily involved. Schmitt himself offered a study of Hamlet, in a rather hyperbolic reading of the play as a coded critique of Stuart family politics. Around the same time, Walter Benjamin's *habilitation* treated Hamlet as a unique figure "capable of striking Christian sparks" in the midst of a literary tendency toward secularized constructions of political sovereignty.[6] Three decades later, Ernst Kantorowicz published his remarkable "Study in Medieval Political Theology," *The King's Two Bodies*, a book which opens with a reading of *Richard II*. Recent experiments in political theology[7] have continued this trend, engaging Shakespeare's plays as the setting

---

5. Carl Schmitt, *Political Theology: Four Chapters on the Concept of Sovereignty*, trans. George Schwab (Cambridge, MA: MIT Press, 1985), 36.
6. Quoted in David Pan's "Afterword" to Schmitt, *Hamlet or Hecuba: The Intrusion of the Time into the Play*, trans. David Pan and Jennifer R. Rust (New York: Telos Press, 2009), 107.
7. Jennifer Rust, Simon Critchley, Jennifer Reinhard Lupton, Ken Jackson, to name just a few of the scholars constructing political theologies with reference to Shakespeare.

for a theory about the questions of the origins of sovereignty and citizenship.

Readings of Shakespeare in these studies tend to fall into two camps. On the one side are those who read him as either naively or intentionally encoding medieval notions of theologically ballasted sovereignty, on the other, those who read him as constructing a visionary secular alternative. Let us briefly consider variant readings of *Richard II*.

Kantorowicz finds the play to be a clear window on a fully embodied medieval theological phenomenon, the doctrine of "the king's two bodies." It was in the fourth year of Elizabeth's reign that the suit against her predecessor and younger brother, Edward VI, came to trial, formalizing the language of the king's "Body natural," the mortal flesh "subject to all the Infirmities that come . . . to the natural Bodies of other People," and his "Body politic," an invisible and immaterial body that does not age or get sick, and is not subject to the human laws that bind his natural body.[8] *Richard II* launches the study as a key document that comes under the eye of the historian gathering evidence for his theory. If a popular Elizabethan play dramatizes the language of the earlier trial, thus implying audience recognition, then we have support for calling this theory *the* political theology of the era. In fact this is just what Kantorowicz finds. The theory is "the substance and essence" of the play: "*The Tragedy of King Richard II* is the tragedy of the King's Two Bodies."[9] The theory finds its ultimate expression at the other end of the set of four plays known as the Henriad, when King Henry V laments his "twin-born greatness" which, though giving him the life of a man, also makes him the repository of all the care of his

---

8. From the Plowden Reports, in Kantorowicz: *The King's Two Bodies: A Study in Mediaeval Political Theology* (Princeton: Princeton University Press, 1957), 7.
9. Ibid., 26.

subjects. This "royal gemination" is Shakespeare's recognition of the two bodies.[10]

Kantorowicz's reading of *Richard II* focuses on three scenes that show the king dissolving from an integral whole into two separate bodies. As the first opens, "there is as yet no split in Richard,"[11] and he associates himself unproblematically with God. The royal—and in fact theo-political—"we" is still intact. But "this glorious image of kingship 'By the Grace of God' does not last."[12] The king passes through a nominalist phase, wondering whether "Richard" is simply a name covering over a mortal and non-regal reality. So a scene that opens with Richard as divine ends with Richard sitting on the ground telling "sad stories of the death of kings" (3.2.52). The second scene that shows the split of the two bodies has him once again affirming his identity with the heavens, only to then depict him falling to a new low: not just a mortal now, but a "frantic man," a fool wallowing in the depths of his own self-pity. The third pivotal scene opens with yet another proclamation that Richard cannot be judged by humankind, as he is "the figure of God's majesty" (IV.1.123);[13] this is the scene that culminates with his auto-decoronation, the "inverted rite" that works the final separation. Where Richard accuses himself of treason, Kantorowicz comments, "That is, the king's body natural becomes a traitor to the king's body politic."[14] Now he is just Richard, or perhaps nameless, since his Christening name was also his regal name. The man formerly known as King Richard is sent to the Pomfret dungeons; long live the king.

The political theology that Kantorowicz finds in the play, and thus in the historical epoch which produced it, is one that associates

10. Ibid., 24–25.
11. Ibid., 27.
12. Ibid., 29.
13. Ibid., 34.
14. Ibid., 39.

the authority of a sovereign immediately with the authority of God. Richard "cascades" from God's deputy to needy mortal to fool precisely as he loses his attachment to the other body, one which is shifting allegiance to Bolingbroke even as it pries itself away from Richard. The medieval theory of kingship, Kantorowicz argues, culminates in the Elizabethan faith in an irrevocable and immediate sovereignty, irrevocable because *that* body, the truly sovereign body, can never die, nor even be the victim of rebellion.

Anselm Haverkamp has challenged this reading by suggesting that Kantorowicz overlooks the subtle ways that the play undermines the stability of the two bodies theory. If the moral authority in the drama shuttles between Bolingbroke and Richard without ever landing securely with either, then to ask which king God wants on the throne—or, which mortal body is the ultimate home of the immortal body—is to ask the wrong question. The "legal subplot" emerges as the true victor in the drama. "Shakespeare redramatizes" an emergent political theory that moves beyond theological foundations, celebrating instead "the force in England's laws." Thus, rather than manifesting a theological principal embedded deeply within the culture, he experiments with a secular one that is just coming into the light. The twinning at work in Richard is opening a space for an inquiry that is no longer interested in either body: "Richard II discovers rather than merely manifests, illuminates rather than illustrates, the doctrine of the king's two bodies at the very moment when its alleged religious force" is reduced from the theological to "workable legal procedures and regulations."[15]

This helps explain some elements of the play on which Kantorowicz remains silent. First, and perhaps most obviously, it sheds light on why Richard's deposing and murder continue to haunt

---

15. Anselm Haverkamp, "*Richard II*, Bracton, and the End of Political Theology," *Law and Literature* 16, no. 3 (2004): 313-26 (316–17).

Bolingbroke and even his son, Henry V, if in fact that is no murder of a king, only of a natural body that is like any other. On Haverkamp's reading, influenced by Agamben's *homo sacer* theory, this haunting is a sign of the growing suspicion, beginning in Richard himself, that darker energies surround any form of human sovereignty.[16] Indeed, more than one monologue of the set of history plays in the series points in this direction, initiated by Richard's association of monarchy with a cult of death in his hollow crown speech. Bolingbrook's own later royal insomnia has more to do with the kingship itself than how he came by it: "[U]neasy lies the head that wears a crown" (*2 Henry IV* 3.1.31). His son comes within a hair's breadth of saying that there is no "second body" at all, just a single mortal one wrapped in "idol ceremony" (*Henry V* 4.1.222).

What this suggests is that Shakespeare may indeed have been up to something new in terms of a political theology in this play. New, but not secular: Haverkamp's reading ignores the complex theological questions that interact with the "legal subplot," for instance the scriptural mash-up with which I began. Surely the difficult religious turn that Richard takes is not immaterial to what the play has to say about politics?

Part of the problem with both the theological and secular readings is they assume Schmitt's definition of politics as secularized sovereignty, and then find Shakespeare to either be prior to or posterior to this conscious secularization. Politics, according to Schmitt, is like theology insofar as it originates in and continually gathers its life force from "the exception," a sublime positing of

---

16. Agamben is more attuned to the religious elements lingering in secularism than is Haverkamp. Though Agamben does not specifically treat Kantorowicz's reading of the play, his critique of the "two bodies" thesis hints, though only negatively, what I here argue positively. Agamben, that is, suggests that kings bear an inhuman sovereignty that cannot be relegated to human authority, without going on to suggest a kind of authority that might be divine without ceasing to be human. See *Homo Sacer: Sovereign Power and Bare Life*, trans. Daniel Heller-Roazen (Stanford: Stanford University Press, 1995), 91–103.

law that cannot itself be rationalized or even accounted for within the terms of what it posits: the state is, in this sense, a kind of miracle.[17] Assuming that the tangle of God and state in *Richard II* is ultimately about the legitimacy of the sovereign, Schmitt's question is suddenly the only obvious one to ask: Is this politics aware of its own theological foundations or not? If not, Kantorowicz is right, and the "King's two bodies" is the essence of the play. If it is aware, then perhaps Haverkamp's reading is the right one: Shakespeare stages the theory at its own twilight, and gestures toward a legitimacy of thoroughly secular origins.

I am not convinced this is the central interest, or most interesting aspect, of the play. In fact, if at first the theological questions serve the political ones—if, that is, characters call on God only to make legitimacy claims—by the end this situation has reversed itself, and the burning question of presence or absence of God has overtaken these political claims. In other words, we miss the most significant theo-political musings of the play if we allow political theology to mean only statecraft consisting of "secularized theological concepts." The remainder of this chapter will attempt to unearth this pre- and post-Schmittian political theology in *Richard II*.

Knowing No "I"

The play opens on the overt question of sovereignty, with a double accusation of treason before the king. Bolingbroke accuses the Duke of Mowbray of stealing the king's money and of murdering the Duke of Gloucester, Bolingbroke's and Richard's uncle, and fifth son of the old King Edward III. Mowbray, for his part, makes nonspecific charges that Bolingbroke is "a villain, a recreant and a most degenerate traitor" (1.1.144-5). In fact, the entire scene is a subtle

---

17. Schmitt, *Political Theology*, 36.

undermining of the king's authority. The charge of murder here is the important thing. Mowbray hints that it was Richard who ordered him to kill Gloucester, and Richard never denies it. Neither does he deny it later, when John of Gaunt, Bolingbroke's father, makes the accusation explicit and to his face. This suggests that Bolingbroke knew it as well, and his accusation against Mowbray was a one-off way of charging the king himself with the murder. Further adding to the challenge to Richard's command here is Mowbray's backwards admission of his innocence by way of guilt: "I neglected my sworn duty" to kill Gloucester (1.1.134), and also the refusal of both parties to throw down the gauntlets they have picked up. "We were not born to sue," Richard complains, "but to command" (1.1.196). But through the opening scene no one seems to be listening.

On the level of the poetry, Richard remains in control, even as the metered replies refuse his command.[18] "Norfolk, throw down!" he calls to Mowbray, referring to Bolingbrook's gage. "We bid; there is no boot." "Myself I throw, dread sovereign, at thy foot," is Mobray's answer. "My life thou shalt command, but not my shame" (1.1.164-66). Even as his subjects limit his command, they cannot help but rhyme with Richard, and repeat his proseless pattern. The play, uniquely, never leaves blank or rhyming verse, adding to the sense that the king, who has the play's first lines, orders the language of the realm. But already, and within his language limits, they are undermining this authority. Richard's kingly authority, on the surface so unshakeable, experiences a subterranean assault from the play's opening lines.

In the second scene, this question of the king's guilt enters the theological sphere. Gloucester's widow calls John of Gaunt, his older brother, a coward for refusing to take action against her husband's

---

18. See E. M. W. Tillyard, *Shakespeare's History Plays* (New York: Macmillan Company, 1946), 246ff.

murderers. Gaunt replies that although his own "part"—an unexplained part—in his brother's blood stirs him toward revenge, yet when the king is both the perpetrator and the realm's ultimate judge, there is no court of appeal but the one in heaven. The Duchess should complain to God, since:

> God's is the quarrel; for God's substitute,
> His deputy anointed in his sight,
> Hath caused his death; the which if wrongfully,
> Let heaven revenge, for I may never lift
> An angry arm against his minister. (1.2.37-41)

Gaunt and the widowed Duchess have here begun to pry open the questions that will soon ravage the realm. Who judges Richard, if he is in fact guilty of the murder? Does the king's command reach so far as justice itself, or is it the other way around, so that heaven will take on the quarrel that the king's subjects cannot? These are questions that Shakespeare also explores in *Richard III* and *Macbeth*, two history plays that, like this one, double as tragedies. In both, the king's increasingly evil acts spur on responses that make the theology more or less clear: there is a justice that rules the realm, and even the creatures and fauna within it, and the king is its subject. Here, Richard's sin forms the background rather than the action of the play, and the judgments of heaven will be much more ambiguous.

In the third scene of the opening act, God is conspicuous in his absence. Unable to convince Bolingbroke and Mowbray to relinquish one another's gages, Richard calls for a trial by combat. Here both will attempt to prove "by the grace of God and this mine arm" (1.3.22) the falseness of the other. Richard, however, finally manages to stop the engagement just before the duel begins, and exiles both men from the kingdom, Mowbray for life and Bolingbroke for six years. God does not get to speak through a victory of might that declares unquestionably the right.[19]

What could God say, though, if the accusation against Richard is true? In that case both men are right to deny their own treason against the realm, but also both "guilty" of treason against the king. Yet, if the ultimate judge is in fact God, it is Richard himself who betrays, and so stopping the combat and banishing the accusers from the realm is a strategy for avoiding divine judgment. John of Gaunt's dying speech will soon broach this accusation for the first time, accusing Richard of "mutiny" against sound judgment (2.1.28) and deposing himself through his own folly (2.1.108). By scene's end, Gaunt's brother York watches Richard seize his now dead uncle's "plate, coin, revenues, and movables" (2.1.162) to fund his Irish wars, and York brashly tells his nephew that his actions "prick his patience" toward rebellious thoughts (2.1.208). Richard's response is to make York governor of the realm while he goes off to fight the Irish! God's name and the king's are just beginning to slip apart here, and Richard is behaving in the interest of neither.

Regarding the halted trial by combat, however, there is something more at work than a plot twist to hide Richard's guilt from God or from exposure by God to the realm. Shakespeare had, in an earlier play (though one that dealt with the later history) crafted a clowning send-up of such a trial, with a master who gets too drunk to defeat his thieving servant (see *2 Henry VI*). There the naive king is the only one—including the audience—who believes God has spoken through the swords. *Richard II* makes a similar point in a more complex way: since no outcome would in fact be a just outcome, the scene calls into question trial by combat itself. The point is not that there is no justice that transcends the king's decree, but rather that the arms of

19. Phyllis Rackin, *Stages of History: Shakespeare's English Chronicles* (Ithaca, NY: Cornell University Press, 1990), 46ff, cites the halting of trial by combat as evidence of Shakespeare's turn from an overtly providentialist to a Machiavellian worldview. It will become clear, I hope, that I take this observation to be exactly half right: this is what the plays turn *from*, but not what they turn *to*.

men are not equipped to determine this justice. Whatever it is that God has to say to Richard, he refuses to be summoned and snookered into a proclamation here. This of course lends a new irony to the Lord Marshal's summoning of the combatants "in God's name and the king's." Who stopped the combat, in the end? Was it Richard, in order to hide his own guilt, or was it God, who was not yet ready to speak?

Also distinguishing the play from Shakespeare's other deposition histories is the deposer himself. *Macbeth*'s Malcolm has an obvious claim to the throne, and can without irony call himself an instrument of the "powers above" (*Macbeth* 4.3.240). *Richard III*'s Richmond has no obvious claim, but Richard's spectacular wickedness calls him forth as an answer to "the prayers of holy saints and wrongèd souls" (*Richard III* 5.6.195). But Bolingbroke, despite his many lines, is almost entirely shrouded in shadow. It is not the looting of his family property that motivates his return from exile, since he is already on his way by this time. He seems simply to be breaking his vow to the king. Upon his return he condemns two of Richard's male companions to death for seducing the king away from the queen's bed, but as this accusation has no other grounding in the plot, the most obvious reading is that he is simply lying.[20] What then was the treason that Mowbray accused Bolingbroke of? Was he perhaps plotting a coup before the confrontation at the play's opening? And was old Gaunt, despite his own sworn fealty, in on

---

20. Kevin Gates, in conversation. I have learned a great deal about the play, and about Shakespeare in general, from Kevin, an Austin-based actor, director, and theater scholar. He has written in an unpublished paper about a remarkable production of the play that he directed, which began with a coin toss to determine which of the two lead actors—he being one of them—would play the role of Richard, and which Bolingbroke. The on-stage toss illuminated the ways in which the two kings mirror one another, and also allowed for dueling interpretations of these two ambiguous characters to radically alter the production. Kevin summarizes the moments prior to the coin toss in a word: "terrifying." Gates, "Casting Richard II by Coin Toss," presented at Blackfriars Conference, 2013.

it, since his fatherly advice at Bolingbroke's sentencing is open to a rather obvious double meaning?: "Think not the King did banish thee,/ but thou the King" (*Richard II* 1.3.256.12-13). Here, at any rate, there will be no divine justice entering on horseback in the fifth act to right the wrongs. If God is speaking through Bolingbroke, he is whispering. And in heavy dialect.

In 3.2, the first of Kantorowicz's "cascading" scenes, Richard returns from his Irish wars already aware the rebellion, which means that he received letters about the kingdom even though he failed to answer them. It is this neglect, more than anything else that loses the kingdom for him, since his forces at home have already dispersed at rumors that he was killed in Ireland. He imagines that the English soil itself will recognize him, and send an army of spiders, snakes, and toads to fight on his behalf. Supporting this earthy army will be a battalion of the heavenly sort:

> For every man that Bolingbroke hath pressed
> To lift shrewd steel against our golden crown,
> God for his Richard hath in heavenly pay
> A glorious angel. Then if angels fight,
> Weak men must fall; for heaven still guards the right. (3.2.54-58)

Richard is still God's, and so has no reason to fear.

This changes though, upon hearing the news of the troops' departure. He despairs, admitting that the "triumph in my face" had more to do with the strength of an army of Welshmen than of angels. It is not simply that Richard has now lost his faith; losing his army has revealed to him that he never had any to begin with. This is the first hint that there is something more than a "two bodies" separation at work here. Richard, whose political authority has been challenged from the outset, is still king of the realm. Now, though, he questions whether that was ever a divinely given authority at all, and not just a heavenly name for earthly power.

At this point something remarkable begins to happen within Richard's language. The first person plural, always the king's prerogative, begins to unravel at exactly the moment that he admits his faith was more in the justice of arms than in that of heaven. His cousin Aumerle embarrassedly admonishes his despair, and Richard replies, "I had forgot myself. Am I not King" (3.2.79)? He means it as an assertion, but the lack of confident plural suggests that heaven may not be on his side after all. Richard's royal "we" is always a theological "we," and losing his grip on the throne is indistinguishable to him from losing God.

Later, in his dramatic confrontation with Bolingbroke, the pronoun shift is even more pronounced. "We are amazed," he calls to the rebellious party,

> and thus long have we stood
> To watch the fearful bending of thy knee,
> Because we thought ourself thy lawful king.
> An if we be, how dare thy joints forget
> To pay their aweful duty to our presence?

No mere human, he continues, can grip the royal scepter, unless he be a usurper, which clearly is what he believes Bolingbroke is about to become. In that case, though, Bolingbroke comes alone, and is acting against the "we" of Richard and God. But here again Richard's language betrays Richard's claim, and he finds himself isolated in spite of his insistence to the contrary:

> And though you think that all—as you have done—
> Have torn their souls by turning them from us,
> And we are barren and bereft of friends,
> Yet know my master, God omnipotent,
> Is mustering in his clouds on our behalf
> Armies of pestilence; and they shall strike
> Your children yet unborn and unbegot,

That lift your vassal hands against my head
And threat the glory of my precious crown. (3.3.71-89)

Even as he insists that there is no distance between God and himself, his grammar tells against him, and he vacillates between the royal/theological we and the isolated singular: the realm has turned from us and we are bereft; God is my master, moving on our behalf; you lift your hands against my head, threatening my crown. Richard's growing sense of his own isolation—from his subjects, his friends, and ultimately from God—causes him to question whether he was ever close to God at all, even in the days when no rebellion threatened the royal we.

In between these two grammatical collapses comes the hollow crown speech, when Richard calls into question not his claim to the crown, but the authority of the crown itself. "For God's sake," he says,

> Let us sit upon the ground
> And tell sad stories of the death of kings—
> How some have been deposed, some slain in war,
> Some haunted by the ghosts they have deposed,
> Some poisoned by their wives, some sleeping killed,
> All murdered. For within the hollow crown
> That rounds the mortal temples of a king
> Keeps Death his court; and there the antic sits,
> Scoffing his state and grinning at his pomp. (3.2.151-59)

Kantorowicz found it difficult to synthesize these lines with his claim that the king's two bodies is the essence of the play, as here the monarchy itself becomes "a little scene" governed by Death. "Throw away respect,/ tradition, form, and ceremonious duty," Richard says, and you will find that I am as "subjected" to hunger, need, grief, and loneliness as anyone: "How can you say to me that I am a king?" No one can answer this question, as they could if the point were simply that the King has a royal body alongside his mortal one. Here, the political question is sharpened. Whereas the previous question consisted of, "Am I the king?," Richard has now asks, "Can any human be?"

This is also the point, though, where the theological question begins to emerge distinctly from the political one, and so the place where Havercamp's reading comes up short. If Richard is an "I" and no longer a "we," and if this is in fact true of all kings, then how does God speak in a realm after all? The play has already rejected the possibility of divine justice manifested in combat. Now it goes further, and rejects the notion of an immediate identification of monarch and God. Richard, meanwhile, goes on speaking of God, now as a mysterious third person.

If God is not revealed in the immediacy of a theo-political plural—regardless of the claim and command of the one uttering it—then how is God revealed? This question begins to press on Richard from the moment he discovers the separation. God was once, so I thought, so close to me that I could open my mouth and his words would issue forth, now I exchange "my scepter for a palmer's walking staff," thus recognizing that God will not be found in the origin of my decree, but at the end of a journey if at all. The gay apparel in which I gave in to flattery I will trade in for an almsman's gown, since I have now seen that it was the flattery itself that held my faith. And "my subjects for a pair of carvèd saints," because I who spoke with God's own voice must learn how to pray to God as a stranger (3.3.148-51).

It is not simply that Richard has become a singular "I" over against a third person divine. The "we" assured him not only that God was with him, but that he was King Richard; as "I," he has lost his own name as well as God's. Thus, when he appears before Bolingbroke to unking himself, his speech is filled with jesting double talk:

Bolingbroke: I thought you had been willing to resign.

Richard: My crown I am, but my griefs are still mine. (4.1.180-81)

"I am willing to resign my crown but not my griefs"? Or "I am my crown, and thus am one with the grief that comes of tearing it away"?

Bolingbroke: Are you contented to resign the crown?

Richard: Ay, no; no, ay: for I must nothing be.
Therefore no, no, for I resign to thee. (4.1.190-92)

"Yes, no, no, yes"? Or "I know no I"? If in fact resigning makes me nothing, then I am no longer a thing that can resign.[21] He imagines himself a snowman, so that his body, like his name, might melt before the heat of the newly crowned Bolingbroke. He asks for a mirror so that he may see "where all my sins are writ, and that's myself" (4.1.265). But the glass can only flatter him as once his companions did, by showing him his youth, beauty, and still regal visage. *It shows him immediately who he is, and thus recalls the false immediacy of the theo-political we.* He shatters the glass, not simply to resist the flattering image, but in fact to destroy his face, since the Richard that it shows him is no more.

This is his condition as he appears in his final scene, the scene that Harold Bloom cites as the prototype of metaphysical poetry.[22] "I have been studying," he says, "how I may compare/ This prison where I live unto the world." In fact, his metaphor is really an attempt to discover himself, the shattered face in the glass, since he is now both nothing and a turmoil of discontented and conflicting wills:

Thus play I in one person many people,
And none contented . . .
. . . But whate'er I be,

---

21. Garber, *Shakespeare After All*, 253–54.
22. Bloom, *Shakespeare: The Invention of the Human* (New York: Riverhead Books, 1998), 266–70.

> Nor I, nor any man that but man is,
> With nothing shall be pleased till he be eased
> With being nothing. (5.5.31-41).

"Any man that but man is"—and even a king, as he has learned, is but a man—will be discontent until he shatters the flattering immediacy of his own self-presence.

In the end, we arrive at the scriptural confusion highlighted at the beginning of this chapter. The highest of his discontented thoughts, thoughts of the divine, are now "mixed with scruples." Richard has not rejected "things divine," but has gathered that the divine presence and even the divine invitation to "come, little ones," will be a mixed blessing, always barbed with the camel's predicament. Indeed, in pasting together these two very different evangelical sentences, Richard is playing out the crisis in which he finds himself at that moment. Accustomed to the immediate identity of "God's name and the King's" (1.3.11), he now commands no one. In fact, he was a rich young ruler, and now is naked and helpless as a child.

Perhaps in the end he is both at once. Since "the breath of worldly men cannot depose/ The deputy elected by the Lord," he continues to be ruler, even as he is the child.

Further, was he not always something of a child when he was king? "The skipping king," Bolingbroke will call him in a later play (*1 Henry IV* 3.2.60), referring to a penchant for flattery and wardrobe that outplayed his responsiveness to the troubles of the realm. So in which of these verses should he find himself addressed? If one is both a rich ruler and a little child, is it difficult or easy to dwell in Christ's presence? This is exactly Richard's dilemma. If the play were an uncritical staging of the two bodies thesis, as in Kantorowicz's reading, the movement from invitation to repellant would be a linear digression: first he was God's king, then he was God's discarded camel. If, as in Haverkamp's reading, it stages a critique of theological politics, then Richard ought, here at the end, to be either the king who gives up on Christ's invitation, or the pilgrim who gives up on kingship. Richard, as we have seen, does neither. Instead, we get a mixture; thoughts "intermixed with scruples." Richard is a mixed character, and his relation to God is of mixed character.

Perhaps he is right to fuse the two biblical passages into one. It is difficult for any ruler to come; only the one who comes not as a ruler at all, but as a child, can hear the invitation. Richard changes his scepter for a palmer's staff because he desires to find the God he once thought he knew. The "scruples" here are the very dissonance that bears a promise. When he was, in the eye of the public at least, still the king, and so commanded in England with the voice of God, he was actually in the place of the gospel's camel: an inhabitant of no kingdom but his own, and stuck outside the kingdom of heaven. Now, helpless as a child, and in the eyes of a public rejected by God, he hears the invitation, at least in mixed form: come, little ones. His time is short. But he has traded in his scepter for a palmer's staff, so perhaps he is already making the journey.

The Coming of the Poet-King

Does any of this constitute a political theology? Obviously, not in so many words. If that were Shakespeare's intention, his play would have been far less ambiguous, and also far less memorable. "Drama has a peculiarly rich capacity to convey several contradictory messages simultaneously,"[23] and here especially we get no clarity about whether God sides with Richard, Bolingbroke, John of Gaunt, the Duchess of Gloucester, or the Duke of York. As it stands, though, the difficulty is precisely what makes it theologically interesting. To take *Richard II* either as a nostalgic play about the lost age of the

---

23. Jonathan Bate and Dora Thorton, *Shakespeare: Staging the World* (London: The British Museum Press, 2012), 101.

divine right of kings or a radical play about the coming secular age is to leave the plot just as it gets interesting. Instead, it is a timely Renaissance play about the emergence of a new craft of theology-rich politics. As Richard becomes less a king, he becomes more a poet,[24] and his language itself becomes his palmer's staff, mediating the distance between himself and God.

If political theology means nothing more than theological justification for political maneuvering, there is plenty going on in this play, as there is throughout Shakespeare. Sovereignty is all over the surface of the play, but the depths seem to care little for questions of which person or family deserves the throne. This is not a political theology that begins in the "miracle" of unwarranted sovereignty, since here it is precisely, and against Schmitt's very thesis, the exception that is called into question. Richard's authority is challenged from the opening lines; Bolingbroke's authority is undermined each time he is upstaged by Richard.

Suppose, though, that Richard never really ceases to be king, because one simply cannot unking oneself. In that case we would expect to find him haunting his successor and his ensuing line. The play ends with Bolingbroke, now King Henry, vowing to take up Richard's palmer's staff and make a penitential pilgrimage to Jerusalem, and calling his nobles to "March sadly after" (5.6.51). In this case it is not that politics is now non-theological, but that Richard has exposed the myth of theological immediacy, and turns toward a new possibility: *the possibility of a kingly reign that is nothing but the gradual, mediated, pilgrim discovery of God.* Perhaps a true ruler would be something of a poet-king. King Richard can see the realm clearly in his mind, and "hammer out" theo-political questions, only after he recognizes that he no longer speaks for God.

---

24. Garber, *Shakespeare After All*, 258ff.

Shakespeare, throughout the histories especially, delights in calling into question the very "miracle" of statehood and its decreed sovereignty. What is England? What is a realm? What constitutes the authority to rule within it? These are radical questions, but clearly radical questions that the public and even the monarchy found worthy pursuits, judging by the success of the plays under the contentious last decade of Elizabeth's reign. A king is "tradition, form, and ceremonious duty," says Richard: a human who tends to be mistaken for something more. Importantly, though, even if a king is nothing more than this—and various plays repeat the same sentiment—he never says a king is nothing because he is this, anymore that we hear him say the poet is nothing because he only uses human words. The question, which seems to me to be one of the key questions of Shakespeare's engagement with royalty, is whether we can give up our expectation that God will rule without mediation, simply and superhumanly, and wager instead on a God who gives himself over entirely to this mediation, ruling nowhere but in the problems, questions, and ambiguities of human "tradition, form, and ceremonious duty." Can states that once depended on the divine right of warrior kings and ceremony come to celebrate the theological possibility of the poet-king?

This is a more difficult pathway to God, and it makes the voice and will of God more difficult to discern. The king no longer owns the power to declare the exception, but only to use human language to invoke the historical community that ceremony and duty names, and together with this community, to lead the state in acts of discernment of divine and human justice. There is authority here, but an authority of mediated seeking rather than one of immediate decree. In this light, *Henry V*, for all its own ambiguities, can be read as the concluding response to the questions that *Richard II* opens. Kingship is, as Bolingbroke's son discovers, not so much about twin bodies as it is about humanly crafted ceremony draping the shoulders of a single human. But this ceremony itself can mediate divine authority: only a powerful authority can call his subjects "band of brothers," and lead them in praying Psalms of penitence. Harry is more Richard than Bolingbroke, his father tells him, and means it as a critique of his son's lack of attention to his royal charge. Perhaps though he is more right than he knows. Harry's prodigal life itself is a kind of pilgrimage that wins the sovereignty neither of his predecessors managed to hold.

Richard II is an exploration of the growing awareness that the king's plurality is not God but only a flattering specter. Though this might lead us toward the evacuation of theology from the political, it does not lead Shakespeare in this direction. If God is not present in the immediacy of the royal "we," then he will not be found at all until the pretense is dropped, the mirrors are shattered, and the palmer's staff is taken up. When palmers do so, we call it a spiritual quest. If kings were to follow them, we would have to call this the beginning of a new "unexceptional" political theology.

10

Ressourcement and Resistance

La nouvelle théologie, the Fathers, and the Bible, against Fascism

Kevin L. Hughes

In November 1942, Nazi armored divisions poured across the border from the occupied zone of northern France into the southern regions, pressing through Lyons and all the way to the Mediterranean port of Toulon in 24 hours. Henri de Lubac remembered the chaos of those days, as Jewish refugees and Christian resistance figures fled or hid in advance of the approaching army:

> "I still remember that morning of November 1942, when, from the d'Ainay basilica, where we were gathered for the opening Mass of the school year, we heard the tanks roll over the quay of the Saone.... The tension was constant. We lived in a fever increased by hunger, by the daily horror of the news, by the next day's uncertainty. And yet, work was carried on, became even more intense. It was at this time that the series *Source chrétiennes* was begun...."[1]

What was the source of this intensity? And why, in specific, was this the time when *Sources chrétiennes,* the series that presents patristic and medieval texts—often biblical commentaries or homilies on scripture—was begun? One might wave off such questions—it's often the case, isn't it, that we throw ourselves into our work in times of trouble, to engage our attention and distract us from the worries that surround us? De Lubac himself suggests as much in the preface to *Corpus Mysticum,* his study of eucharist and the church in the early middle ages: "At that time storm clouds were gathering over Europe: this occupation provided me with a haven of peace."[2] So perhaps this is how we should understand the work on *Sources chrétiennes,* as the kind of diversion one seeks to console oneself in times of strife?

De Lubac certainly had many other things on his desk. The most directly threatening work de Lubac undertook—and likely the immediate cause of the Gestapo's pursuit of him in 1942 and 1943—was the clandestine publication of *Les Cahiers du Temoignage chrétien,* the "pamphlets of Christian witness," which de Lubac and a few collaborators snuck off to remote areas to edit for publication. These pamphlets contained manifestos such as Gaston Fessard's "*France, prends garde de perdre ton âme!*" [France, take care not to lose your soul!] and essays against anti-Semitic laws and other matters of policy or culture.[3] Such pressing matters would seem to place *Sources chrétiennes* at a certain scholarly ivory-tower remove. But to suppose this would be to mistake the basic shape of de Lubac's argument for Christian "spiritual resistance" from the beginning. I want to suggest in this essay that de Lubac's thought, before the war and after,

---

1. Henri de Lubac, *At the Service of the Church,* trans. Anne Elizabeth Englund (San Francisco: Ignatius Press, 1993), 50.
2. Henri de Lubac, *Corpus Mysticum: The Eucharist and the Church in the Middle Ages,* trans. Gemma Simmonds, CJ (London: SCM Press, 2006), xxiii.
3. Henri de Lubac, *Christian Resistance to Antisemitism: Memories from 1940–1944* (San Francisco: Ignatius Press, 1988), 131–35.

suggests a continuous argument, advanced in word and in deed, to address the very particular political and cultural ills of his society in a time of deepest crisis.[4] For de Lubac, the recovery of spiritual exegesis was a spiritual re-armament for an underground battle, beneath the political and military maneuvers, for the soul of the church and the heart of the world. In particular, facing the rising storm of fascism, de Lubac argued that the renewal of scriptural interpretation was the necessary theological foundation for Christian resistance. The very spiritual interpretation of scripture which seemed to the critical scholarly eye to signal the nostalgia for the backward past was for de Lubac an essential tool for his present age.

Spiritual Warfare

With the collapse of the French war effort against Germany in 1940,[5] Henri de Lubac and his Jesuit confreres discovered that they, as Catholic spiritual leaders in their community, would be a target for the German invasion force, and so they fled on foot into the mountains of Ardeche to escape capture and imprisonment.[6] When the demarcation line and the Nazi-friendly rump regime of Vichy was established under Marshall Petain, these Jesuits returned to their school at Fourviere and were able to continue their work in the classroom. Only a few of these, including de Lubac, were taken into the confidence of French resistance leaders, and they began to plan strategically how to get their voices heard. Throughout 1941, a small group of resistance leaders worked to organize a clandestine

---

4. This contribution is dedicated to my graduate students in my 2014 *Ressourcement* seminar at Villanova University. Daniel Baker, Hadassah Bergstrom, Eric DeMeuse, Austin Detwiler, Jeffrey Mayer, Ryan O'Connell, Claudia Petruncio, and Carl Vennerstrom all contributed insights to this piece as we worked our way through de Lubac. I am grateful for their insight, wit, and wisdom.
5. For a full discussion of de Lubac's war years, see the exhaustive biography of Georges Chantraine, *Henri de Lubac,* 4 vols. (Paris: Cerf, 2007-2013), vol. 3.
6. de Lubac, *Christian Resistance,* 125.

distribution network for *Les Cahiers du Temoignage chrétien* (TC) throughout the southern regions of France and to delegate responsibilities for its production. De Lubac served as managing editor and (sometimes) anonymous author,[7] moving around to remote country homes or rectories to edit each volume, avoiding any risk of exposure. Returning to Lyons from one of his editorial excursions, de Lubac was tipped off that he was on a Gestapo arrest list and was able to stay away until the arrest fever had passed. From 1940 to 1944, de Lubac worked in constant vigilance—sometimes able to appear publicly, sometimes disappearing into hiding during one crackdown or another—all the while working away piece by piece on TC, and on *Sources chrétiennes* and its related monograph series, *Théologie*. *Sources chrétiennes*, as mentioned above, produced editions of patristic texts, many of which were homilies and scriptural commentaries from the Greek patristic tradition. *Théologie* offered theoretical discussions of traditional Christian scriptural and doctrinal principles. De Lubac's zeal to bring *Sources chrétiennes* and *Théologie* to press in the face of Nazi occupation came from their shared conviction that these deep patristic and scriptural resources were all the more vital to a church faced with persecution, what de Lubac did not hesitate to call "spiritual warfare."

From his earliest published writings in the 1930s, de Lubac opposed any direct authority of the church in politics. At a time when the right-wing Action Française party rallied conservative French Catholics into a kind of militant Catholic political wing, de Lubac rejected the conflation of the Church's spiritual authority with direct temporal power. Temporal affairs will often contain within them deep moral and spiritual concerns, and in these matters, the Church must speak: "There can be no question of closing off any area of

---

7. Ibid., 126–27.

thought or human activity from the Church, because there is no activity or thought—however profane in appearance—in which, in one way or another, faith and morality cannot be involved."[8] But she must speak *as the Church*, using the spiritual authority proper to her, and so she "operates from within: to proclaim the *non licet,* she addresses herself to men's consciences."[9] The Church's responsibility requires that she may intervene spiritually in temporal matters, but without temporal authority or jurisdiction. Neither usurping temporal power for her own ends nor retreating into a separatist political quietism, the church's spiritual authority may very well invite martyrdom rather than Machiavellian machinations, and yet it is her solemn duty to speak the truth. And if this is true for the church as a whole in its authoritative offices, it is true as well for the faithful in proper measure: "Each one of the faithful must strive to make this ideal and these means his own, following all the rules of prudence and Christian obedience, according to the situation, according to his lights."[10] These words, spoken in 1931, are carried into practice less than a decade later. Without direct political or temporal action, de Lubac and his collaborators endeavor to risk martyrdom in stirring the consciences of the faithful under a hostile regime.

In an essay entitled "Spiritual Warfare," published during the war in *Cité nouvelle* in 1943, De Lubac argues that the battle with fascism "is no longer a problem of the historical, metaphysical, political, or social order. It is a *spiritual* problem [sic]. It is the total human problem. Today, the fight against Christianity . . . is aimed directly at the heart. The Christian concept of life, Christian spirituality, the inner attitude which, above any particular act or any external

---

8. Henri de Lubac, "The Authority of the Church in Temporal Matters," in *Theological Fragments,* trans. Rebecca Howell Balinski (San Francisco: Ignatius Press, 1989), 199-233 (211).
9. de Lubac, "Authority," 213.
10. Ibid., 232–33.

gesture, defines the Christian: this is what is at issue."[11] His writings throughout this period manifest his immediate and deeply held conviction, in the wake of the Nazi seizure of power, that the rise of fascism was, indeed, an "anti-Christian revolution." "The end," he says, "is less to destroy Christianity completely than to debase it."[12] Indeed, de Lubac concedes that Christians themselves had already done much to debase it themselves.

De Lubac sees the contempt with which the Nazis treat Christian faith; in their view, it is already debased and needs now simply to be swept out to the dustbin of history. Indeed, it is not in their view alone: "To how many of us does Christianity appear in fact 'like something great, expansive, to which we can surrender ourselves entirely with joy and enthusiasm'?" De Lubac cites Jacques Rivière, writing to Paul Claudel, to assess the signs of the times for Christian faith in France:

> I see that Christianity is dying. . . . We do not know what these spires, which are no longer the prayer of any of us, are still doing over our cities; we don not know what these great edifices mean that today enclose stations and hospitals and from which the people themselves have chased the monks; we do not know what these turgid stucco crosses of a revolting art demonstrate on tombs.[13]

Before fascism ever arose as a political force, Christians have distanced themselves more and more from the root and sources of their own faith, falling into "formalism and routine," "blaspheming every day a little more the Lord with whom it claims kinship outwardly while understanding him less and less."[14] Christian faith has become

---

11. Henri de Lubac, "Spiritual Warfare," *Theology in History*, trans. Anne Englund Nash (San Francisco: Ignatius Press, 1996), 488-501 (489).
12. Henri de Lubac, "Letter to my Superiors, April 1941," in *Theology in History* (San Francisco: Ignatius Press, 2014), 428-39 (431-32).
13. de Lubac, "Spiritual Warfare," 496. De Lubac is citing the correspondence between Rivière and Paul Claudel from 1907.
14. Ibid., 497.

anemic: "As we practice it, as we think about it first, it is a weak ineffective religion; a religion of ceremonies and devotions, of decoration and vulgar consolation, without serious depth, without any real grasp of human activity, at times even without sincerity."[15] So debilitated, so debased, Christian faith falls all too easily under the contempt of its opponents, and even of its own sons and daughters, themselves tempted to 'cast longing eyes,' as the prophets once said, on the side of the new paganism, in order to steal something of that strength and that life with which it appears to be suffused."[16] Without direct attack, the Nazi (or Nazi-friendly Vichy) regime easily erodes and undermines fundamental elements of Christian self-understanding.

Faced with such a precipitous collapse, de Lubac's French Catholic peers seem drawn to revert to old temptations, seeking a politically engaged Christianity that betrays its spiritual authority in the service of temporal power: "If we want to discover a strong Christianity, that 'high-powered Christianity' of which there has been so much talk, our first concern must be not to let it be shifted, as is threatened today, into the direction of a Christianity of power."[17] Such a temptation distorts Christianity and thus weakens it further. Instead, de Lubac proposes, "it is a matter of returning to Christianity its power in us, which means, above all, of rediscovering it such as it is in itself, in its purity and authenticity." Here, he proposes *ressourcement* not simply as a program for *theological* renewal reserved for professors and seminarians, but as a strategy of *spiritual warfare* against fascism for every Christian: "[T]o the degree we have let ourselves lose it, we have to rediscover the *spirit* of Christianity. To do so, we have to

---

15. Ibid.
16. Ibid., 497–98.
17. Ibid., 498. It is striking how political and theological alliances broke: Garrigou-Lagrange initially supported Action Française (prior to its condemnation by the Holy See) and was a staunch supporter of the Vichy regime during the war.

steep ourselves in its sources, and above all in the gospel."[18] De Lubac calls his fellow Christians to rediscover Christian faith by steeping themselves in its sources, especially Christian scripture. Only through this deep and foundational re-sourcing of Christian faith will allow Christians to bear witness with integrity and charity in the face of Nazi neopaganism.

Scriptural Exegesis and the Spiritual Life

From his first book in 1938, before the war began, de Lubac argued for a central role for scriptural interpretation in the re-sourcing and renewal of Christian faith. In particular, he looks to the tradition of spiritual exegesis of scripture to give essential shape to the Christian spiritual life itself. While, he admits, it is often demeaned in our latter-day critical fashions as fanciful invention, the spiritual exegesis represented in the traditional "fourfold sense" of the fathers and medieval doctors is a spiritual pedagogy that draws the events of biblical history into the light of Christ and then integrates this light into the moral and spiritual life of the faithful reader. It is this insight that de Lubac finds captured in the schoolteachers' rhyme handed down through the Middle Ages:

> *littera gesta docet, quod credas allegoria*
> *moralia quod agas, quo tendas anagogia*
> [The letter teaches events; allegory, what you should believe.
> The moral, what you should do, and anagogy, where you should be headed]

Scripture, for all its variety of genres and historical contexts, nevertheless, *as scripture*, centers around "the essential fact: the mystery of Christ [*allegoria*], prefigured or rendered present in facts [*littera*], interiorized by the individual soul [*moralia*], and

---

18. de Lubac, "Spiritual Warfare," 499.

consummated in glory [*anagogia*]." The spiritual interpretation of scripture is not simply a theological hermeneutical strategy; it is a formative practice of the spiritual life itself: "The entire Bible thus appears as a 'mirror,' where man learns to know himself with his misery and his sin while getting to know the perfection for which God destines and calls him. The facts that the Bible relates are also interior events, the *processus animae.*"[19] Such a way of proceeding makes scripture the central point of convergence of Christian personal and ecclesial identity.

With the literal sense, or "the letter," the scriptural reader studies the events of salvation history and the words used to describe them, seeing God's work in the world as objectively present and then as taken up into words. The *gesta Dei,* the "mighty deeds of God" in the history of the People Israel emerge for the Christian reader as covenant promise. This promise is then taken up and brought to fruition in *Christ* and in the *Church,* which are the subject of the *allegorical* sense of scripture. As the Old Covenant is taken up in the New, so Christ completes or fulfills that life, both in his own life and in the community of believers, the social Body of Christ, which he has invited and founded. When the *allegorical* sense is discovered, the scriptural reader then brings the insights of these senses into his/her heart, such that s/he can be ordered to Divine Life more fully and completely in his/her ordinary life. Thus, the "moralia" or moral sense is not simply rules for conduct or exemplary lessons. The moral sense of scripture represents the personal, spiritual internalization of the truth of Christ and membership in the Church, connecting the past of salvation history to the soul's present life, and thus pointing forward to the last sense, *anagogia.* The anagogical sense

---

19. Henri de Lubac, "On an Old Distich: The Doctrine of the 'Fourfold Sense' in Scripture," *Theological Fragments,* trans. Rebecca Howell Balinski (San Francisco: Ignatius Press, 1989), 109-27 (115).

carries forward the personal and corporate moral understanding of the *viator*, the Church-in-pilgrimage, toward its divine and heavenly end. *Anagogia* concerns both the movement of the soul into mystical union and the eschatological movement of the church and soul toward the Heavenly Jerusalem. To read scripture according to the fourfold sense is to place oneself against the horizon of the length of salvation history and the breadth of the corporate Body of Christ, the Church, and to deepen one's own intimacy with Christ. Scripture's fourfold sense thus offers more as much formation as information; it becomes a foundation stone of Christian spiritual identity. Modern readers will tend to consider "eisegesis," reading an interpretation *into* the text, or, at best, a kind of 'jazz improvisation' around and about the text, picking up a term or phrase and exploiting it for one's own theological ends. "The Alexandrians," according to de Lubac's contemporary René Cadiou, "easily *sacrificed history* in their desire to impose symbolism, even though Christian revelation is, in the first place, an historical event."[20] For de Lubac, the nature of spiritual exegesis is precisely the opposite. Rather than usurping the biblical text for one's subjective ends, it is a handing over of oneself to be conformed to and formed within the world of the scriptures.

But spiritual understanding is not an uncritical yielding in some manner of "blind faith." Instead, it is a vigorous critical engagement with the text that "set up an often subtle dialectic between historical reality and spiritual reality, between society and the individual, between time and eternity. It contains, as one might say today, a whole theology of history, which is connected to a theology of Scripture."[21] Moreover, such spiritual understanding is not

---

20. René Cadiou, *La Jeunesse d'Origene* (1936), 54, cited in Henri de Lubac, *History and Spirit: The Understanding of Scripture According to Origen* (San Francisco: Ignatius Press, 2007), 9 [Emphasis mine].
21. Henri de Lubac, *Medieval Exegesis: The Fourfold Sense of Scripture*, vol. 1, trans. Marc Sebanc (Grand Rapids: Eerdmans, 1998), xix.

undertaken to the exclusion of historical study. While the two reading strategies will come into tension, it is this very tension that holds each method in proper relation: "[B]efore interpreting the Old Testament spiritually by the New, it is indispensable to have understood the New historically by the Old. It is nonetheless of great importance . . . not to confuse the disciplines. Their union is desirable, even necessary, but it is delicate."[22] Historical/textual work roots the scriptural texts in the life and culture that gave it birth, but in order to read the scriptural text *as scripture,* the believer is attuned through spiritual reading to the resonant relations between the two covenants, and then between these two and the his own soul.

De Lubac turns to the fathers and medieval doctors to remember or relearn the disciplines of spiritual understanding, but he does not imagine that he, or we, can return to their own practice. As the science of textual criticism—and our critical consciousness itself—develops over time, our scriptural reading will have to develop, too.

No less attentive than they themselves were to the mystery signified in the history, we will perhaps be more attentive to the historicity of the figure or, at least, more aware of the approach that the precise knowledge of that historicity requires. And we will thus strive to unite our modern 'historical sense' to that profound 'sense of history' that their spiritual exegesis was able to bring out.[23]

But such an adaptive spiritual exegesis will not come to birth of its own accord; instead, it will require the disciplined recovery of the practice of the Fathers and Doctors, wedded to a disciplined re-engagement of our own symbolic imagination, to resist the "very different direction that the spirit of the age carries us," into an "anti-symbolism," a "dreadful inversion" that will make God the symbol

---

22. de Lubac, *History and Spirit,* 454.
23. Ibid., 492.

of man, his image objectified."²⁴ In other words, scriptural exegesis becomes for de Lubac the path of spiritual resistance to modern fascism's neo-pagan colonization of the imagination.

"A Christian Explanation of our Time"

Henri de Lubac was convinced that the recent fascist ascendancy was only the latest and most visible evidence of a broader and deeper crisis in the Christian imagination, and he set himself to the task of helping to reawaken and reinvigorate the Christian convictions of his fellow French Catholics. In January 1941, he had been invited to give two lectures to the Catholic faculties at Lyons on "The Theological Foundation of the Missions." The first lecture drew upon *Catholicism* and argued for the mandate of the Church to be a "light for the revelation of the nations." In it, he sketches the trajectory of this universal mission from the Old Testament to the New: Christ takes up and fulfills the vision already present in the promise to Abraham and in the proclamation of the prophets. This long history informs the present Church, and the church only knows itself to be the church when it is in mission to the nations, continually presenting the Gospel to the world. This lecture, though it raised the censors' eyebrows, was published later in 1941. The second lecture, however, was de Lubac's "Response to Objections." Here de Lubac first tackles a sort of blasé bourgeois "live and let live" objection: why not let people be in their own faith? But then he turns to a more serious—and more imminent—threat to the Church's missional identity. "I must now approach, in this second part, a subject that is impossible for me to pass over in silence without betraying the cause of the missions, I would even add: without betraying the Church. . . . We are referring, as you have guessed, to the racist objection."²⁵

---

24. Ibid., 494.

Mission to lesser races, it is argued, are a waste of time; even worse, Christianity's universal mission "inherited from Israel, would lead Europe to ruin if it were to triumph."[26] In response, de Lubac offers some fundamental critiques of the philosophy and science behind racial theory, but then he concedes that, given the wide systematic and programmatic claims race theory makes, "it is a faith.... In truth, the debate is neither scientific nor even philosophical. A refutation cannot suffice because it is only negative. To faith, one must oppose faith. To the racist faith, our Christian and Catholic faith."[27] In these bold strokes, de Lubac struck his first public blows against the rising totalitarian tide. The same themes prevail: only a positive movement of Christian faith and identity will be equipped to respond to the threat of Nazi neopaganism. Of course, this second lecture would not see print until after the war was over. In his memoir of the period, he confesses, "In my naïveté, I still believed at that time that I was expressing the common sentiment of a very large part, if not all, of French Catholicism."[28] The resistance he encountered to this second lecture took him aback, and he quickly regrouped and changed strategy.

De Lubac expressed his deepening concern in a confidential memorandum to his Jesuit superiors. He describes the convergence of themes that will continue to appear, in cleverly cloaked forms, in his subsequent publications: Hitler's Germany represents the vanguard of an anti-Christian revolution, persecuting the Church at every turn, attacking its universalist claims for mission and, in the very same breath, attacking the Jews with an anti-Semitism that is "rampant in its most contemptible form."[29] Paradoxically, an attack on the

---

25. Henri de Lubac, "The Theological Foundation of the Missions," in *Theology in History*, trans. Anne Englund Nash (San Francisco, Ignatius Press, 1996), 367-427 (407–8).
26. Ibid., 409.
27. Ibid., 418.
28. de Lubac, *Christian Resistance*, 25.

very particular identity of the Christian Church is always at the same time an attack on the Jews. And Christians find themselves diminished in their own internal resources, unable and/or unwilling to resist: "In the face of so tragic a situation, how can we fail to be surprised to perceive only so few signs of uneasiness in Catholic and even ecclesiastical circles? Without stopping their intrigues in other respects, the Nazis seek to put our vigilance to sleep, and nearly everything is taking place as if they were succeeding. It seems that we have become, in large measure, dupes of the necessity in which we find ourselves of participating in the official lie. . . . Is this not a sign that souls are not in a state of resistance?"[30]

If faith must be opposed by faith, de Lubac looks at his fellow Frenchmen and finds no faith on the earth to oppose Nazi neopaganism. What is required, then, is a full-fledged project of re-evangelization; "[A] more deeply and integrally lived Christianity, offering less of a hold to the caricatures of the adversary, presupposing perhaps more of reform in our habits and methods, must constitute the sole complete safeguard."[31] But this "more deeply and integrally lived Christianity," is unimaginable apart from a deeper integration of the scriptures into Christian life. Faced with the shocking realization of the anemic faith of his fellow French Christians who are easily tossed by every wind of Nazi propaganda, de Lubac seems intent on launching a comprehensive assault on the banality of Christian faith and practice even as he endeavors to renew it from within with the deep resources of scriptural understanding.

In late 1941, de Lubac began to test the limits of the censors with a series of more and more provocative articles with this end in mind. The first, "A Christian Explanation of Our Times," scrupulously

---

29. de Lubac, "A Letter to My Superiors," 432–33.
30. Ibid., 434–35.
31. Ibid., 438.

avoids any explicitly political tones, but it points to the emergence of the present crisis and collapse of the French social order in a series of four stages: (1) The internal weakening of Christian faith through habitualization and privatization, and (2) the inability, therefore, of Christians to respond adequately to rapid social and technological change, leaves few resources to resist (3) a general sentiment of metaphysical despair, and so Christians are left vulnerable to (4) the "substitute faiths" that step in to fill the vacuum.[32] In this first test of the censors, de Lubac does not name any particular "substitute faiths," but the implicit indictment of fascist mythologizing is clear. As he goes on to describe the centrality of the Gospel in the historical formation of French national identity, one can almost sense him cautiously treading over a sensitive line and then quickly backing off: "[T]o the Gospel we owe our very idea of man. If we deny the Gospel, we are lost. . . . Now (to say in passing) the Gospel is the flower and supreme blossoming of the Bible. The God of Jesus is the God of the prophets. . . . Jesus has not come to reject but to carry out the heart of the message of which the people of Israel were the bearer."[33] The lines of the argument are clear—to respond to our present crisis, we must revive our culture. To revive our culture we must renew our Christian identity. To renew our identity, we must return to the Bible. And to return to the Bible is to rediscover our debt and affiliation with the Jewish people. When this article was published, Fr. Victor Dillard wrote to de Lubac how "surprised" he was "at all you were able to say." He continued: "It is necessary to fight at this moment. . . . we must use all the freedom that remains to us in order to write and to cry out."[34] De Lubac had begun to push the limits of the censors to summon French Christians to a deep

---

32. Henri de Lubac, "A Christian Explanation of Our Times," in *Theology in History*, trans. Anne Englund Nash (San Francisco: Ignatius Press, 1996), 440–56 (441–44).
33. Ibid., 447.
34. Henri de Lubac, *Christian Resistance*, 103.

spiritual resistance, not simply to the eclipse of the Christian identity of France, but particularly, to the wedge forced between Christians and Jews by Vichy apologists.

The success of this initial article emboldened de Lubac. But his next intervention, the working title of which was "A Defense of Christ and the Bible," was in press with the journal *La Chronique sociale* when the censors intervened to prevent its appearing. Despite the appeal efforts of Fr. Dillard and others, carrying the case to the national censor's office, permission to publish was refused. Fr. Dillard confided to de Lubac in a letter in December 1941, "I have the impression that we could have spoken about these questions several months ago, but the noose is tightening. 'If we let this article go by,' they said to me, 'we would immediately have a reaction from the occupying power.'"[35] De Lubac's Jesuit superior took to his defense and managed to get the piece published in *La Vie spirituelle* in 1942, and then de Lubac revised the article and published it in Switzerland with three other articles by confreres. This little volume, entitled *Israël et la foi chrétienne,* was smuggled back into France; it circulated in secret for the rest of the war, and, according to historian Jean-Marie Mayeur, its effect was "considerable."[36]

With a new title, "A New Religious 'Front,'" and beyond the reach of the Vichy censors, this intervention represents de Lubac's most overt and ardent appeal to his fellow French Christians to defend both themselves and the Jews; for de Lubac, attacks on the latter are attacks on the former: "France was Christian, which comes back to saying that it was Jewish."[37] De Lubac defends first the Jewishness of Jesus and early Christianity, and then he proceeds to

---

35. Ibid., 104–5.
36. Ibid., 108.
37. Henri de Lubac, "A New Religious 'Front,'" in *Theology in History,* trans. Anne Englund Nash (San Francisco: Ignatius Press, 1996), 457-87 (471).

defend the Old Testament itself. Like the ancient Valentinians, Nazi theorists attempt to split the Old Testament from the New and discard it, a "Semite Old Testament" stripped off from an "Aryan New Testament."[38] To the contrary, de Lubac writes, "we maintain the indissoluble bond between our two Testaments, always in the final analysis, interpreting the Old by the New, but also always basing the New on the Old. . . . There is only one single Scripture for us, which, as an entire whole, is sacred to us."[39] De Lubac understands that the war against the Jews is being fought at the level of theory, in the dismantling of a tradition-soaked scriptural hermeneutic, and so in the dismantling of a full-throated Christian proclamation. On this new front of spiritual warfare, de Lubac invites his readers to return to scripture, to the spiritual interpretation that establishes the relationship between the Old Testament and the New. Perhaps it is no accident that the publication of "A New Religious Front" comes within months of the publication of the first volume of *Sources chrétiennes*, St. Gregory of Nyssa's *Life of Moses*, an exemplary instance of patristic spiritual interpretation. Nine more volumes of *Sources chrétiennes* would appear between 1942 and the end of the war, including Gregory's *Creation of Man* and Origen's *Homilies on Genesis*. What de Lubac argues in his essays and addresses he aims to teach through the exemplary case of Gregory of Nyssa. The surest form of spiritual resistance to the totalitarian flood is to sink one's roots more deeply into the soil of Christian faith—into the scriptures.

---

38. Ibid., 486. De Lubac is citing the terms of Edmond Picard, *Synthese de l'antisemitisme* (Brussels, 1941). Picard attempted to write the history of Europe since ancient Greece as the war between Aryans and Semites.
39. Ibid., 486.

Conclusion: "Resistance to Anti-Semitism"? Or Defense of the Church?

In the midst of war and occupation, out-maneuvering the censors in public even as he evaded the Gestapo with his covert publications, Henri de Lubac waged his "spiritual war" against the invasive Nazi counter-faith. It must be conceded that de Lubac's first and most intense effort was directed at the defense of Christian faith and the freedom of the Church. For de Lubac, the Anti-Semitic Laws and the persecution of the Jews that followed were symptoms and consequences of an internal failure of the Church rather than the chief scandal, as we might see it. Is it even fitting, then, to see de Lubac's efforts as "Resistance to Anti-Semitism," as the title of his wartime memoir suggests? For all his courage, is Henri de Lubac still a nostalgic "soldier of the Great War," an aristocratic gentleman fighting for the defense of a latter-medieval Christendom?[40] It is certainly true that de Lubac always defends the Jews and the Church together; for him, Pius XI's rallying cry, "Spiritually, we are Semites!" united the Church and the Jews in a spiritual solidarity. But is this solidarity nevertheless reducible to a subordination of Jews to the superseding Christian Church in the New Covenant? Is the spiritual interpretation de Lubac commends a kind of covert oppression—a kinder, gentler anti-Semitism?

De Lubac's defense strategy might strike us as somehow less than a full-throated theoretical defense of the Jews on their own terms, but we must ourselves take to heart his own critique of the scholars

---

40. Such, I think, is the implication of Robin Darling Young's article, "A Soldier of the Great War: Henri de Lubac and the Patristic Sources for a Premodern Theology," in *After Vatican II: Trajectories and Hermeneutics,* ed. James L. Heft (Grand Rapids: Eerdmans, 2012), 134–63: "Most hauntingly, there is no acknowledgment of the ongoing presence of the Jews as claimants to the Hebrew scriptures and their interpretation. The latter is especially mysterious in light of de Lubac's theory of human unity, and, while under the Vichy government, his perilous criticism of Anti-semitism." (142).

of his own age. For de Lubac, the scholarly engagement of the "Old Testament" on its own historical terms, separated from the integral theology of Christian scripture, seems intended to grant Israel and its scriptures a certain fitting autonomy, but it is this very act of separation that has deprived the Church of its deepest internal reasons to defend the Jews. The supposed academic neutrality of the "Hebrew Scriptures" is easily converted into the mode of contrast and division, of "Semitic Old Testament" from "Aryan New Testament." As Christians erase or forget their own "spiritual Semitism," they all too easily reject Semitism of any sort at all as the alien other. While enlightened sensibilities suggest that neutrality is the first step toward tolerance and respect, de Lubac suggests that it is in deepening our own particular commitments as Christians that we—strangely, perhaps—discover a deeper affinity with, a deeper filiation to the people Israel.

It is through the retrieval and revival of Christian spiritual exegesis of scripture that Christian hands are best trained for spiritual warfare. The movement of the soul from the events of salvation history, to their illumination in Christ and the Church, to their personal appropriation and internalization in the soul's own present moral life, pointing toward their final rest in God's saving presence, becomes the key to holding paradoxes in fitting tension. In this scriptural integration, Jew is connected to Christian, past is connected to present and future, the individual soul is connected to the destiny of the saints, and the Alpha is connected to the Omega. If de Lubac's own revived spiritual interpretation may still be examined for elements of supersessionism that we might wish now to overcome or recast, it will be examined along the trajectory that he established, through a deepening rather than a distancing.[41] Indeed, de Lubac

---

41. Indeed, I would suggest that the success of the Scriptural Reasoning movement points to a (surprising) sequel to de Lubac's own work of retrieval. As Jews, Christians, and Muslims

frankly admitted that these scriptural modes must develop and change. But such development and change will come in unexpected ways. As he himself said, "We can take it for sure beforehand: he who will best answer the needs of his time will be someone who will not have first sought to answer them. It is what is found in the depths of ourselves, for ourselves, which has the chance of becoming the topical remedy and the essential sustenance for others."[42] For de Lubac, the self-defense of the Church, using the deepest resources of the traditions of scriptural interpretation, is at one and the same time the fiercest offensive assault on the Anti-Semitism that lies at the heart of the false faith of the Nazi regime. If scriptural interpretation is not quite "political" in the strict sense, it is all the more powerful as spiritual warfare against the principalities and powers that float above, or beneath, the regimes of the world.

---

meet to share study of their scriptures out of the wellsprings of their own traditions, they serve as mutually corrective without calling each other to compromise their deepest traditions. In fact, this shared study allows the traditions to discover sources for their correction within their own respective traditions. And the effect is, quite definitely, "theopolitical." See, for example, Peter Ochs and William Stacy Johnson, eds., *Crisis, Call, and Leadership in the Abrahamic Traditions* (New York: Palgrave Macmillan, 2009). For a preliminary exploration of the relationship between de Lubac, Vatican II, and Scriptural Reasoning, see Kevin L. Hughes, "Deep Reasonings: *Sources chrétiennes, Ressourcement*, and the Logic of Scripture in the years before—and after—Vatican II," *Modern Theology* 29:4 (October 2013): 32–45.

42. Henri de Lubac, *Paradoxes of Faith*, trans. Paule Simon, Sadie Kreilkamp, Ernest Beaumont (San Francisco: Ignatius Press, 1987), 111–12.

11

Inhabiting Scripture

Wesley's Theopolitical Reading of the Bible

D. Stephen Long

John Wesley's reading of holy scripture was less a method for interpretation and more a lived social practice that required constant interaction with others inside and outside the church. Because the Beatitudes formed the center of the Christian life, the purpose of reading scripture entailed inhabiting them, or—perhaps better put—having the Holy Spirit inhabit us by drawing us into the life of Christ, which will always be characterized by the Beatitudes. Nowhere can this understanding of reading scripture be better understood than in Wesley's General Rules. They formed the heart of the Wesleyan movement and provided a communal context not only to hear scripture, but more importantly, to inhabit it. Anyone could know the bare sense of scripture: do good and avoid evil. Wesley acknowledged that and called it "the righteousness of a Pharisee" and the "religion of the world." But to inhabit scripture entailed something different; it required "heart religion."[1] For this reason, Wesley took passages from the Ten Commandments and beatitudes from the Sermon on the Mount and set them within a social context so that they might be lived.

Wesley's social inhabitation of scripture was not a hermeneutical method for understanding; nor was it a program for adjudicating difficult cases of conscience. It may have been a "method" in the more ancient sense (and thus the "Methodists" were properly named), a sense that Pierre Hadot identifies in his *Philosophy as a Way of Life*.[2] Here method is *met' hodos* (along the way). Method is not the search for an indubitable, or even dubitable, foundation upon which one can build, but a journey—a movement "along the way."

"Method," however, seldom signifies this more ancient sense when it comes to reading scripture. Now it means the proper source(s) for knowledge. Once this understanding of "method" takes precedence over the lived social practice of reading scripture, then the Bible becomes either an epistemology or a guidebook for ethics. Unfortunately, with the invention of the so-called "Wesleyan Quadrilateral," scripture became a source for a method rather than a lived practice. For it to be the latter requires the social context of the class meeting. If they do not exist, Wesley's social reading of scripture cannot occur. This essay first addresses how fitting Wesley's use of scripture into a method that seeks the right order of sources in order to attain doctrinal essentials, fails to illumine his more social, or better "catholic," contribution. Then, it establishes a more proper context for reading scripture in the Wesleyan way. Finally, it turns to his

---

1. Wesley, "The Great Privilege of Those Who Are Born of God," in *The Works of John Wesley*, ed. Albert C. Outler, 24 vols. (Nashville: Abingdon Press, 1985) vol. 1, 431-43: 442.
2. Pierre Hadot, *Philosophy as a Way of Life* (London: Wiley-Blackwell, 1995).

interpretation of the Sermon on the Mount in order to show how he offered a theopolitical reading of the Bible.

Scripture as Method: The Failure of Interpreting Scripture Well

What is the place of scripture in Wesley and the Wesleyan tradition? Ken Brower states, "The Bible is the only authoritative text for Wesleyans. While reason, tradition and experience are foundational for theology, Wesleyans accept the Reformation principle of Scripture alone."[3] Brower is, of course, correct, but the statement requires nuance. He is correct in what he implicitly opposes with his statement—the idea that Wesleyan theology should be founded upon a "quadrilateral" of sources: scripture, tradition, reason and experience. He is also correct in what he affirms. Wesley affirmed the Reformation's *sola scriptura*.

But the statement misses something significant. Much of the modern discussion on Wesley's use of scripture focuses on it as an epistemological method. The question put to it is how do we know what is authoritative? What are the methodological sources for this knowledge? Are there four sources or one? If there are four, how are they to be related? This quest predominated the Wesleyan tradition at least since the 1970s, as it did many other Christian traditions as well.

Since its beginning, Methodism has seen fits and starts where it tries to justify itself as a church by claiming some distinctive. That distinctive often gets presented as a unique approach to Protestant Christianity that refuses to make confessions, such as those found in the Reformed and Lutheran traditions, central to its identity. Often this approach draws on Wesley's sermon, "A Catholic Spirit," in order to affirm modern pluralistic arrangements. It concludes that what

---

3. Kent Brower, "Wesleyan Approach to Scripture," in Al Truesdale, ed., *Global Wesleyan Dictionary of Theology*, (Kansas City: Beacon Hill Press, 2013), 488.

makes the Wesleyan tradition distinctive is its approach to theology, an approach that draws on a pluralism of sources where scripture is one among many, albeit the most central. This approach came to be known as "The Wesleyan Quadrilateral," and drew upon Wesley's sermon, "Catholic Spirit" for its justification. This interpretation of the Wesleyan "Catholic Spirit," then, has nothing to do with the Catholic tradition; it has to do with a pluralistic approach to resourcing modern theology that states one can begin with any of the four sources, scripture, tradition, reason and experience, and from them derive what is essential for Christian identity.

The Wesleyan Quadrilateral was invented at United Methodism's 1972 General Conference. It created a new, lengthy hermeneutic to the Wesleyan standards of doctrine—the Articles of Religion, Confession of Faith and General Rules—called "Our Theological Task," which can be found in Methodism's *Book of Discipline*. Since its founding in 1784, the *Discipline* begins with a historic statement about the rise of Methodism, followed by "The General Rules" and the "Articles of Religion." It also included the "Order for the administration of the Lord's Supper," as well as for Baptism, Funerals, and Ordination. Gradually the liturgical orders were removed from the *Book of Discipline* and after 1972 a new section, "Our Theological Task," was placed after the General Rules and Articles. "Our Theological Task" became the hermeneutic by which to interpret the standards of doctrine. This new hermeneutic drew on Wesley's expression, "the catholic spirit," and set it forth in two, contradictory ways.[4] On the one hand, it was supposed to be understood as connecting the Wesleyan tradition to the larger catholic tradition, to a "common heritage." On the other, it supposedly characterized a Wesleyan distinctive—Methodism was not a "confessional" church

---

4. Ibid., 73.

(despite having a "Confession of Faith" and "Articles of Religion")[5] but allowed for a "pluralism" of theological approaches via the hermeneutical method the Wesleyan Quadrilateral provided.

The Wesleyan Quadrilateral immediately became controversial. Robert Cushman, dean of Duke Divinity School, argued it misrepresented the Wesleyan tradition and led to a "theological indifferentism." Many Methodists rallied to defend or challenge the Wesleyan Quadrilateral as Methodist General Conferences wrestled with how the four sources related. From 1972 to 1984 General Conference interpreted the Wesleyan "catholic spirit" in terms of the second interpretation: a "theological pluralism" as an "alternative" to any confessional tradition. The result was an unstable tension, which the 1984 General Conference was tasked to resolve. The 1984 General Conference was charged with addressing "the proper understanding of the catholic spirit, which is often spoken of today as pluralism."[6] It clarified what was meant by a catholic spirit through a more careful articulation of sources and their interrelations for theology. The 1984 General Conference highlighted the first interpretation of the Wesleyan Quadrilateral as setting forth a "Catholic Spirit" that connected the Wesleyan tradition with other Christians in a common heritage. It stated, "United Methodists never undertake the task of theologizing as a totally new venture. We share a common heritage with all other Christians everywhere and in all ages." But following Wesley, General Conference interpreted this "common heritage" primarily in terms of a minimum of doctrine to be believed:

With them [other Christian churches] we acknowledge belief in the

---

5. For an affirmation that Methodism is "confessional," see my *Keeping Faith: An Ecumenical Commentary on the Articles of Religion and Confession of Faith in the United Methodist Church* (Eugene, OR: Wipf & Stock, 2012).
6. Richard Heitzenrater, "Doctrine and Theology in the U. M. C.," in Langford, ed., *Doctrine and Theology in the United Methodist Church* (Nashville: Kingswood Books, 1991), 94.

triune God—Father, Son and Holy Spirit. We hold common faith in the mystery of salvation in and through Jesus Christ. We proclaim together that, in our willful alienation God judges us, seeks us, pardons us, and receives us, only because he truly loves us. We therefore believe that the Holy Spirit prompts us to respond in faith and enables us to accept God's gift of reconciliation and justification. This sense of common Christian heritage is rich in our hymnody and liturgies.[7]

General Conference identifies a "catholic spirit" as belief in the Trinity, salvation in Christ and the Spirit's work in reconciliation and justification. It notes, but never explores, that the "common heritage" is found in "our hymnody and liturgies." It never asks if our ability to read scripture well depends upon the hymnody and liturgy and vice versa.

The 1984 General Conference continued to speak of four sources, but emphasized scripture's preeminence. Its clarifications, for all their improvement over the so-called Wesleyan quadrilateral and the theological fragmentation it entailed, nonetheless failed. It did not produce a substantive catholic spirit or address the pressing question how scripture, doctrine, worship and life interact. The 1984 General Conference shared in common with the 1972 General Conference that catholicity is primarily a matter of minimal doctrinal essentials derived from a theological method that needs to establish the proper relationship among four sources. Although it made considerable advances over the 1972 invention of the "Wesleyan Quadrilateral," the terms of the debate remained the same. The pressing question remained: How is scripture to be used in order to establish the proper authority that can identify doctrinal essentials Wesleyans must affirm in order to maintain a catholic spirit? As long as this is the question, Wesley's best use of scripture will be ignored.

Wesley himself is to blame, in part, for such an impoverished

---

7. *The Book of Discipline of the United Methodist* (Nashville: United Methodist Publishing House, 1984), 73–74.

catholic spirit and use of scripture. Wesley opened the door to this fragmentation. In his sermon "Catholic Spirit," he stated that a 'catholic spirit' did not mean, "'Embrace my modes of worship,' or, 'I will embrace yours.'" Such a statement readily lends itself to the pluralistic, "alternative to any confession," interpretation. But the context for Wesley's argument should not be forgotten. He was speaking to members of the Wesleyan movement who came from different churches. He was not addressing members within a common church, which is obvious in what comes next in his sermon, which seldom gains a hearing. He wrote, "This also is a thing which does not depend either on your choice or mine. We must both act as each is fully persuaded in his own mind."[8] Note the apparent contradiction in this sentence. Worship does not depend upon individual choice, but each must be "fully persuaded" as to worship style. If the latter point gets emphasized without attention to the former, then Wesley's statement easily gives the impression that each individual Christian or congregation should chose those modes of worship they find persuasive, but this overlooks the first part of his sentence. Worship does not depend on individual choice. His point is not that each congregation, lay member or minister should pursue the worship style he or she determines to be authentic. His point is that members of the Wesleyan movement from churches other than the Anglican did not need to follow Anglican worship styles to be part of the movement, and most importantly, the government should not establish a church and require uniformity of worship. Each church represented in the movement had a set worship and if a member of that church was persuaded by his or her church's worship, then such persons should not use the apparatus of government to impose their mode of worship. They could still seek holiness

---

8. John Wesley, *The Catholic Spirit*, in *The Works of John Wesley*, ed. Albert C. Outler, 24 vols. (Nashville: Abingdon Press, 1985), 2:79-95 (89).

together. Nonetheless, the mode of worship is not a function of individual choice. Within a church, it is not in the realm of "think and let think."

If Wesley thought a church, grounded in a catholic spirit, could have as diverse worship styles and practices as currently exist in Methodism or Protestantism in general, he never would have affirmed Article XXII, "Of the Rites and Ceremonies of the Church" in the Methodist "Articles of Religion," an article that continues as a "standard of doctrine" to this day. It provides a better understanding of a "catholic spirit" than the minimum, doctrinal essentials the Wesleyan Quadrilateral produces. That article states:

> It is not necessary that rites and ceremonies should in all places be the same, or exactly alike; for they have always been different, and may be changed according to the diversity of countries, times and men's manners, so that nothing be ordained against God's Word. Whosoever, through his private judgment, willingly and purposely doth openly break the rites and ceremonies of the church to which he belongs, which are not repugnant to the Word of God, and are ordained and approved by common authority, ought to be rebuked openly, that others may fear to do the like, as one that offendeth against the common order of the church, and woundeth the consciences of weak brethren. Every particular church may ordain, change, or abolish rites and ceremonies so that all things may be done to edification.

Rites and ceremonies are not subject to "private judgment;" they are a matter of "common authority." Each minister cannot choose for her or himself how to baptize, preside at the Eucharist or celebrate the liturgical year. To turn such matters into "private judgment" decided by a minister is an egregious form of clericalism that violates communal agreements. Wesley assumes there are "rites and ceremonies . . . ordained and approved by common authority," but if a church exists that has no such "rites and ceremonies," then all we have is private judgment.

Interpreting Scripture as a Political Act

What does the above foray into Methodist polity have to do with reading scripture as a theopolitical act? If scripture is reduced to an authoritative source within a method to identify basic doctrinal essentials, then it cannot be read well. If it is read outside of the common liturgical context in which it makes most sense it can only become a function of private judgment. Scripture is neither a "how to" book for constructing a theological position nor a rulebook for adjudicating difficult cases of doctrine and ethics. It is the living word of God intended, like all words, to communicate such that the One communicating inhabits our life and we his. For that to occur, the social and catholic context within which scripture gets read makes all the difference. Scripture may be *sola* in the Wesleyan tradition, but does not function alone; it functions within a liturgical and social context that allows it to *communicate*. That is, it produces a communion, a common worship, doctrine and life that identifies God so God can be worshipped and God's life participated in. All three are necessary to read scripture well.

Note for instance how central the proper teaching on God's nature and attributes are to Wesley. He discusses them in his sixth sermon on the Sermon on the Mount in the context of properly hallowing the Lord's name and thus fulfilling scripture. Although his interpretation of God's nature and agency are clear and brief, he has drawn upon a rich catholic tradition of the perfectly, simple Triune God. He writes:

> The name of God is God himself—the nature of God so far as it can be discovered to man. It means, therefore, together with his existence, all his attributes or perfections—his eternity, particularly signified by his great and incommunicable name Jehovah. . . . His "fullness of being," denoted by that other great name, "I am that I am;" his omnipresence;—his omnipotence;—who is indeed the only agent in the material world, all matter being essentially dull and inactive, and moving

247

only as it is moved by the finger of God—his Trinity in Unity and Unity in Trinity.[9]

Wesley placed doctrine in the context of Beatitude, just as he did worship. If any of these three forms of communication (doctrine, worship life) are deficient, our reading of scripture will be as well.

Let me now focus on how the Christian life contributes to our reading of scripture, noting that for Wesley the Christian life cannot be divorced from proper worship of God, which will of course require doctrine so that we can identify, as much as can be identified, the God worthy of worship. If we cannot identify God at all, then worship would be impossible. But the point of doctrine is never to solve a puzzle; it is to worship God so that we can be drawn into the life God announced as blessed. Indeed, beatitude characterizes Christian life.

In his sermons on the Sermon on the Mount, John Wesley wrote, "I shall endeavor to show that Christianity is essentially a social religion, and that to turn it into a solitary relation is indeed to destroy it."[10] This quote often gets misrepresented. It does not refer to "social justice," a term made famous by Pius XI in his *Quadragesimo Anno*. I am confident Wesley would affirm much that is present in the "social justice" tradition, but his affirmation that Christianity is a "social religion" has little to do with it. He explains what he means by first defining "Christianity" and then "social religion." He writes, "By Christianity I mean that method of worshipping God which is here revealed to man by Jesus Christ." The first context for his claim that Christianity is a social religion is worship. He then explains "social religion:" "When I say this is essentially a social religion, I mean not only that it cannot subsist so well, but that it

---

9. John Wesley, "Upon Our Lord's Sermon on the Mount VI," in *The Works of John Wesley*, 1:572-91 (580-81).
10. Ibid., 1:533.

cannot subsist at all without society, without living and conversing with other men."[11] Society is essential because the life of Beatitude, which is the heart of the Christian religion for Wesley, cannot be exercised in solitude. He identifies meekness and peacemaking as examples of "dispositions" that can only be exercised in the presence of others. He acknowledges the hermit can become meek, but "as it implies (which it no less necessarily does) mildness, gentleness, and long-suffering, it cannot possibly have a being, it has no place under heaven, without an intercourse with other men." Likewise peacemaking entails conversing with others.[12]

Notice how Wesley uses scripture here. He takes two beatitudes, meekness and peacemaking, and asks what the social conditions are for being able to exercise them. He answers that they require communication with others. If we were not placed in social conditions where peacemaking was necessary or meekness possible, then there would be no real possibility for us to inhabit those holy dispositions. Reading scripture well, then, requires not merely the act of reading scripture, but reading it so that it takes root in our social interactions. Where do such social interactions occur? It is no coincidence that the early Methodist movement placed people in "societies" and gave the rules to follow in all their interactions. The place to begin to think well about Wesley's reading of scripture is his "General Rules." They provide the foundational social interaction that allows a reading of scripture that is less a "source" within a method and more a "way" into the life of God.

Wesley's use of scripture is best understood as a social reality found in the *General Rules for the United Societies*. Methodism and the Wesleyan tradition accidentally became a church; others have noted that unfortunate historical reality. Methodism makes more sense as

---

11. Ibid., 1:533–34.
12. Ibid., 1:534–35.

a lay order within the church in which persons come together to live by a "rule." From early on, the Methodist *Book of Discipline* began with its General Rules followed by its confession (Articles of Religion). It sought to bring together life and doctrine. A doctrine that is not lived is ideology; a Christian life that is not doctrinal is mere sentimentality. The former has the form but not the heart of religion. The latter has the heart but lacks form. At his best, Wesley sought to bring the two together. He affirmed their co-joining in his preface to his *Sermons on Several Occasions*:

> And herein it is more especially my desire, first to guard those who are just setting their faces toward heaven (and who, having little acquaintance with the things of God, are the more liable to be turned out of the way) from formality, from mere outside religion, which has almost driven heart-religion out of the world; and secondly, to warn those who know the religion of the heart, the faith which worketh by love, least at any time they make void the law through faith, and so fall back into the snare of the devil.[13]

Note the important interplay in Wesley's preface between "law" and "faith." For Wesley, faith establishes the law; it never dissolves or supersedes it. Even more interesting and controversial, law can promote faith. Wesley's emphasis on the General Rules explains how. He refers to the General Rules as "the religion of the world" and "the religion of the Pharisees."[14] The latter is a reference to the "law," but Wesley did not dismiss the law or set grace against it. He argued that law and grace were never a contradiction. While references to the religion of the world and of the Pharisees would usually be considered negative, they are not negative for him. They identify a "formal" religion, a religion where persons "obey" the law, but

---

13. John Wesley, "Preface," in *The Works of John Wesley*, 1:103-7 (107).
14. John Wesley, "Upon Our Lord's Sermon on the Mount V," in *The Works of John Wesley*, 1:550-71 (565–67). See D. Stephen Long, *John Wesley's Moral Theology* (Nashville: Kingswood Books, 2005), 149.

do so merely as a formality. The same can occur with participation in the sacraments, confession of creeds and affirmations of doctrine. Each of them can be nothing more than "mere outside religion." True religion occurs when the law, the sacraments, confessions and doctrine are not only formally affirmed but also inhabited. They become not "external" but "internal." This language could easily produce nothing but sentimentality. It could lead to the blithe response that what matters is authentic faith and love of God, not following laws, observing sacraments or confessing creeds. But notice again from the above quote how far that would be from Wesley's intention. There is both a "formality," a "mere outside religion," that provides false consciousness, but there is also a "heart religion" that wrongly "makes void the law" by thinking it can dispense with the formal. The point of the Wesleyan movement as a lay order committed to a rule was to bring the two together.

> The structure of the Methodist *Book of Discipline* illustrates this intention. The introduction to it first states that in 1739 "eight or ten persons, who appeared to be deeply convicted of sin, and earnestly groaning for redemption, came to Mr. Wesley in London." Then it reminds the readers what Wesley did. He "appointed a day when they might all come together; which from thenceforward they did every week." Wesley did not feed them pious sentimentalities, but formed societies and gave them a rule. The introduction states, "There is only one condition required of those who desire admission into these Societies—'a desire to flee from the wrath to come and to be saved from their sin'." This single condition, however, quickly expanded; for the introduction then states that such a desire "will be shown by its fruits." What are those fruits? Obedience to the General Rules. The following words precede the listing of the General Rule, "It is therefore expected of all who continue therein that they shall continue to evidence their desire of salvation. . . ."
>
> *First*: By doing no harm, by avoiding evil of every kind especially that which is most generally practiced, such as. . . .

Second, By doing good: by being in every kind merciful after their power: as they have opportunity doing good of ever possible sort, and as far as possible to all men:. . . .

Third, By attending upon the ordinances of God; such are. . . .

Under each of these general rules, specific rules are then listed, thirteen under do not harm, five under do good and six under attending upon the ordinances. Each of these general rules can be traced to a biblical passage. Let me provide some examples.

The first two specific rules under "do no harm" are "The taking of the name of God in vain" and "The profaning the day of the Lord, either by doing ordinary work therein or by buying or selling." These specific rules are, depending on how one counts them, the third and fourth of the Ten Commandments. The General Rules begin with the first table of the Ten Commandments ordering our faith and love to God. But the second table is also represented. Two other specific rules prohibit "Slaveholding: buying or selling slaves" and "The giving or taking things on usury—that is unlawful interest." The latter is a prohibition found in several passages of the Old Testament, but both are also understand as violations of the seventh commandment, "You shall not steal."

The biblical resonances are not only found in the prohibitions; they are also present in the affirmations of doing good. The first specific rule for doing good draws on Matt. 25 and requires members of the societies to do good to all people: "To their bodies, of the ability which God giveth, by giving food to the hungry, by clothing the naked, by visiting or helping them that are sick or in prison." The fifth specific rule is an obvious reference to Heb. 12:1-2: "By running with patience the race which is set before them, denying themselves, and taking up their cross daily." Likewise all the rules to attend upon the ordinances of God have biblical precedent: worship, proclamation, communicating at the Eucharist, prayer, searching the scriptures, fasting and abstinence.

One positive affirmation in the second General Rule shows the connection between them and Wesley's understanding of "heart-religion;" something easily misunderstood. That specific rule commands Methodists to do good: "To their souls, by instructing, reproving, or exhorting all we have any intercourse with; trampling under foot that enthusiastic doctrine, that 'we are not to do good unless *our hearts be free to it*'." This specific rule puts to rest any understanding of "heart-religion" as an inward, pietistic existentialism. Wesley does not divide external observance from internal disposition. He understands that both need each other. One obeys the General Rules whether or not one has a heartfelt disposition to do so. By extension, given that each finds a place in the General Rules, the same holds for confession, sacramental observance and obedience to liturgical worship styles authorized by one's church. Of course external observance is not yet "heart religion." It is at most a condition that contributes to the latter's possibility.

Jennifer Herdt's work, *Putting on Virtue: The Legacy of Splendid Vices*, most closely approximates Wesley's intention. She defends the tradition of imitating acquired virtues for the purpose of happiness even when one's imitation may not yet be "authentic." She only makes one reference to Wesley in her important work, but it is telling. She notes that Wesley, along with "French devout humanism" and "Cambridge Platonism" could resource "modern theological ethics" with "mimetic virtue."[15] Wesley's imitation of virtue would, I think, be more "ecclesiocentric" than her account seeks to be, but Herdt has nonetheless pointed out something important in the Wesleyan tradition of Christianity. It is less

---

15. Jennifer Herdt, *Putting on Virtue: The Legacy of the Splendid Vices* (Chicago: University of Chicago Press, 2008), 285.

concerned with modern conceptions of authenticity that refuse to act virtuously if one has not truly inhabited virtue and are overly frightened of hypocrisy. Wesley's heart religion is not an attempt at authenticity; it is faith fulfilling the law through holy dispositions where one puts on these dispositions (for after all they belong first and foremost to Christ) even if our hearts are not yet "free to it." Of course, if virtue remains only a "putting on" it will be inadequate; it is preferable not to putting on virtue but it is not yet virtue's fullness.

To do good, avoid evil and attend upon God's ordinances as an external observance was necessary but insufficient. What more should be done? The more is the "religion of the heart," and here is Wesley's most interesting and at the same time most traditional understanding of the relationship among scripture, doctrine and life. The religion of the heart, or true religion as he put it, is a life of beatitude.[16] It had little to do with a warm-hearted conversion to Jesus as one's personal savior. It was instead the indwelling of the Holy Spirit in the believer such that the life Jesus pronounced blessed became not only one's own, but socially embedded in the world. True religion, the religion of the heart, is the law established by faith such that it bears the fruit of poverty of spirit, meekness, mournfulness, righteousness, mercifulness, purity of heart, peacemaking, and possibly, as it brought for Jesus himself, persecution for righteousness sake.

For Wesley, the heart of holy scripture culminates in the way of life Jesus pronounces as blessed in his Sermon on the Mount. It is how Jesus fulfills the law. He reads scripture through the juxtaposition of two mountains and their revelations, the Law given to Moses and the Blessed Life Jesus announces. It brings happiness and completes the "innate instinct" humans have to be happy. In his introduction

---

16. To understand how it is traditional see Servais Pinckaers, *The Sources of Christian Ethics* (Washington, DC: The Catholic University of America Press, 1995).

to the Beatitudes in his "Explanatory Notes on the Bible," Wesley wrote: "To bless men, to make men happy, was the great business for which our Lord came into the world. And accordingly he here pronounces eight blessings together, annexing them to so many steps in Christianity. Knowing that happiness is our common aim, and that an innate instinct continually urges us to the pursuit of it, he in the kindest manner applies to that instinct and directs it to its proper object. Though all men desire, yet few attain happiness, because they seek it where it is not to be found."[17] The proper object of happiness is the life of Christ; the beatitudes are self-descriptions of his human agency in its perfection. To be ordered to that perfection is to find happiness. The Beatitudes fulfill the law.

For Wesley, the two mountains, like the two testaments, need each other for their intelligibility. If we do not have the Mosaic Law then we cannot understand the Blessed Life and vice versa. Let me provide an example of how this works. Take for example the command "Thou shalt not kill." Let us assume our neighbors keep this command but only externally—they fear punishment, loss of reputation or status. Perhaps they even do a cost-benefit analysis and decide it would be better not to kill their neighbor. Is such a bare observance keeping the law? The answer is yes and no. Yes, the law has not been violated. Neighbors have not been killed and that is good. An external observance is better than no observance at all. Nonetheless, the law's true purpose has not been fulfilled; for its purpose is not primarily negative—do not violate a precept—but positive—inhabit the Blessed Life. "Peacemaking," then, is the fruit of the law's command. The "religion of the heart" is the believers' participation in the life of Christ through the Holy Spirit so that rather than the law not being violated, it becomes a "principle

---

17. John Wesley, *Wesley's Notes on the Bible*, ed. G. Roger Schoenhals (Grand Rapids: Francis Asbury Press, 1987), 407.

within." For this reason Wesley gave those seeking to flee from the wrath to come "General Rules" and said observe them whether your "hearts be free to it" or not. The grace of mere observance can become an inhabitation of the Spirit turning it into "heart religion."

Reading the Bible as a Political Act

Notice what Wesley accomplished. He did not provide a hermeneutical method for interpreting scripture. He provided a rule filled with scripture that fit within a social context first of discourse among members of the societies and second within social engagement broadly understood. The two "societies," the local society of the class meeting and the larger society of everyday interactions, fed into each other. How could we read scripture well? The first place to examine that question was in the class meeting by asking each other: "Were you stealing from others by the way you made your living or profiting from others' misery? Were you fighting with each other, taking each other to court and living as enemies and strangers rather than friends?" In the class meeting one was free to confess how the scripture was and was not being fulfilled in one's life. One waited upon God to bring about such fulfillment, but the waiting was never quietist. One tried to "put on" the holy dispositions that would bring beatitude even if one did not yet inhabit them. The very act of putting them on, of observing the religion of the world and of the Pharisees could be a means of grace by which the fulfillment of the rules—the life of Beatitude—came as the gift it is. The purpose of the law fulfilled by faith was not, however, to be construed individualistically. Christianity is a social religion. What became inhabited in the local society was to be extended into the larger society. The purpose of the society was not the cultivation of individual piety, but "social" Christianity, even across ecclesial divides. Moreover, Wesley hoped it might be present across national divides as well. The Beatitudes, if they are truly the Beatitudes, will produce a Catholic Spirit, something Wesley found missing in his own day. Their purpose ultimately is to bear the fruit of the love of God and neighbor. Learned in the local society, this love should then be extended to the larger society, even if it did so negatively. That is, it helps us identify what is amiss. Wesley identified it in his own day without mincing words: "See how *these* Christians love one another!"

These Christian kingdoms that are tearing out each other's bowels, desolating one another with fire and sword! These Christian armies that are sending each other by thousands, by ten thousands, quick into hell! These Christian nations that are all on fire with intestine broils, party against party, faction against faction! These Christian cities where deceit and fraud, oppression and wrong, yea, robbery and murder, go not out of their streets! These Christian families, torn asunder with envy, jealousy, anger, domestic jars—without number, without end! Yea, what is most dreadful, most to be lamented of all, these Christian churches!—churches ('Tell it not in Gath;' but alas how can we hide it, either from Jews, Turks or pagans?) that bear the name of Christ, 'the Prince of Peace,' and wage continual war with each other.[18]

The question the Wesleyan tradition puts before us for reading scripture well is not if we have the proper method, but if scripture inhabits our society. It is a "method" only in the ancient sense; it is to be used in everyday life as a way to be followed. Of course, modern methods of interpreting scripture remain important and are often illuminating, but Wesley was on to something significant. Scripture is finally God's self-communication so that a people can live

---

18. John Wesley, "Upon Our Lord's Sermon on the Mount II," in *The Works of John Wesley*, 1:488–509 (507–8).

in communion with God and one another. If that does not occur, we may be interpreting a text but we are not yet reading scripture.

12

The Scriptural Logic of Barmen and the Jewish Question

Susannah Ticciati

A frequent refrain in retrospective reflection on the Barmen Theological Declaration is its lack of explicit comment on the National Socialist measures against the Jews. Thus, Eberhard Busch: "It is correct and profoundly fateful that the Barmen Declaration, particularly in its first thesis, does not imply in any way that it stands and must stand in an essential bond with the Jews."[1] John de Gruchy registers the critique that "Barmen was not only ambiguous but silent with regard to the plight of the Jews."[2] Rowan Williams, in recognition of Barmen's limitations as dogma, acknowledges: "It

1. Busch, *The Barmen Theses Then and Now: The 2004 Warfield Lectures at* Princeton Theological Seminary, trans. Darrell and Judith Guder (Grand Rapids: Eerdmans, 2010), 30.

is, notoriously, silent on the Jewish question, even though this, as it affected the Church, was so significant a part of Barmen's agenda."[3] And Barth himself later wrote to Eberhard Bethge, "I myself have long felt guilty that I did not make [the Jewish] problem [*Die Judenfrage*] central [*entscheidend*], at least public, in the two Barmen declarations of 1934 which I had composed."[4]

While noted and lamented, this lacuna, so obvious and glaring with hindsight, has not been sufficiently interrogated. In this essay I want to offer an essentially affirmative reading of Barmen as a political use of scripture, but I want to do so with a view to the Jewish lacuna. I will explore, on the one hand, why it was so difficult or even impossible—theologically speaking—to confront the Jewish question head on. I will ask, on the other hand, how with the benefit of hindsight we might go beyond Barmen but still in the spirit of it, making good its lack. I will suggest that it is—ironically—precisely

2. John W. de Gruchy, *Bonhoeffer and South Africa: Theology in Dialogue* (Grand Rapids: Eerdmans, 1984), 126.
3. Rowan Williams, "Beginning with the Incarnation," in *On Christian Theology* (Oxford: Blackwell, 2000), 79-92 (87).
4. Eberhard Bethge, "Troubled Self-Interpretation and Uncertain Reception in the Church Struggle," in *The German Church Struggle and the Holocaust*, ed. Franklin H. Littell and Hubert G. Locke (Detroit: Wayne State University Press, 1974), 167-84 (167). For the full text of the original letter, see *Evangelische Theologie* 28 (1968), 555–56. The first Barmen Declaration does in fact raise the issue (at least in terms of racism in the church), as Rolf Ahlers points out. See Rolf Ahlers, *The Barmen Theological Declaration of 1934: The Archeology of a Confessional Text* (New York: Edwin Mellen Press, 1986), 248 n. 20. The first Barmen Declaration was approved by the First Free Reformed Synod on 4 January 1934 in the city of Barmen. The second, more famous, Declaration (which is the subject of this essay) was agreed upon at the First Confessional Synod of the German Evangelical Church, a federation of Lutheran, Reformed, and United churches, on 31 May 1934, also in Barmen. The latter marked the official birth of the Confessing Church, which separated from the "German Christians"—adherents of Hitler, through whom Hitler was attempting to control the official German Evangelical Church—in the belief that only by doing so could it represent the true German Evangelical Church. The principal author of both declarations was Karl Barth. But while he wrote the first single-handedly, the second Declaration went through several versions before it reached its final form, first in discussion between the members of the theological commission given the task of drafting the declaration (Karl Barth, Hans Asmussen, and Thomas Breit), and finally in response to its reception by the Synod of Barmen. However, the first full draft discussed by the commission was in fact composed entirely by Barth. See Ahlers, *The Barmen Theological Declaration*, for a detailed account of the genesis of the text of the Declaration.

the theology of Barmen (among other things[5]) that makes way for the clarity with which we see Barmen's own failure today. Even today this clarity needs sharpening, and this essay hopes to offer a small contribution towards that end.

The essay will be structured as follows. The first section will articulate what Barmen did well, delineating the way in which it uses scripture, and the theological understanding of scripture that undergirds this use. The second section will ask what this enabled in respect of the Jewish question, concluding that it was not enough. The third section will probe this deficiency, asking after the forces that shaped the theology of the time, within whose strictures the Barmen authors were bound to operate. The final section will move towards a theological repair of Barmen in the light of intervening history, asking what a responsible and robust theological response to the Jewish question might look like today. While we are in a very different place historically speaking from the National Socialist Germany of the 1930s, the question raised for Christians by the Aryanism of the Nazis remains a pressing one: What is the significance of Jews (whether Christian or non-Christian) for Christians, and in relation to the God of Christ?

What Barmen Did Well

The first of the Barmen theses sets the parameters for the remaining five. It makes the Declaration, in Barth's later estimation, "the first confessional document in which the Evangelical Church has tackled the problem of natural theology."[6] The thesis is a comment on John

---
5. See p. 278.
6. Karl Barth, *Church Dogmatics*, 4 vols. (Edinburgh: T& T Clark, 1936-1969), 2/1, 172 (hereafter *CD*). Barth clearly saw natural theology as the fundamental problem to which Barmen was a response. According to Jordan J. Ballor, this is where Bonhoeffer departs from Barth, regarding the Aryan Clause as a much more central threat, not just a symptom of a deeper theological problem. In keeping with this, Bonhoeffer read Barmen differently, as a call to concrete ethical obedience (Jordon J. Ballor, "The Aryan Clause, The Confessing Church, and the

14:6 and John 10:1, 9. As do all the theses, after citing scripture, it offers an expository affirmation followed by a rejection. The text runs: "Jesus Christ, as he is attested to us in Holy Scripture, is the one Word of God which we have to hear and which we have to trust and obey in life and in death. We reject the false doctrine, as though the Church could and would have to acknowledge as a source of its proclamation, apart from and besides this one Word of God, still other events and powers, figures and truths, as God's revelation."[7] In his short commentary on this first thesis in the second volume of the *Church Dogmatics*, Barth spells out the logic of this rejection of natural theology. I will explicate it here, highlighting its potency in the face of the Nazi regime. In the following sections we will see that its potency is also its weakness.

Barth shows how the "also" of natural theology always ultimately presses for an "only." When anything else is placed alongside Jesus Christ, attested in scripture, as divine revelation that is normative for the church (whether it be reason, conscience, history or nature), that other revelation will eventually exclude Jesus Christ, becoming the only revelation.[8] It does so (we can infer from Barth, who leaves the reason implicit) because anything creaturely, when stamped with divine authority, is an idol. And God cannot be worshiped alongside an idol. Rather, when anything creaturely is absolutized, the result is an enslaving and oppressive ideology.

We see this with horrific clarity in the Nazi ideology. The "definite

---

Ecumenical Movement: Barth and Bonhoeffer on Natural Theology, 1933–1935," *Scottish Journal of Theology* 59, no. 3 ([2006], 263–80). The Aryan Clause was issued by the National Socialist government on 7 April 1933, excluding those of Jewish descent and those married to Jews from holding office in the state (including, therefore, the office of ministry within the church).

7. The translation is that of Arthur C. Cochrane, which appears in the Constitution of the Presbyterian Church (USA), *Book of Confessions* (see Arthur C. Cochrane, *The Church's Confession Under Hitler* [Philadelphia: Westminster Press, 1962], Appendix VII, 238–42). I will follow this translation throughout.

8. Barth, *CD* 2/1:173.

and new form of natural theology"[9] that arose here was the hailing of the historical events surrounding the rise of National Socialism, of Hitler himself, and of German blood and soil as new embodiments of divine revelation alongside scripture. But as Barth points out, "[a]ccording to the dynamic of the political movement, what was . . . intended . . . was the proclamation of this new revelation as the only revelation, and therefore the transformation of the Christian Church into the temple of the German nature- and history-myth."[10]

Barth interprets Barmen as a miraculous witness to the fact that despite this all-consuming assault on the church, which carried to its logical conclusion spelt its destruction, "the Word of God still remained" in and for the church, "after all other grounds had crumbled under [its] feet."[11] What is brought to light in Barmen's first thesis is the fact that the Word of God has been and will remain the church's "secret 'only,'" "in the face of the 'also' of invading natural theology."[12] Barth argues that Barmen, in its first thesis, exposes and rejects not only its most immediate enemy in the natural theology of the Nazis, but along with it the natural theology that he deems to have held sway within the church in one form or another throughout the previous two centuries (Schleiermacher and Ritschl come in for special mention). The German Christian "error" is the latest in this long line of errors; it is more obviously repugnant to those looking on from outside, but no different in its basic logic.[13]

The ideological pull of the "also" has been made clear. But what is the logic of the scriptural "only"? How is it that scripture itself does not become another enslaving ideology? How is its revelation different from the natural revelations that it has so often been usurped

9. Ibid., 173.
10. Ibid., 73.
11. Ibid., 176.
12. Ibid., 173.
13. Ibid., 174–75.

by? Is it just a matter of its usurping them in turn? The first important point here is that scripture itself is only a witness, or that which "attests" (in the terms of Barmen's first thesis). Thus it does not, as human, fallible word, arrogate to itself divine authority. There is no absolutization of its human form. When understood in this way, scripture cannot itself, in other words, become an ideology. But second, and more importantly, that which it attests is Jesus Christ. Again, while there is always the possibility of a "Jesuolatry,"[14] Christ as God incarnate cannot become the possession of any human community (even that community of which he is the head), and so cannot become the slogan for another form of human mastery. As Thesis 6 puts its: "We reject the false doctrine, as though the church in human arrogance could place the Word and work of the Lord in the service of any arbitrarily chosen desires, purposes, and plans." On the contrary, Jesus' lordship stands in judgment over all worldly claims to lordship.

This is the force also of the third thesis's definition of the church as "the congregation of the brethren in which Jesus Christ acts presently as the Lord in Word and sacrament through the Holy Spirit." The critical bite of this is brought out in the rejection: of "the false doctrine [that] the Church [be] permitted to abandon the form of its message and order . . . to changes in prevailing ideological and political convictions." In other words, Christ's lordship is that on which all human ideologies come to grief.[15]

In short, Barmen's appeal (to paraphrase its first thesis) to "Jesus

---

14. This is my own term rather than Barth's.
15. This is in keeping with the conclusions of de Gruchy, who offers helpful reflections on Barmen's appeal to Christ's lordship, sensitive to its potential ambiguity. Thus, on the one hand, it might be taken as a "symbol of male dominance, of hierarchical sovereignty." On the other hand (and this is how he understands it to be intended), that Jesus is Lord means, among other things, "a rejection of all ideologies that dehumanize"; "solidarity with all those he came to 'seek and save'"; and *"freedom* for the church to be the church in the world and not the captive of any ideology" (de Gruchy, *Bonhoeffer and South Africa*, 128).

Christ, attested in Scripture, as the one Word of God to be trusted and obeyed," does not undergird an alternative (scriptural) ideology, but becomes instead the grounds for a life of continual repentance. The church, as "the Church of pardoned sinners," (Thesis 3) will again and again be seduced by other lords, such that the only form its acknowledgment of Christ's lordship can take is one of repentance. The potency of this witness in the face of Hitler's totalitarianism is brought out in Thesis 2. Insofar as Jesus is "God's mighty claim upon our whole life," there is no area of life that escapes the radical critique of his lordship and thus the radical call to repentance. This precisely exposes the problem of totalitarianism, which by definition excludes all voices of criticism, whether from within or without. To appeal to Christ is to critique this attempted insulation from all critique.

By contrast with its political and theological target, Barmen models openness to criticism even in its form. By heading up each thesis with a scriptural quotation, it takes on the posture of witness to scripture, and invites its readers to scrutinise its claims in the light of the scripture to which it points. Indeed, in the preamble to all the declarations, resolutions and motions adopted by it,[16] the Synod says: "*Try the spirits whether they are of God! Prove also the words of the Confessional Synod of the German Evangelical Church to see whether they agree with Holy Scripture and with the Confessions of the Fathers.* If you find that we are speaking contrary to Scripture, then do not listen to us!"[17] Barmen's use and understanding of scripture will unfold more fully as we turn from its strengths to its more questionable aspects.

---

16. The Synod put forward not only the Theological Declaration, but also declarations concerning the legal status and practical work of the German Evangelical Church, among other subordinate resolutions and motions. For the full set of texts adopted, in English translation, see Cochrane, *The Church's Confession*, Appendix VII, 237–47.
17. Ibid., 237 (emphasis original).

READING SCRIPTURE AS A POLITICAL ACT

Barmen and the Jewish Question

Barmen's political bite has already begun to emerge. Especially in the rejections there are clear points of targeted attack, despite the general terms in which this attack is mounted. It is worth spelling these out further in order to highlight, by contrast, where Barmen does "lack concreteness," as de Gruchy puts it.[18] Thesis 1 rejects the acknowledgment of "other events and powers, figures [*Gestalten*] and truths, as God's revelation." As Cochrane points out, "*Gestalt*" connotes a person with historical influence who attracts a following, and thus the use of the term here cannot help but bring Hitler to mind.[19] Thesis 4 rejects the appointment within the church of "special leaders vested with ruling powers [*besondere, mit Herrschaftsbefugnissen ausgestattete Führer*]." The target here seems to be the replication of the *Führerprinzip* within the church, as the State government bypasses normal church election processes in order to select church authorities who will effectively operate as its puppets.[20] The critique of Hitler's embodiment of the *Führerprinzip* is not far in the background.

Finally, Thesis 5, which clarifies the relation between church and state, contains potential political polemic, depending on how it is interpreted. The church has the task, it reads, of "[calling] to mind the Kingdom of God, God's commandment and righteousness, and thereby the responsibility both of rulers and of the ruled." If taken in the spirit of Dietrich Bonhoeffer's critique of the Aryan clause[21] (written in 1933),[22] this task takes a politically active form when the state flouts its God-given responsibility. According to Bonhoeffer,

---

18. de Gruchy, *Bonhoeffer and South Africa*, 126.
19. Cochrane, *The Church's Confession*, 239 n. 2.
20. See Hans Asmussen's address in ibid., Appendix VIII, 248–63 (259–60).
21. See n. 6.
22. Dietrich Bonhoeffer, *No Rusty Swords by Dietrich Bonhoeffer*, trans. Edwin H. Robinson and John Bowden (London: Collins, 1965), 221-29.

this happens when "the state fails in its function of creating law and order," which it does, for example, when it "[deprives] any group of subjects . . . of their rights."[23] By contrast, Hans Asmussen's address (accepted by the Barmen Synod together with the Barmen Declaration as its authoritative interpretation)[24] downplays any hint of political activism, stressing a more conservative version of the Lutheran two kingdoms doctrine.[25]

This proviso notwithstanding, it is clear that the strongly scriptural-theological stance taken by Barmen did not prevent it from carrying sharp political implications. Moreover, the fact that, in natural theology, it targets a much broader theological error with deep roots, does not prevent it from singling out and confronting the present and most recent manifestation of this error in Hitlerism.

What, then, of its lack? In the context of what it does achieve, as just outlined, the most surprising omission is any mention of the Aryan clause itself. True, it talks of "ideologies" in the most general terms; but it would not have stepped outside its own theological parameters if it had given, as an example of such dehumanising ideologies, Hitler's racial nationalism and its exclusion of the Jews. Indeed, while Barth later laments his failure to make the Jewish question central in the two Barmen declarations of 1934, he did in fact condemn the racism of the Aryan clause, at least as it pertained to the church, in the first Barmen Declaration of 4 January (although not centrally, to be sure).[26] He had also singled it out for attack in his theological pamphlet of 1933, *Theologische Existenz Heute!*, referring specifically to the exclusion of Jewish Christians from the church.[27]

---

23. Ibid., 225.
24. The full text, in English translation, can be found in Cochrane, *The Church's Confession*, Appendix VIII, 248–63.
25. Ibid., 260–61.
26. For the full text of the first Barmen Declaration, see Rolf Ahlers, *The Barmen Theological Declaration*, 124–29, translated from K. D. Schmidt, *Die Bekenntnissse des Jahres 1934* (Göttingen: Vandenhoeck & Ruprecht, 1935), 22–25. The condemnation comes in 5.3b.

Why this specific condemnation dropped out of the second Barmen Declaration is an interesting question, one possible reason being its need to satisfy the Lutherans as well as Reformed church members.[28] Whatever the reason (or reasons), I want to argue that the real lack does not lie simply in the omission of a specific condemnation of the Aryan clause. This could have been included without any distortion of Barmen's intent. Rather, we can start to probe Barmen's deeper deficiency in respect of the Jewish question when we focus on the contours of its theology.

First, when Barmen appeals to holy scripture, it nowhere specifies that this comprises both Old and New Testaments. Indeed, all its scriptural citations are from the New Testament. The latter *could* be circumstantial, and the former a result of the demand for brevity. Indeed, the longer Barmen I *does* specify that scripture comprises the twofold witness of Old and New Testaments, rejecting any sidelining of the Old (2.2). Nevertheless, there is a formalism to Barmen II's appeal to Christ as attested in scripture, and its elision of specific mention of the Old Testament only exacerbates this.[29] The suspicion

---

27. Karl Barth, *Theologische Existenz Heute!*, ed. Hinrich Stoevesandt (Munich: Christian Kaiser Verlag, 1984), 59–60.
28. On the one hand, it had a Lutheran political conservatism to contend with. On the other hand, the difference might have to do with a contrast between Lutheran and Reformed understandings of the nature of confession, in which the Reformed view is more accommodating of temporally contextual critique. See Ahlers, *The Barmen Theological Declaration*, 133–35, for this contrast. While neither declaration calls itself a confession, that is what both effectively were and became, as accepted by official (and more than local) church bodies. On Barmen I as confession, see ibid., 122–23. On Barmen II as confession, see Cochrane, *The Church's Confession Under Hitler*, 182ff., and Busch, *The Barmen Theological Declaration*, 4–5.
29. Busch plays up the twofold nature of the scriptural witness as understood by Barmen (*The Barmen Theses Then and Now*, 23–25). But he can only do so by appeal to other texts. Moreover, he cites from Barth's lecture entitled "The First Commandment as Theological Axiom," given in March 1933 (found in Karl Barth, *Theologische Fragen und Antworten: Gesammelte Vorträge*, vol. 3 [Zürich: Zollikon, 1957], 127–43), in evidence of Bath's claim that the God of humanity is the God of Israel (Busch, *The Barmen Theses Then and Now*, 23). However, the context is again an attack on natural theology, and Barth's aim is to place the first commandment in a soteriological, and ultimately christological, context.

is raised that Barmen is operating with a monolithic understanding of scripture as witness to God's eternal Word spoken to us in time. In the next section, I will argue that for Barth, and by implication Barmen, Christ is the revelation of God not as one who is embedded and caught up in the vicissitudes of history, but as one who cuts through these vicissitudes from without, calling the church to a recognition of its provisionality, as it "[testifies] in the midst of a sinful world" (Thesis 2). This christological standpoint is in part what gives Barmen its force as a critique of all human ideologies. But it also makes it all too blunt an instrument.

Second, and closely related to the first point, in a text which has the Aryan clause at least implicitly in view it is amazing that there is no mention at all of Israel—God's chosen people. In this important respect Barmen's critique remains general: it does not draw on the particularity of the scriptural message as this attests to Jesus' history within and at the culmination of the history of the people of Israel. By doing so it might have found theological grounds for making Nazi antisemitism its particular target. Instead, the latter falls within its critique only as an example of human ideologies more generally, albeit a particularly pernicious one.

Barth's theology did in fact find room for a doctrine of Israel. His fullest treatment of it was in *Church Dogmatics* 2/2, published in 1942. Israel is paired with the church as the twofold form of the one community of God elected in Jesus Christ, Israel as its passing form, witnessing to the divine judgment, the church as its coming form, witnessing to the divine mercy.[30] The anti-Jewish implications of this are ambivalent from the perspective of the history of Christian supersessionism,[31] but however they may be assessed, the utility of

---

30. See Barth, "The Election of the Community," §34, *CD* 2/2:195–305.
31. Barth is a significant figure in Jeremy F. Worthen's *The Internal Foe: Judaism and Anti-Judaism in the Shaping of Christian Theology* (Newcastle: Cambridge Scholars, 2009), especially 174–88. Worthen's evaluation is that Barth challenges and overcomes the liberal anti-Judaism of his

this doctrine for Barmen's critique of Nazi antisemitism remains limited. We will see why in the following sections, but to anticipate, we can say that Barth's Israel is a theological abstraction in relation to his Jewish contemporaries suffering at the hands of the Nazis.

We have highlighted the generalism of Barmen's critique. We see a similar generalism in the critique it enables in its wake. Thus, in a memorandum submitted to Hitler on 4 June 1936 by the Provisional Board and Council of the Confessing Church,[32] Nazi antisemitism is condemned on the following two theological grounds: first, the making of "blood, race and nationality" into "qualities that guarantee eternity" is contradicted by the First Commandment; and second, hatred of the Jew is prohibited by the "Christian injunction to love one's neighbour."[33] These may be sound theological refutations as far as they go, but they do not get to the bottom of the particular evil of divinising race, and the even more particular evil of the hatred of Jews. In *Theologische Existenz Heute!* Barth's condemnation of the Aryan clause was similarly general (as well as being confined to its implementation in the church): "The fellowship of those belonging to the Church is not determined by blood, therefore, not by race, but by the Holy Spirit and Baptism."[34] True, this specifically targets racism, but it fails to single out anti*semitism* in particular, and thus to reflect on why Jews might be of special significance for the church.[35]

---

time, but re-inscribes traditional Christian anti-Judaism in a new way. Cf. R. Kendall Soulen, *The God of Israel and Christian Theology* (Minneapolis: Fortress Press, 1996), esp. 81–106, which similarly understands Barth to have offered important resources for the overcoming of supersessionism while perpetuating it in modified form.

32. See Cochrane, *The Church's Confession*, Appendix X (for the text of the Memorandum) and 207–10 (for the historical context).
33. Ibid., 275.
34. Barth, *Theological Existence To-Day!*, 52.
35. Interestingly, Barth himself, in a radio talk given on 13 December, 1949, entitled "The Jewish Problem and the Christian Answer," suggests (in keeping with the critique offered here) that an appeal to love of neighbour is not an adequate response to the problem of antisemitism because it is not "specifically Christian" (Karl Barth, *Against the Stream: Shorter Post-War Writings, 1946-52* [London: SCM Press, 1954], 193–201 [200]). While his own answer here, in keeping

Returning to Barmen in the light of these other documents, we see its generalism all the more clearly—but also its distinctiveness in targeting the general sin of *natural theology*. We thus begin to appreciate the problem of Barth's critique of Nazism primarily under the banner of that much broader error. While such critique sheds important, indeed indispensable, light on it, to classify it thus does not get to the roots of the perniciousness of Hitler's program. Instead, antisemitism is treated as just a brand of racism, and racism as a just a form of natural theology. But it is not arbitrary that Hitler hates the Jew, just as Israel is not just one nation among many for the Christian. Hitler's Aryanism, we might hazard, is a parody of Christian theology.[36] Where the latter discovers universal truth in the particular life of Jesus of Nazareth, who witnesses to the God of a particular people, Israel, Aryanism—as the purging of all Jewishness—reaches for a universalism by elimination of the particular roots of the church. It ends up, of course, promoting its own German particularism. This, even more obliquely, might be understood as itself a parody of Judaism, replacing Judaism's "non-competitive particularity" with its own crushing, totalitarian particularity. To speak of Judaism in these terms is both to go beyond Barth, and to anticipate this essay's constructive proposal vis-à-vis the Barmen Declaration.

The Theological Limits of Barmen

In sum, Barmen's real failure in respect of the Jewish question lies in its generalism. This prevents it, not from explicitly mentioning the Aryan clause—it might have done so even though it does not, but

with his doctrine of Israel developed in the context of his doctrine of election in *CD* 2/2, is "specifically Christian," it is ambivalent in the same way as the latter with respect to the problem of supersessionism.
36. This invites the qualification "*good* Christian theology," since Hitler's Aryanism arguably builds on and is in continuity with some earlier forms of Christian supersessionism.

from mounting a theological critique of the specific sin of hating Jews (whether Christian or non-Christian). How might we account for this failure in terms of Barmen's wider theological-historical context?

I will attempt to answer this question from a standpoint internal to Barth's theology. In other words, I will assume that he is right in his diagnosis of the problem of natural theology—as far as this goes. To recall, his claim is that the "and" of natural theology inexorably pushes towards an "only," ultimately displacing and excluding the revelation of Jesus Christ, as attested in scripture, altogether. We analysed the logic of this above, but we can uncover another layer of it in this new connection. The problem with the "and" in any of its various forms is that it is foundationalist in its pretensions: theological conclusions are built on it (whether it be reason, history, science, human experience etc.) as a sure foundation that cannot be brought into question from other standpoints. Indeed, it has divine authority. But for this reason it contains within itself an implicit universalism: its findings are valid for everyone irrespective of time and place.[37]

To counter this foundationalist universalism, Barth must reach for a non-foundationalist particularism.[38] He finds this, as we have seen, in Jesus Christ, as attested in scripture. Jesus fits the bill: he is thoroughly particular; and while he is a "sure foundation," he is not a foundation like others. He is not a foundation we build for ourselves from within our own human resources. He is not a premise we can comprehend and move on from, drawing our own incontrovertible conclusions. He is not at our disposal in this way, but again and again

---

37. Such universal validity has variously been claimed for unchanging reason, universally shared human experience, the empirical findings of the natural sciences or of historical research, and so on.
38. Which is, at the same time, a non-foundationalist universalism. Indeed, the issue is not so much particularism *or* universalism, as it is the relationship between them. The problem with the Nazi ideology (as diagnosed above) is its opposing of universalism and particularism, seeking the former by way of its exclusion of Jewish particularity. A non-foundationalism will, by contrast, overcome the binary opposition.

challenges the conclusions we draw. He is a living foundation who will always invite us to think and act anew.

However, this answer, in which the potency of Barmen lies, harbours within it the danger of theological abstraction—wherein lies its weakness. Barth does not deny for a moment the historically fragmented, untidy and vulnerable nature of the scriptural witness, nor the historically questionable and shadowy nature of the life of Jesus itself. But the historical character of scripture and of the life of Jesus is utterly trumped by the dynamic of divine revelation into which God catches them up. The revelatory power of their witness is not contained in the historical particulars themselves. It is as if God lifts them out of their human vulnerability as he speaks in and through them. In short, while Barth arrives at a particularism, it is an exclusively theological particularism in which the particulars of history have negligible place.[39] The result is an abstractive theological particularism; and this is what underlies the *generalism* of Barmen's theological critique.

In his theological-historical context, I venture, Barth could not have argued otherwise. He is forced down the road of theological abstraction, I suggest, because the road of historical particularism is squarely closed off to him. And this is because history has been harnessed to a historical foundationalism from which it cannot be swiftly extricated in order to serve Barth's alternative (non-foundationalist) theological ends. This is a large claim which I can

---

39. This is certainly true of Barth's earlier theology (up to and including the first volume of the *CD*). See Rowan Williams, "Barth on the Triune God," in *Karl Barth: Studies of His Theological Method*, ed. S. W. Sykes (Oxford: Clarendon Press, 1979), 147–93 (152–58), for a classic and sophisticated critique along these lines. But it is arguably still the case in his later theology. For a paradigmatic example of the complete overshadowing of historical contingency by the dynamics of divine redemption, see *CD*, 4/1:283–357. Lessing's "ugly ditch" pales in comparison with the ugly ditch that God overcomes in Christ between God and sinners; indeed, we preoccupy ourselves with the former in order to flee from our encounter with God as judge (ibid., 287–94).

only put forward as a hypothesis in this essay. Its testing would require a thorough interrogation of Barth's scholarly context in its light. I will limit myself to some observations regarding one particularly powerful force in this context: the historical theology of Adolf von Harnack.

I will look, in particular, at the Harnack-Barth correspondence published in 1923 in *Christliche Welt*.[40] This is a telling snapshot of the dividing lines in respect of which Barth's theology is etched. The first three of Harnack's "Fifteen Questions to the Despisers of Scientific Theology" are focused on the necessity of "historical knowledge and critical reflection [*geschichtliches Wissen und kritisches Nachdenken*]"[41] for determination of the content of the gospel, correct understanding of the meaning of the religion of the Bible, and as the basis for preaching. The last two questions make explicit the foundationalist pretensions only implicit in the first three. So well do they capture what is at stake that I will cite them here almost in full:

> (14) If the person of Jesus Christ stands at the centre of the gospel, how else can the basis for reliable and communal knowledge [*die Grundlage für eine zuverlässige und gemeinschaftliche Erkenntnis*] of this person be gained but through critical-historical study [*kritisch-geschichtliches Studium*] so that an imagined Christ is not put in place of the real one? What else besides scientific theology [*wissenschaftliche Theologie*] is able to undertake this study?
>
> (15) ... Is there any other theology than that which has strong ties, and is in blood-relationship, with science [*Wissenschaft*] in general? ...[42]

The revelatory character of Jesus Christ is subordinated here to the

---

40. See H. Martin Rumscheidt, *Revelation and Theology: An Analysis of the Barth-Harnack Correspondence of 1923* (Cambridge: Cambridge University Press, 1972), 29–53, for the full text in English translation. For the German, see Karl Barth, *Theologische Fragen und Antworten: Gesammelte Vorträge*, vol. 3 (Zürich: Zollikon, 1957), 7–31.
41. Rumscheidt, *Revelation and Theology*, 29; Barth, *Theologische Fragen und Antworten*, 7.
42. Rumscheidt, ibid., 31; Barth, ibid., 9.

results of historical research, which are the "sure foundation" of real knowledge of him. Thus theology as a discipline is rooted in and built upon the more general discipline of history. To free theology of these ties, Barth must look for its scientific character elsewhere. And to avoid yet another foundationalism he must find it in the subject matter of theology itself. His answer to Harnack's very first question tells us that

> the communication of the content of the gospel . . . can be accomplished only through an act of this 'content' itself. . . . The 'scientific character' [*Wissenschaftlichkeit*] of theology would then be its adherence to the recollection that its object *once was subject* and must become that again and again."[43]

And his answer to the last question appeals to the "*Sachlichkeit* [concrete objectivity]" to which theology is accountable.[44]

The only place left for critical-historical study in this context is a self-eliminating one:

> Critical-historical study [*kritisch-geschichtliches Studium*] signifies the deserved and necessary end of *those* 'foundations' [*Grundlagen*] of this knowledge [of Jesus Christ] which are no foundations at all since they have not been laid by God himself. Whoever does not yet know . . . that we *no* longer know Christ according to the flesh, should let the critical study of the Bible [*kritischen Bibelwissenschaft*] tell him so."[45]

Harnack's foundationalism goes together with a sought-after universalism (as is implied in the title of his acclaimed lectures published in 1900 as *Das Wesen des Christentums*[46]). He seeks a message that is free from historically circumstantial baggage and can

---

43. Rumscheidt, ibid., 31–32; Barth, ibid., 10.
44. Rumscheidt, ibid., 35; Barth, ibid., 13.
45. Ibid.
46. Adolf von Harnack, *Das Wesen des Christentums*, 3rd ed. (Tübingen: Mohr Siebeck, 2012). For the English translation, see Adolf von Harnack, *What is Christianity?*, trans. Thomas Bailey Saunders, 5th ed. (London: Ernest Benn, 1958).

therefore speak across the centuries. He calls this "the simple gospel" [*das schlichte Evangelium*]⁴⁷ and equates it with "the love of God and the love of one's fellow."⁴⁸ However, it becomes clear that for Harnack some cultural moments come closer to this message than others. In question 8, he asks Barth: "If Goethe's pantheism, Kant's conception of God or related points of view are merely opposites of real statements about God, how can it be avoided that these statements are given over to barbarism?"⁴⁹ Lurking only just below the surface of Harnack's questions is an insidious bid for cultural supremacy, dressed up as an innocent universalism.

Harnack's covert bid for cultural supremacy comes to forceful expression in his historically argued case for the uniqueness of Christianity, and specifically for the historical superiority of Christianity over Judaism.⁵⁰ The "husk" of which the "kernel" of Jesus' message must be divested, according to Harnack, is precisely Judaism.⁵¹ The universalism of Christianity is contrasted with the particularity of Judaism: it is *Jewish* particularity of which Christianity must free itself if it is to come to consummate expression.⁵²

If it is this same logic that we see carried to extreme conclusions in National Socialism, then "universalism" has in the latter become an undisguised bid for racial supremacy, with the ultimate goal of total domination and eventual extinction of other races. Jewish particularity remains the threat, we can speculate—again anticipating our movement beyond Barth—because it does not play by the same rules. Israel is divinely chosen and holy, but not because of any

---

47. Rumscheidt, *Barth-Harnack Correspondence*, 37–38; Barth, *Gesammelte Vorträge*, 15–16.
48. Rumscheidt, ibid., 30; Barth, ibid., 8.
49. Ibid.
50. See Jeremy F. Worthen, *The Internal Foe*, 159–67, on Harnack's place in the wider historical trajectory of the argument for the historical superiority of Christianity, and for a concise account of the anti-Jewish contours of Harnack's theology.
51. Harnack, *What is Christianity?*, esp. 132.
52. See Worthen's judicious summary in *The Internal Foe*, 163.

national supremacy, and not with the consequence that it seeks to dominate or wipe out other nations. The Aryan race, as God's new chosen people, is—in its despotic particularity—a parody of the people of Israel.

It is, I hope, becoming clear why it is that in order to avoid being sucked down this trajectory, Barth had to resort to what we have called a "theological abstraction." Not only was historical research entrenched in a foundationalist ideology, but the results of this research (at least among some of his Christian colleagues) made Christian uniqueness dependent upon its contrast with Judaism, and therefore upon an implicit anti-Judaism.[53] In short, Barth had to free theology from its historical moorings if he was going to free it from its ideological capture.[54] This, in practice, meant relativising the results of historical research in their relevance for theology. The uniqueness of Christianity, or better, of Christ, is not a historical one.

However—and it is in this sense that Barmen's potency is also its weakness—this abstraction from history makes Barth's theology incapable of a specific confrontation with the Jewish question. Whatever else it requires, the latter demands a careful treatment of the relations *and distinctions* between biblical Israel, first-century Judaism(s), and contemporary Judaism—and the relation of each to the Christian church. And these are historically charged matters. Barth's theology arguably only has room for the biblical Israel, considered theologically as the passing form of God's one elect community, and without further reflection on its relation with contemporary Judaism, it remains a theological abstraction.

---

53. While Barth's theology perpetuates an anti-Judaism of its own, it successfully leaves behind an account of the historical superiority of Christianity over Judaism, as two species of religion.
54. The force of this "had to" is practical rather than logical. Given Barth's immediate intellectual context, it would have been very difficult for him to put historical research to a different, non-foundationalist, use. And if he had done, there is no saying that he would have been correctly heard.

Furthermore, without reflection on its continuation in first-century Judaisms, it remains unclear how biblical Israel relates to the church.

Beyond Barmen

Since Barth (and arguably in part because of him) it has become possible to do theology that is once more informed by historical research, but that is not built upon its foundations in the manner of Harnack's historical foundationalism. There is a case to be made that Barth's freeing of theology from a foundationalist history contributed to freeing it for another, rather different relationship with history. That story is, of course, bound up in the much broader one of the emergence of "postmodern" modes of thinking more generally, involving the convergence of several shifts in intellectual history—within the natural sciences and history, among other disciplines, as well as within theology. But whatever the historical causality, the following can be conceded. In broadly postliberal circles, which are also post-Barthian, there is the recognition that history is told from particular perspectives, and thus the embrace of a variety of histories. Once a dominant historical narrative has been displaced in favour of a plethora of historical voices, theology is free to listen to these voices in an ad hoc way without having to buy into any one historical vision hook, line, and sinker. Instead, self-consciously situated within the context of a particular theological tradition, the theologian can allow her traditional understandings to be sharpened, challenged and revised by historical findings, lending history an internal critical voice.

I want to suggest, in this final section, that "internal critical voice" is one helpful way of conceiving of the role of recent historical trends in Biblical Studies and related scholarship: specifically, the New Perspective on Paul, and related literature involved in the re-envisioning of first-century Judaism(s), and the renarration of the origins of Christianity and its eventual emergence over against Judaism—as late as the fourth century.[55] While not all its contributors are Protestants (or even Christians), it is possible to argue that the New Perspective has a broadly Protestant frame of reference: its main target is the Lutheran reading of Paul and its perpetuation in later thinkers such as Rudolf Bultmann and Ernst Käsemann.[56]

Even more specifically in its sights is the anti-Judaism of the Lutheran Paul.[57] And this is where the New Perspective becomes especially relevant for this essay. Barmen was written at a time when it was assumed that already in the writings of Paul Christianity stood over against Judaism as one monolithic religion over against another. Christ was rejected by his own people, the Jews. Those who believed in him formed a new people, the Christian church. The Jews, consigned to the past, were supplanted by the Christians; Israel was superseded by the church; Judaism was replaced by Christianity. It is this story which, on the one hand, underpins the argument for the historical superiority of Christianity (of which Harnack is a

---

55. Two of the key landmarks in the emergence of the so-called New Perspective on Paul are Krister Stendahl's "The Apostle Paul and the Introspective Conscience of the West," *Harvard Theological Review* 56 (1963): 199–215; and E. P. Sanders's *Paul and Palestinian Judaism: A Comparison of Patterns of Religion* (London: SCM Press, 1977). For a helpful summary of shifts in scholarship regarding Christian origins and Jewish-Christian differentiation, see Adam H. Becker and Annette Yoshiko Reed, "Introduction: Traditional Models and New Directions," in *The Ways That Never Parted: Jews and Christians in Late Antiquity and the Early Middle Ages*, ed. Adam H. Becker and Annette Yoshiko Reed (Tübingen: Mohr Siebeck, 2003), 1–33.

56. This is how it is framed, for example, in Stephen Westerholm, *Perspectives Old and New on Paul: The "Lutheran" Paul and His Critics* (Grand Rapids: Eerdmans, 2004).

57. Although such anti-Judaism is arguably reproduced in a different key by some of the New Perspective writers. If Luther's brand of anti-Judaism is the accusation of legalism, James Dunn's and N. T. Wright's brand is the accusation of ethnocentrism or nationalism. See, for example, J. D. G. Dunn, *Romans 9–16*, WBC 38b (Dallas: Word, 1988), 593; and N. T. Wright, *What Saint Paul Really Said: Was Paul of Tarsus the Real Founder of Christianity?* (Grand Rapids: Eerdmans, 1997), 84. This is picked up and addressed by adherents of the so-called "radical New Perspective." See, for example, Lloyd Gaston, *Paul and the Torah* (Vancouver: University of British Columbia Press, 1987), Stanley Stowers, *A Rereading of Romans: Justice, Jews and Gentiles* (New Haven: Yale University Press, 1994), and John Gager, *Reinventing Paul* (Oxford: Oxford University Press, 2000) (which argue variously for a two-track salvation, one for Jews and one for Gentiles).

supreme representative). And it is this story which, on the other hand, severely limits the possible Christian arguments against antisemitism, because it undergirds a biblically-based, theological anti-Judaism.

Developments in and beyond the New Perspective have issued in a fundamental challenge to this old model, putting a spoke in the wheels of the "historical superiority" argument, and undermining an ingrained, biblically-argued, theological anti-Judaism. The new historical perspectives are internally diverse, but we need only follow their broadest trajectory in order to articulate this challenge. First, rather than a monolithic Judaism, it is truer to talk about a variety of Jewish sects or "Judaisms"[58] in the first century. Second, the emerging group of Christ-followers was itself "a Judaism" in this sense. Third, Judaism and Christianity in something resembling the form in which we now know them did not exist until possibly as late as the fourth century, but gradually emerged from a jumble of competing voices as they gained mutual and antagonistic definition.[59] This third insight deftly does away with the "historical superiority" argument: Christianity cannot be said to supersede Judaism as the historically new over against the historically past; rather they emerge contemporaneously, sharing the same inheritance but interpreting it differently in response to the tumultuous events of the early centuries.

The theological anti-Judaism targeted by the early New Perspective writers, with reference to the writings of Paul, is that

---

58. To talk about "Judaisms" is knowingly anachronistic, but it has heuristic value in suggesting both variety and family resemblance, by contrast with a spurious, monolithic religion over against which Christianity sets itself.

59. For a portrait of competing Jewish schools in the first century, and the place of Christ-followers among them, see, for example, Luke Timothy Johnson, "The New Testament's Anti-Jewish Slander and the Conventions of Ancient Polemic," *JBL* 108 (1989): 419–41. For a fourth-century dating of decisive Jewish-Christian differentiation, see, for example, Daniel Boyarin, *Border Lines: The Partition of Judaeo-Christianity* (Philadelphia: University of Pennsylvania Press, 2004). In their introduction to the edited volume, *The Ways that Never Parted*, Becker and Reed suggest the need to challenge the model of a "single and simple 'Parting of the Ways,'" in favor of a "variety of different 'Partings' at different times and in different places" (22).

which opposes Christian grace to Jewish legalism. However, this is but one specific form of an opposition which assumes a monolithic Judaism over against which Christianity can set itself.[60] In the light of the "new story," the anachronism of any such opposition is evident. To reiterate, there is in Paul's time no one thing called Judaism, nor is there any "Christian" standpoint outside it: "Christianity" is itself "a Judaism" (to embrace a double anachronism). Specifically, Paul is arguing as a Jew with his fellow Jews, taking his place amongst a variety of competing Jewish sects. He does not speak from outside his Jewish identity as something he now rejects; he finds it, rather, to be fulfilled and transformed in an unexpected way in Christ. If many of his fellow Jews reject Christ, this is not because there is something intrinsic to "Judaism" which sets it in opposition to Christ. In short, there is no theological anti-Judaism to be found within Paul, whether in terms of Jewish legalism or something else. It is only some way down stream that Christian anti-Judaism becomes a possibility—in the course of later polemical developments in which a largely Gentile church seeks to distinguish itself from "Judaism," and non-Jesus-Jews from "Christianity." These later struggles for definition must not be retrojected into Paul.

The undermining of the "historical superiority" argument and of a biblically-based (and specifically Pauline), theological anti-Judaism: this is the negative legacy of the new historical perspectives. But they also have a positive legacy in the particular arguments they make way for against anti-Judaism and antisemitism. We have argued that the problem of Barmen in the face of the Jewish question was its theological generalism. We have shown how this was unavoidable in the context of a historical foundationalism. What the new perspectives contribute to is the possibility of a historically sensitive,

---

60. The charge of ethnocentrism falls into the same trap. Cf. n. 57.

theological response to National Socialism, which specifically targets its antisemitism.

We have identified the eradication of Jewish particularity in the name of a Christian (totalitarian) universalism as the logic of the anti-Judaism that is taken to extremes by National Socialism. It is not enough in the face of this to say that Christianity has its roots in Judaism, or that Jesus and Paul were Jews. Such arguments were available to those at Barmen. But they would not have overturned an insidious Christian totalitarian logic. In a further, critical step, the new perspectives teach us that "Christianity" was itself "a Judaism." To follow Christ is not by definition to leave behind one's Jewish identity. In other words, whatever else a genuine Christian universalism involves it does not involve the eradication of Jewish particularity.

To pursue constructively what it might involve, we need to address a question that has not yet been raised in this general account of the new historical perspectives—albeit only briefly and suggestively as this essay draws to its conclusion. That question is as follows: What are the implications for Israel of the inclusion of Gentiles in the people of God? If Israel is simply redefined as the church of Jews and Gentiles, then a replacement theology is effectively reintroduced, and the way is opened for Jewish identity to become irrelevant within the church. An alternative answer can tentatively be developed by way of the analogy of the olive tree in Romans 11. Gentiles are grafted in to the olive tree of Israel. But they remain unnatural branches, having been grafted in contrary to nature (11:24). If some of the natural branches (Jews) are cut off, they are the exception, since they are precisely natural branches with a natural claim to belonging (11:20). In other words, Israel retains its fundamentally Jewish identity. The coming of Christ makes it possible for Gentiles to be included without becoming Jews, but only as secondary and derivative. This is quite the opposite of a picture in which Jewish Christians are anomalous members of a largely Gentile church. Rather, it is Gentiles who are anomalously included in the people of Israel. It follows that Gentile identity is forever secondary to Jewish identity, defined only in relation to it. A Christian universalism informed by Romans 11, far from eradicating Jewish particularity, defines all else in relation to it.

The secondariness of Gentiles is easy to forget in today's largely Gentile church, and even more so in a context in which the identity-marker "Gentile" has almost entirely fallen out of use, and in which "Christian" has superseded any theologically meaningful distinction between "Jewish Christian" and "Gentile Christian." In such historical circumstances, unforeseen by Paul, the Gentile members of the church are arguably dependent on those Jews who are not in the church—whose Jewish particularity is therefore especially evident—for a reminder of their secondary and derivative existence. If this is the case, then it is arguable in turn that "Judaism," as a religion defined over against Christianity (as it has come to be), is the only antidote to a totalitarian Christian universalism. Without tangible Jewish particularity, the church will forget its Jewish-Gentile makeup, and its resultant universalism without difference will tend towards the cultural imperialism we have diagnosed above. It will become, in other words, a particularism in disguise, seeking to wipe out particularities which do not conform. Conceptually speaking, therefore, a genuine Christian universalism goes hand in hand with a non-competitive Jewish particularism. In a time in which Judaism and Christianity are two distinct religions, it follows that Christianity is in need of Judaism for its own integrity (whether this is true the other way round is an interesting question). A Christian anti-Judaism is superseded by a Christianity "distinct from but inseparably in relation"[61] to Judaism.

Conclusion

This is a portrait of the relationship between Christianity and Judaism that was simply not available to those involved in producing the Barmen Declaration. The question is whether such a portrait is a faithful development of Barmen's intent in new historical circumstances. I would argue that it is so insofar as it plays in a new key Barmen's "universal particularism." First, it recapitulates and intensifies Barmen's critique of Nazi totalitarianism by pinpointing its roots in the eradication of Jewish particularity. Second, it recapitulates and intensifies Barth's theological particularism by way of a historical particularism which recognizes that the particularity of Jesus Christ is theologically and historically inseparable from the particularity of the Jewish people, both in the first century and today. This does not involve any retreat into natural theology, since the historical insights serve an internally critical rather than foundational role, operating as they do within a theological framework informed by Barmen and the theology of Barth. More speculatively, it is possible that the portrait we have sketched in which Christianity finds its complement in Judaism is in some form a reworking of Barth's complementary pairing of the church and Israel. But that is for the exploration of another essay.

---

61. For this terminology I am indebted to Nicholas Adams, *The Eclipse of Grace: Divine and Human Action in Hegel* (Malden, MA: Wiley-Blackwell, 2013), see e.g. 22-23.

13

The End of Sacrifice

John Howard Yoder's Critique of Capital Punishment

John C. Nugent

John Howard Yoder repeatedly engaged the topic of capital punishment throughout his prolific literary career.[1] Central to Yoder's position is the idea that both biblically and culturally, from ancient society until today, capital punishment is an inherently cultic or ritual practice.[2] For Yoder, Christ's death fulfills the ultimate

---

1. Yoder began publishing on capital punishment in 1959 and continued exploring and articulating his position until his death in 1997. Over the course of these four decades, we see no significant change in his position, although he deepens and broadens it at points. His first published piece was "The Death Penalty," in *The Mennonite* (Nov 1959): 724–25. His last piece was an unpublished addendum in 1997 to a work he published online through Shalom Desktop publications, titled "You Have It Coming: Good Punishment. The Legitimate Social Function of Punitive Behavior" (1995). These essays, as well as Yoder's other works on this topic, have been assembled, edited, and published as *The End of Sacrifice: The Capital Punishment Writings of John Howard Yoder*, ed. John C. Nugent (Scottdale, PA: Herald Press, 2011).
2. This is why Yoder's final work on capital punishment, an engagement of the cultural role

purpose that the death penalty first served: to atone for the "cosmic, ritual, religious evil" of taking the life of a fellow human created in God's image (Gen. 9:6).³ Since Christ's sacrifice atones for such evils it also forbids and makes obsolete all future bloodletting that seeks to atone for sin (Heb. 9:26-28).⁴ Yoder's theological challenge to the morality of the death penalty brings a level of hermeneutical sophistication and interdisciplinary awareness to the topic in a way that provokes fresh insight and casts due suspicion on long held positions.⁵ Indeed, it is ultimately Yoder's theological reading of

---

of punishment (*The End of Sacrifice*, ch. 5), is not merely tangential to Yoder's project. By unmasking the sacrificial component of the public practice of capital punishment, Yoder is calling Christians to own up to their core theological commitment to the finality of Christ's sacrifice to atone for sin.

3. Ibid., 101.

4. During a dissertation defense at which I was present, Richard Mouw once quipped that Yoder had no theology of atonement, by which he meant no notion that the cross did anything to deal with human sin. Despite knowing Yoder quite well, having written and even traveled with him, Mouw seems to have assumed this because so many of Yoder's writings focus on showing that Christ's death means more than simply atonement for sin. It also means, for example, an end to enmity between Jews and Gentiles and victory over the powers and principalities. This is typical of Yoder's work. He paid more attention to neglected matters in theology than to those that have received adequate treatment. The publication of *The End of Sacrifice* should put to rest the notion that Yoder had no theology of atonement.

5. Unfortunately, few readers have taken note of Yoder's important work on this topic. Stanley Hauerwas offers the most sustained engagement in "Punishing Christians: A Pacifist Approach to the Issue of Capital Punishment," in *Religion and the Death Penalty: A Call for Reckoning*, eds. Erik C. Owen, John D. Carlson, and Eric P. Elshtain (Grand Rapids: Eerdmans, 2004), 57–72. Recent works that also recognize his work in this area include Darrin W. Snyder Belousek, "Capital Punishment, Covenant Justice and the Cross of Christ: The Death Penalty in the Life and Death of Jesus," in *Mennonite Quarterly Review* 83, no. 3 (2009): 375–402; Millard Lind, *The Sword of Sheer Silence and the Killing State: The Death Penalty and the Bible* (Telford, PA: Cascadia, 2004), 141–44; Glen Stassen, "Biblical Teaching on Capital Punishment," *Review and Expositor* 93 (1996): 485–96; and Michael L. Westmoreland-White and Glen H. Stassen, "Biblical Perspectives on the Death Penalty," in *Religion and the Death Penalty*, 123–38. Most works, however, ignore Yoder altogether. See, for example, most of the articles in *Capital Punishment: A Reader*, ed. Glen H. Stassen (Cleveland, OH: Pilgrim Press, 1998); *Religion and the Death Penalty*; and two recent books whose basic arguments have not taken seriously the position Yoder articulates: Ron Gleason, *The Death Penalty on Trial: Taking a Life for a Life Taken* (Ventura, CA: Nordskok Publishing, 2008); and Oliver O'Donovan, *The Ways of Judgment* (Grand Rapids: Eerdmans, 2005). Gleason's exegetical leap from Gen. 9:6 to Rom. 13 is a classic example of the sort of undisciplined hermeneutical sleight of hand that Yoder exposes throughout his works on capital punishment. Though far more disciplined, O'Donovan's approach continues to operate with a division of spheres mentality that, while

scripture that enables him to show why liberal approaches to abolishing capital punishment have failed and why adherence to specific Christian convictions remains the most viable and relevant alternative.[6] This essay demonstrates how Yoder's disciplined hermeneutical method, careful biblical exegesis, and penetrating cultural analysis enabled him to mount a substantial theological critique of the practice of capital punishment.

A Canonical-Directional Hermeneutic

No biblically grounded case for or against capital punishment stands without a specific hermeneutic that accounts for how the Old and New Testaments relate to one another. Capital punishment advocates often accentuate the continuity between the testaments in an effort to make their case with Old Testament passages that seem to require it. Opponents of capital punishment routinely accentuate discontinuity between the testaments in order to brush aside unsupportive passages as irrelevant. Still, others bracket one part of the Old Testament witness (for example, the Mosaic covenant) and base their case *for* capital punishment on another part (for example, the covenant with Noah). They deem the latter as timelessly relevant and the former as pertinent only to Old Covenant Israelites. Yoder rejects all three of these strategies and replaces them with what I am calling a "canonical-directional" approach.[7]

Though Yoder never claimed to be a Bible scholar, he draws

---

claiming with Yoder that Christ's reign is relevant to all spheres of life, nonetheless enjoins Christian politicians to do the opposite of what Christ taught as a sort of reverse prophetic statement.

6. Yoder does not presume to be original in asserting the implications of Christ's death for the death penalty; he credits Karl Barth for expressing similar sentiments. Ibid., 103, 182.

7. I have adapted much of the material in this section from my book, *The Politics of Yahweh: John Howard Yoder, the Old Testament, and the People of God*, Theopolitical Visions Series (Eugene, OR: Cascade Books, 2011), 10–13. I provide case studies that illustrate Yoder's use of this canonical-directional hermeneutic in the appendix, 211–15.

valuable insights from Old and New Testament scholars to demonstrate how passages in one Bible book inform another and still another until a discernible trajectory emerges from Genesis to Revelation. He sees this trajectory as a crooked developmental line but an organic line, nonetheless.[8] Yoder's particular way of reading passages together as a coherent overarching narrative and then applying them to questions of theology and social ethics sets his work apart and makes unique contributions to political readings of scripture.

Yoder's approach to scripture incorporates the insights of two distinct hermeneutical methods. The designation "canonical-directional" captures the particular way he melds them together. The term "canonical" emphasizes Yoder's biblical realism with its preference for working with the final form of the canonical text. The term "directional" emphasizes Yoder's conviction that the Old Testament should be interpreted as pointing to and finding its fulfillment in Christ. Though I separate these methods for the purpose of analysis, Yoder blends them together seamlessly in his exegesis.

Yoder associates his canonical approach to scripture with the biblical realism movement of his time.[9] Biblical realists, according to Yoder, are those who approach scripture with the best available tools for interpreting an author's original intent and who trust that all texts in their canonical form actually hang together and present a coherent message.[10] Though biblical realists make no effort to insulate scripture from careful scrutiny, they also see no need to

---

8. John Howard Yoder, "To Your Tents, O Israel: The Legacy of Israel's Experience with Holy War," *Studies in Religion* 18, no. 3 (1989): 345-62 (354).
9. Yoder did not pioneer this approach, but acknowledges his dependence on Otto Piper, Paul Minear, Oscar Cullmann, and Karl Barth in *Christian Attitudes to War, Peace, and Revolution*, eds. Theodore J. Koontz and Andy Alexis-Baker (Grand Rapids: Brazos Press, 2009), 310.
10. Yoder "The Message of the Bible," in *To Hear the Word*, 2nd ed. (Eugene, OR: Cascade Books, 2010), 155-77.

perpetuate the common text critical bias against the historicity of biblical events and the suspicion that the original authors and editors routinely committed pious fraud. They thus pay scant attention to theories of authorship and underlying sources, and focus instead on the final form of the text as if it were bequeathed directly to them by the original authors.

Biblical realism should not be confused with naïve biblicism. Yoder insists that it is a post-critical phenomenon: "What is at stake is not whether the Bible can be interpreted at a great distance without linguistic and hermeneutic tools, but whether, at those points where it is clear in what it says, we are going to let that testimony count rather than subjecting it to the superior authority of our own contemporary hermeneutic framework."[11] This means carefully scrutinizing both the biblical text and our modern biases. Following Paul Minear, Yoder argues that biblical realism aspires to what has always been the scholar's highest goal: to allow the object under investigation to dictate the appropriate method of interpretation.[12]

Yoder was equally committed to reading scripture "directionally." This means reading scripture forward—from Old Testament to New and not vice versa—as well as reading Old Testament persons and events in light of the New Testament. In Yoder's words, "The Bible is a story of promise and fulfillment which must be read directionally. The New Testament, by affirming the Hebrew Scriptures, which Christians have come to call the Old Testament, also interprets them. Abraham and Moses are read through Jesus and Paul."[13] How can Yoder read Abraham and Moses in light of Jesus and Paul without compromising his commitment to reading scripture directionally? He does so by affirming scripture's unique promise-fulfillment

---

11. Yoder, "The Use of the Bible in Theology," in *To Hear the Word*, 77-93 (89).
12. Yoder, "Message of the Bible," 176.
13. Yoder, *Priestly Kingdom: Social Ethics as Gospel* (Notre Dame, IN: University of Notre Dame Press, 1984), 9.

structure. Since Jesus is the fulfillment of a soteriological trajectory that begins in the Old Testament, he is the critical key for discriminating between positive developments within the Bible story that constituted genuine progress for God's people and negative ones that needed to be overcome.

This ability to interpret earlier events in the canon in light of later developments is critical to Yoder's ability to narrate all of salvation history in a cohesive way.[14] Since the New Testament freely appropriates the Old Testament as its antecedent tradition with no system-induced anxiety about violating dispensational boundaries, Yoder saw continuities between the testaments where others presumed discontinuity. What God was doing in the world and through the chosen people in Genesis is simply an earlier stage in a canonical movement that culminates in the Gospels and finds its consummation in the return of Christ and restoration of the cosmos. In granting the benefit of the doubt to the conceptual world of the texts as they stand, Yoder found himself submitting to scripture's judgment rather than presiding over it.[15]

It is also important for our purposes to recognize Yoder's conviction that the New Testament's witness to Jesus is the most complete revelation of God—the God of creation, flood, and Old Covenant. This means that scripture is not a compendium of competing ethical codes, but the gradual formation of a people that

---

14. Though Yoder traces his directional approach to early Anabaptism, he also identifies it as a practice that the wider believers' church heritage shares with the Reformed tradition. See Yoder, *Anabaptism and Reformation in Switzerland: An Historical and Theological Analysis of the Dialogues between Anabaptists and Reformers* (Kitchener, Ontario: Pandora Press, 2004), 169–72; "The Hermeneutics of the Anabaptists," in *To Hear the Word*, 217–37; *Preface to Theology: Christology and Theological Method* (Grand Rapids: Brazos, 2002), (373); and Yoder and Mouw, "Evangelical Ethics and the Anabaptist-Reformed Dialogue," *Journal of Religious Ethics* 17, no. 2 (Fall 1989): 121-37 (132-33).
15. It is becoming increasingly common for scholars to judge scripture and find several parts lacking. For example, Eric A. Seibert, *The Violence of Scripture: Overcoming the Old Testament's Troubling Legacy* (Minneapolis: Fortress Press, 2012).

faithfully embodies the ethics of its creator as revealed in Jesus. We must read New Testament passages concerning capital punishment as if they were completing the movement of the Old, and Old Testament passages as if they were paving the way for the New.[16]

A Biblical Case Against Capital Punishment

Yoder's biblical critique of capital punishment begins with what is perhaps the most critical text in the debate, God's postdiluvian pronouncement to Noah in Gen. 9:5-6: "For your own lifeblood I will surely require a reckoning: from every animal I will require it and from human beings, each one for the blood of another, I will require a reckoning for human life. Whoever sheds the blood of a human, by a human shall that person's blood be shed; for in his own image God made humankind." For capital punishment advocates, this command is simple and decisive: even before the Mosaic covenant, God legislated that all creatures of the earth must be held accountable for taking life. Even if God did not reinforce this edict by mandating capital punishment all throughout Torah, there is sufficient evidence in this passage alone to convict.

This line of thinking is too simplistic for Yoder because it does not sufficiently engage the full context of Genesis 9. The first necessary layer of context is Genesis 4–6, which begins with God's decision to protect the life of the first human to shed another human's blood. In

---

16. Though this hermeneutical approach may prove too forward-looking for a pure biblical exegete and too backward-looking for a theological interpreter of scripture, its sincere attempt to find common ground and listen respectfully to each camp warrants a like hearing. See Stephen E. Fowl, *Engaging Scripture: A Model for Theological Interpretation* (Malden, MA: Blackwell Publishers, 1998); Daniel J. Treier, *Introducing Theological Interpretation of Scripture: Recovering a Christian Practice* (Grand Rapids: Baker Academic, 2008); and Todd J. Billings, *The Word of God for the People of God: An Entry to the Theological Interpretation of Scripture* (Grand Rapids: Eerdmans, 2010). Yoder likely fits more comfortably among theological interpreters of scripture, but leans much more heavily upon biblical studies and expresses more suspicion toward allegorical approaches that ignore scripture's directional movement. See Yoder, *Priestly Kingdom*, 9.

Gen. 4:8-15, after killing Abel, Cain does not fear divine retribution. Rather, he fears the vengeful reflex of wider society to kill him. God agrees with Cain's assessment and promises to avenge Cain sevenfold should others take his life into their own hands. We therefore see in this passage that, independent of divine influence, humans gravitated toward a primitive form of death penalty that God immediately condemned.

Yet, divine condemnation was not enough to prevent further bloodshed. Shortly thereafter, in Genesis 4, Cain's near-descendent Lamech kills a man for harming him and usurps God's role by escalating the threat of vengeance, saying, "If Cain is avenged sevenfold, truly Lamech seventy-sevenfold." Violence escalated to such an extent that by Noah's day, "every inclination" of the human heart was "always evil continually" (Gen. 6:5). In fact, the earth was so filled with violence that God deemed it necessary to purge it completely with a flood (Gen. 6:11, 13).

The second layer of context is the immediate text within which God's postdiluvian pronouncement to Noah is situated. Gen. 9:1-7 reads:

> God blessed Noah and his sons, and said to them, "Be fruitful and multiply, and fill the earth. The fear and dread of you shall rest on every animal of the earth, and on every bird of the air, on everything that creeps on the ground, and on all the fish of the sea; into your hand they are delivered. Every moving thing that lives shall be food for you; and just as I gave you the green plants, I give you everything. Only, you shall not eat flesh with its life, that is, its blood. For your own lifeblood I will surely require a reckoning: from every animal I will require it and from human beings, each one for the blood of another, I will require a reckoning for human life. Whoever sheds the blood of a human, by a human shall that person's blood be shed; for in his own image God made humankind. And you, be fruitful and multiply, abound on the earth and multiply in it."

Yoder makes several important observations about this passage. First, this passage is not foremost about the death penalty. It is about the sacredness of lifeblood—both animal and human. The antediluvian violence that warranted the flood apparently involved killing and consuming animals with no regard for the sanctity of life. God therefore reins in this practice by informing Noah and his descendants that all lifeblood is God's exclusive possession. Though humans may now consume animals, perhaps as a sort of concession, they must acknowledge that all life belongs to God alone by draining animal blood before eating. Whether humans acknowledge it or not, all bloodshed is a ritual sacrifice and may only be performed according to specific guidelines prescribed by God. These guidelines, of course, anticipate the Israelite sacrificial system as spelled out in Torah.

As an extension of this ritual practice, God also reins in human bloodshed. If animal blood may be shed only under carefully prescribed, divinely mandated conditions, how much more the blood of those who bear God's image? When people usurp God's exclusive right to human blood, they violate God's order and commit a sacred offense that must be rectified. To put this in theological terms, atonement is necessary. It is fitting that this ritualistic violation of sacred blood be met with an equally cultic practice that begins and ends with the slayer's blood. It is important to note, Yoder insists, that God is not here introducing humanity to a new practice. Humans were inclined to execute killers since Cain and Lamech's day. Rather, in response to the escalating vengeance of Lamech and the rampant violence of antediluvian culture, God affirms the need for atonement, makes explicit its sacrificial nature, and limits the shedding of blood to the single life of the slayer.[17]

---

17. This should not be interpreted as contradicting God's desire to spare the first murderer's life, but as a concession God is making to the sinfulness of humanity. God has already made several such

The remainder of the Old Testament furnishes the third layer of context. God's desire to restrain the human tendency to escalate vengeance permeates the Law and the Prophets. The Decalogue proscribes killing, which Yoder interprets as taking life when God has not authorized it. The sacrificial system makes the shedding of animal blood a priestly affair. The *lex talionis*, or law of equal recompense (that is, "eye for eye" and "life for life"), continues God's desire to limit retaliation in ways proportional to the original offense—nothing more. The cities of refuge, which were presided over by priests, were instituted to protect the life of a killer who did not kill on purpose. The need for multiple witnesses to secure a conviction and the transference of responsibility for prosecution from the next of kin to community leaders and judges, places further restraints upon capital punishment. The practice of Yahweh War,[18] both to secure the promised land and to maintain it, is defined in ritual, sacrificial terms and requires divine authorization through priests (Deut. 7:2-6; Josh. 6:17-21).[19] In the Torah and the Prophets,

---

concessions. For example, killing an animal to clothe Adam and Eve after they sinned, using the threat of revenge to protect Cain's life, flooding all creation in order to keep humans from destroying this world altogether, and allowing humans to eat animals (and not just vegetation) after humans introduced death into the world. Genesis portrays a God who so loves humans that he chooses to get blood on his own hands to provide for fallen humanity's ongoing survival.

18. "Yahweh War" is a term Yoder uses to distinguish between the warfare God authorized the Israelites to wage and other forms of warfare that were typical of the nations. The most defining characteristic of Yahweh War is that God fights the battle on behalf of Israel and that Israel is required to follow God's often bizarre instructions for how they ought to participate. The emphasis of Yahweh War is that the battle belongs to God—and not to Israel.

19. The ritual nature of warfare is graphically illustrated in the fall of Saul from the kingship. Rather than wait for Samuel, the priest, to ritually consecrate his battle (every Israelite battle had to be consecrated by a priest to ensure God's approval and presence, see Num. 10:8-9), Saul took it upon himself and was severely rebuked by Samuel and God (1 Sam. 13). Shortly thereafter, Saul violates the sacredness of warfare by disregarding God's command to kill all of the designated humans and animals as a whole burnt offering (1 Sam. 15). That these chapters have to do with the sacredness of blood is evident in the intervening chapter (1 Sam. 14), in which Saul has to deal with his soldiers eating animals with their lifeblood in them and when he subsequently spares his son's life after unwittingly vowing to give him over to God.

God continues the trajectory of reining in bloodshed even further than Gen. 9:6.

It thus comes as no surprise when Jesus, immediately after claiming to fulfill rather than abolish the Law and the Prophets, cites the *lex talionis* formulations and then commands his followers *not* to repay evil for evil. Instead, they are to turn the other cheek, love their enemies, and pray for those who persecute them (Matt. 5:38-42). Jesus' teaching can only be regarded as fulfilling these laws if, in their original contexts, they were intended to restrain or delimit retaliation. Jesus also addresses the death penalty in John 8 when the teachers of the law bring before him a woman who was caught in adultery and therefore guilty of a capital offense. His response is twofold: to challenge the self-righteousness of her would-be executioners and to proclaim his moral authority to grant forgiveness, even to civil offenses such as this.

On the cross, Jesus reveals God's ultimate response to human sin. In Yoder's words, "Vengeance was never God's highest intent for men and women's relations with one another; permitting it within the limits of justice (that is, of equivalent injury) was never really his purpose. What God always wanted to do with evil and what he wants humans today to do with it is to swallow it up and drown it in the bottomless sea of his crucified love."[20] Though the wages of sin is death (Rom. 6:23), in going to the cross in Barabbas's place, Jesus died so that all capital offenders might live. In going to the cross as an innocent man, Jesus exposed the selective justice of Caiaphas, Pilate, Herod and all religious and political powers who claim the authority to take life.

According to Yoder, the sacrificial or atonement language that the New Testament letters use to interpret Jesus' death is crucial (Rom.

---

20. Yoder, *The End of Sacrifice*, 43.

3:25; Heb. 2:17; 9:26; 10:12; 1 Cor. 5:7; Eph. 5:2; 1 John 2:2; 4:10). Such language underscores the pertinence of the cross for all Old Testament sacrifices, both animal and human, whether performed by religious specialists or public servants. Since the death of Jesus brought a decisive end to sacrifices for sin, Christians should proclaim its abolition and death penalty advocates should no longer claim biblical validation. In Yoder's words:

> It is the clear testimony of the New Testament, especially of the Epistle to the Hebrews, that the ceremonial requirements of the Old Covenant find their end—both in the sense of fulfillment and in the sense of termination—in the high-priestly sacrifice of Christ. "Once for all" is the good news. Not only is the sacrifice of bulls and goats, turtledoves and wheatcakes at an end; the fact that Christ died for our sins, once for all, the righteous one for the godless (Heb. 9:26–28; 1 Pet. 3:18), puts an end to the entire expiatory system, whether it be enforced by priests in Jerusalem or by execution[ers] anywhere else.[21]

From beginning to end in scripture, the shedding of blood is a ritual or cultic action that requires divine authorization. When such authorization is not provided, the resulting breach in the cosmic moral order requires some sort of divinely authorized atonement. Those who by faith acknowledge Jesus as God's sacrifice to end all sacrifices therefore possess no biblical grounds to justify the continuing practice of capital punishment.

Cultural Engagement of Capital Punishment

It is common today for theologians to assume that because Yoder was a Mennonite he must have advocated an insular, sectarian ethics

---

21. Ibid. 102–3. The title of this essay and Yoder's collection of capital punishment writings derives from the double entendre that Yoder identifies in this quote. It is not clear here or elsewhere, as far as I can tell, what exactly Yoder makes of the abiding role of Jewish practices such as circumcision, Sabbath, and food laws. He states in *Jewish-Christian Schism Revisited* (Grand Rapids: Eerdmans, 2003), that he would approach practices like Sabbath from a posture of fulfillment rather than abolition (93), but he does not unpack what that might look like.

with little or no bearing on the public realm. Yoder did theologize as a Mennonite, but he did not simply seek to justify the stance of his own tradition. Rather, he made his case with a keen eye toward challenging problematic tendencies within his tradition. Toward this end, he rejected the false choice between articulating a faith-based position and speaking relevantly into the realm of world governance. He refused to espouse an official position for Christians and then leave it to unbelieving public authorities to establish their own position without having the opportunity to receive guidance from the church. On the contrary, Yoder insisted that it is the church's responsibility to proclaim Christ's lordship and its implications to all people since all people live under Christ's jurisdiction, regardless of whether they submit to his lordship. We proclaim Christ as prophet, priest, *and king* because his jurisdiction encompasses all social, religious, and political realms. Consequently, the end of sacrifice is not only true for Christians and binding on the believing community; it is true for the cosmos and binding on all rulers and authorities, powers and principalities.

Yoder insisted that we should not be derailed by the consequentialist fallacy. Those who oppose capital punishment are often confronted by the question "where would this lead?" The assumption behind this question is that if legitimate power bearers cease striking fear into the hearts of would-be killers with the threat of execution, anarchy will ensue. To ask the state to forgive offenses, the logic goes, is to ask them to shut down the whole state apparatus. Though Yoder suspects this question is merely rhetorical, he takes it seriously by appealing to scripture. The world's rebellion, which Christ declared would endure until his return (for example, Matt. 24, Mark 13), guarantees that Christian social critique will not lead so far that the world relapses into antediluvian violence and chaos. The world may therefore be challenged, one point at a time, to take one step in the right direction and to move up one more notch toward God's righteousness as revealed in Jesus. Just as God, in scripture, strives to limit vengeance and bloodshed, our witness should be to continue that movement by pulling this limitation tighter and tighter.[22]

For this reason, Yoder advocated that Christians stay informed about capital punishment legislation, awaken public opinion by speaking to neighbors and writing to newspapers, witness to legislators when capital punishment is on the table (among other times), support local and denominational efforts to publish conference resolutions and create other channels of testimony, and pray for kings and all who are in high places (1 Tim. 2:1-2).[23] Rather than positing dual realms with different moral codes or trying to legislate morality for unbelievers, we should speak to the authorities on a case-by-case basis about what it means to be decent and human. We cannot posit an ideal state, for that would be the kingdom of God, and we are under no obligation to propose a pattern for society that would work according to our convictions, for that would be the church. Yet, in each case we say no to the state's misguided attempts to secure justice not because a disciple should not do such a thing, but because an intelligent statesman should not. We must not witness to state representatives on the basis of faith commitments that they have not made, but on public commitments that they *have* made.

Yoder made this case for the Christian witness to the state since his earliest writings on capital punishment. In the last few years of his life, however, he returned to this subject with fresh insights in "You Have It Coming."[24] In this work, Yoder investigates why, at the end of the twentieth century, capital punishment had begun to

---

22. Yoder, "The Christian and Capital Punishment," in *The End of Sacrifice*, 37-61 (47-48).
23. Ibid., 60–61.
24. Ibid., ch. 5.

make a legislative comeback in the United States. Drawing upon and extending the work of René Girard and Émile Dürkheim, he comes to the conclusion that capital punishment will not go away altogether because it remains socially functional. From Dürkheim, he learns that punishment conforms to a sociological pattern that obtains in all societies. The practice of punishment is (a) vengeful and not performed for health or rehabilitation, (b) supported by transcendent validation, (c) deemed indispensable for society even without the moral approval of social scientists, and (d) reinterpreted by societies so as to hide the primitive simplicity of the drive behind more respectable reasons.[25] From Girard, he learns the relevance of scapegoating to the current practice of lethal justice. According to Girard (a) vengeance is a primitive thoughtless reflex that propagates itself though imitation or mimesis, (b) at the origins of civil organization it was deemed necessary to redirect the escalating cycle of violence by channeling it against one victim, (c) the scapegoat is sometimes a leader and other times an outsider (whether gypsy, witch, or Jew), (d) the foundational sacrificial event is commemorated and ultimately covered up by myth and ritual, and (e) the Hebraic worldview as fulfilled in Jesus finally broke the cycle of scapegoat based cultures.[26]

According to Yoder, Girard betrays his liberal sensibilities by narrating the primitive drives behind scapegoating as an embarrassment that needs to be hidden. By way of contrast, Yoder explores various understandable motives behind punishment, including maternal (asserting authority over a child), filial/oedipal (moving lame-duck predecessors out of the way), governmental (showing the public who is boss), victim vindication (meeting the psychic need of victims to return pain for pain), and tectonic shift

25. Yoder, "You Have it Coming," in *The End of Sacrifice*, 153–238 (159–60).
26. Ibid., 167–68.

(marking a major transition in cultural meaning through dramatic punitive events). Yoder observes that the point behind these motives is not that equal compensation is necessary to level the playing field, but that more than equal measure is needed to drive the point home that the offender is no longer in charge. He then suggests that scapegoating is not simply an artifact of the primeval past, but a paradigm for the present.[27]

Previous liberal attempts to abolish the death penalty have failed precisely because they did not adequately account for the cultic or ritual function of capital punishment. This function rests upon neither due process nor democratic fairness. Rather, it rests upon the perceived transcendental need to right a wrong. Though Yoder himself had previously made numerous practical and moral arguments against the death penalty—including its exorbitant expense, failure to rehabilitate or deter, social inequity, infallibility of judicial systems, inconsistency in application, jury tampering, prison problems, dehumanizing effect on society, violation of the sanctity of life, and murder of innocents—he now observes that liberal Enlightenment cannot ultimately prevail against capital punishment because it fights the wrong battle.[28]

Yoder concludes that Christians ought to empathize with their neighbors' need to punish rather than reject with moral outrage the notion of vindictive demand. We must grant the truth that the divine order demands pain for pain and acknowledge with the letter to the Hebrews that this legitimate demand was met on the cross of Jesus Christ, once and for all. Though the current practice of lethal punishment is neither morally satisfying nor ultimately redemptive, it cannot be abolished altogether because it continues to be functional for those who have rejected the message of Jesus.

27. Ibid., 233.
28. Ibid., 180–87.

At the end of the day, Yoder's assessment of capital punishment ends where it begins. Sociology has confirmed what theology should always have affirmed: taking life is a cultic and atoning ritual act. Yoder's later reflections express considerable regret that liberal Christian efforts to abolish capital punishment have failed precisely because they catered to modern sensitivities rather than stand by the theological message that the world desperately needed to hear. In Yoder's words, "The way the impact of the death of Jesus can enter the social process is not that it does away with punishment, but that it offers a paradigm whereby, in one place at a time, the awareness that 'this is too much' can break through." Though wider society's attempts to curtail violence cannot usher in the reign of Christ, "each of them partakes in a fragmentary way of the victory of resurrection and Pentecost, thus offering to others elsewhere, noncoercively, the power to replicate reconciliation."[29] Though Yoder never backs down from his conviction that the way of Jesus is the standard by which all institutions will be judged, he gravitates toward a form of witness that is realistic about the world's rebellion while remaining explicit about its theological commitments. Apart from such witness the world will never be able to recognize and confess Jesus Christ as the end of sacrifice.

---

29. Ibid., 233.

14

A Broken Body Reads Mark

Craig Hovey

It is by now widely acknowledged that every reading of the Bible is a political reading, that is, every reading reflects the interests, power, location, and context of the interpreters. Even so, we still must ask what kind of text we are reading if we hope to read it rightly. In this essay, I focus on the Gospel of Mark. Mark alone claims to have written a *Gospel*, a story with a very specific purpose: not to entertain but to convert.[1] And although John wrote a "book," he is also rather upfront about his strategy: it is written so that you might believe that Jesus is the Messiah, the Son of God (John 20:30-31). Gospels confront our prejudices and challenge our way of life through an encounter with another way of life.

---

1. Siegfried Schulz, "Mark's Significance for the Theology of Early Christianity" in William Telford, ed. *The Interpretation of Mark* (Philadelphia: Fortress Press, 1985), 197–206.

Even so, it is not enough to identify the kind of text we are reading. In the Gospel of Mark, we *existentially* become aware of whether and how our living accords with how we are reading, seeing, and understanding what we read and see. While we may not perceive what we see or understand what we hear (Mark 4:12), Mark has actually woven the possibility of misunderstanding into the text as an entailment of the gospel of Jesus, especially as the gospel involves risks and dangers for disciples whose broken bodies influence their reading. Misunderstanding is not likely to be overcome using even the best exegetical methods. Rather, right reading requires right living—living in ways the text anticipates. Apart from this attention to right living, it is still possible to interpret the text, but not to understand it. In this sense, the text involves *us* in the process of interpreting.

There is nothing particularly new in this hermeneutic. Jesus used a similar strategy when he taught in parables. The parable of the sower explains why Jesus taught in parables—it is possible to be close to the kingdom and not perceive it. In fact, God has deliberately obscured it. The secret of the kingdom of God has been given to those who come to Jesus asking what it means; "but for those outside, everything comes in parables; in order that 'they may indeed look, but not perceive, and may indeed listen, but not understand; so that they may not turn again and be forgiven'" (4:11-12). The deliberate obscuring of the message of Jesus in the Gospel of Mark is political in so far as it forces readers of Mark to participate in the politics of the broken body of Christ. They must participate in this broken body in order to gain understanding of the text. Finally, the nature of their participation, which is to say, the nature of the politics of the broken body, is eucharistic, or so I will argue.

Seeing

What does it mean to read politically? We might discern a writer's aims or assumptions as political. We might go out of our way to look for political applications of what we read. Here, in Mark, the text has political potential that will be worked out by those who read it. We might also ask how our political situation as readers leads us to draw certain conclusions about what we read that we might otherwise miss. The content may not be especially political, but our *reading* will nevertheless still be political because it reflects our political circumstance.[2] Additionally, we might move between the text and our lives to see how each is influenced by the other. The text creates readers who cannot help but read *that same text* differently the next time they read it. This is a combination of the first and third approaches. Perhaps there are multiple groups of readers for whom the text will in part function to unite them with others—the reading of texts can create communities that act on each other in ways that bring them together and transform them. These four different modes differ somewhat in how they handle the elusiveness of the text's political meaning.

I contend that Mark is actually counting on his readers missing quite a lot of what his book has to offer, and not only its politics. Since this strategy is part of the gospel of Jesus, Mark has made his Gospel to reproduce that effect in the lives of hearers. As we look to examples of this strategy, we need to recognize the inherent limitations in what we are doing: Mark and Mark's Jesus are deliberately elusive; Jesus runs ahead; he answers questions with further questions; he refuses to give people what they "seek" in him. If we look to identify the politics of Jesus, it will always remain in large

---

2. This is what liberation theology and other contextual theologies mean by *praxis*.

measure, and by design, hidden except to eyes of faith. Our academic endeavors are foiled before we even begin.

Mark begins in an unusual way: "The beginning of the good news of Jesus Christ, the Son of God" (1:1). Some have noticed that this is not a complete sentence (it lacks a verb) but instead functions as the book's title. Here, "beginning" doesn't refer to the start of the *book* but the start of the *gospel* itself. Mark's book is only the beginning! In the same way that Jesus in John's Gospel says that his followers will do greater things than he did (John 14:12) and that the world itself couldn't contain every book about Jesus if everything he did was written down (21:25), Mark is saying that his book is only the start of greater things. This is how the kingdom of God starts—like a mustard seed—and grows and grows (Mark 4:30-32).

But if Mark's book about Jesus is, for readers, only the beginning of the gospel about Jesus, how does it *end*? *When* does it end? Does it end at 16:8 or in another place? There is a single-verse ending and an eleven-verse ending, both of which many modern scholars believe are interpolations.[3]

However, I want to point out that a debate about endings is anticipated, in a way, at the very beginning. If 16:8 is indeed the original ending, it could be said to function abruptly for a reason. The reader never "sees" the resurrected Christ. Unlike all three of the other gospels, Mark only *shows* us an empty tomb and a young man who reissues the call to discipleship: "*Look*, there is the place they laid him. . . . He is going ahead of you to Galilee; there you will *see* him" (16:6-7). Then the book ends on a disquieting note with the women not telling anyone out of fear, which for Mark is the opposite of the faith that provides sight.

So, how do we read Mark politically? We must recognize that, for

---

3. See Beverly Roberts Gaventa and Patrick D. Miller, eds., *The Ending of Mark and the Ends of God: Essays in Memory of Donald Harrisville Juel* (Louisville: Westminster John Knox, 2005).

Mark's readers, approaching Jesus is a *political act that is part of their reading*. It does not simply arise out of the text through more careful exegesis or better historical or background cultural knowledge, or better execution of literary analysis. Instead, right-readers of Mark are given the secret of Jesus' meaning—the kingdom itself—by their bodily movement. As Philip Berrigan says, "Hope is where your ass is."[4] Where are you *physically* when you read? What do you have? How much do you own? What are you defending? What do you have to lose? Rather than follow Jesus, the rich man goes away sad "for he had many possessions" (Mark 10:22). Yet a rich woman "wastes" her wealth by anointing Jesus' head with costly ointment (14:3-9). The narrative about the rich woman turns around the question: What do you have to *gain*? Everything.

The questions are also different under different material conditions: What do you lack? Where is your hope? A poor widow (12:41-44) becomes the spiritual sister of the anointing woman through their material practice of *giving* and *sharing* when she also gives everything. Certain readings are enabled by particular ways of living; other ways of living disable true readings. The truth, therefore, is not simply *in the text*. Nor is it in the political circumstance, struggle, and context of the readers. It is found in between; it is located in the reading community's struggle to be who the text is requiring it to be in order to hear the truth. If the Bible isn't simply another text to be read and interpreted, this should not be a surprising hermeneutic. The old systematic language of *illumination* refers to the Spirit's role in opening the eyes and minds of readers to God's truth in such a way that *moves* through the text but that *comes* from God.

As I have already described, a current fashion is to point to political and economic conditions that influence interpretation (postcolonial

---

4. Cited in Ched Myers, *Who will throw away the Stone?* (Maryknoll, NY: Orbis, 1994), 158.

hermeneutics). But such materialistic readings do not go far enough in their emphasis on lived experience. The economies of sharing in Mark go beyond the sharing of wealth to include the spiritual conditions that either enable or disable it. What is the difference between the rich man who goes away sad and the rich woman who anoints Jesus? It is that the woman believes that Jesus is the messiah ("anointed one") even though she may not understand that she is anointing his body for suffering and burial (14:8).

Indeed, Mark acknowledges the subjective side of how people respond in faith and how readers respond with eyes to see primarily by hinting that Christian suffering is a prerequisite for right reading. To illustrate this point, I want to briefly discuss Portuguese Marxist interpreter of Mark, Fernando Belo, and his 1970 book, *A Materialist Reading of the Gospel of Mark*. I want to advance a eucharistic reading of Mark's bread/body theme in spite of Belo's objections that this spiritualizes the materialist (economic) dimension and is the work of bourgeois, capitalist exegetes. He writes that we need to "invert the process followed in current exegesis. That is, it is not 'the Eucharist' that enables us to read the bread sequences. . . . On the contrary, it is the bread sequences that will enable us to read 'the Eucharist.'"[5] Although Christian eucharistic practice can be "read" anew by better exegesis, I want to complicate what strikes me as a too-simple "A to B" way of reading. We read *through* the Eucharist no matter how corrupt that practice may be, which means that it is a much riskier project than Belo allows.

The church's eucharistic practice has sometimes been a way of fostering solidarity between those whose bodies are being broken and those whose aren't. This *sharing* in the body of Christ has had a double-meaning: the sharing *of* Christ's body is a sharing *in* Christ's

---

5. Fernando Belo, *A Materialist Reading of the Gospel of Mark*, trans. Matthew J. O'Connell (Maryknoll, NY: Orbis, 1981), 211.

body, in his own suffering and in his collective body, the church. When one member suffers, all suffer with her (1 Cor. 12:26). But the Eucharist doesn't initially point to suffering in general. For Christ's suffering was at our hands; we caused him to suffer. So the Eucharist not only unites sufferers with each other and with non-sufferers within the church; it also confronts us with the extremity of the human capacity to make others suffer. If God has "used our sin to save us from that sin," writes Mark Heim, he did it "so that victims of such acts would never be invisible—they look too much like Jesus."[6] At its best, Christian eucharistic practice really does unite sufferers in the body of Christ.

Even so, let's not pretend that the Eucharist always and everywhere does this; very often it doesn't. It may even work against these goals. In the next section, I will show how a better Eucharist is both required and advanced by the Gospel of Mark. In saying that Mark requires it, I mean that we will not understand the book without it. In saying that Mark advances it, I mean that text and sacrament work together to fix what is broken.

Sharing

The first feeding scene is set in the desert where there is nothing to eat (6:34). Jesus has the crowd remain in the desert, which is being transformed into a green pasture ("grass") where they will be fed. Recalling Psalm 23, Jesus the shepherd makes the sheep lie down in green pastures. It is not that there is nothing in the desert; there is just not enough. The disciples offer to buy two hundred denarii worth of bread (6:36-37) but Jesus instructs them to feed the crowds from their own supply. Jesus' provision has nothing to do with the

---

6. S. Mark Heim, "Saved by What Shouldn't Happen: The Anti-Sacrificial Meaning of the Cross" in *Cross Examinations: Readings on the Meaning of the Cross Today*, ed. Marit Trelstad (Minneapolis: Fortress Press, 2006), 211–24 (224).

typical economic order of buying and selling; the disciples had just returned from a mission in which they had been explicitly told not to take bread or money (6:8). Ultimately, Jesus provides through sharing what there is.

For Belo, capitalistic exegesis tends to read these feeding stories sacramentally, which for him amounts to a bourgeois habit of neglecting material and economic meanings. Belo's critique is instructive because it alerts us to a more basic, modern tendency to believe that we need to choose between a materialist and a sacramental reading of the text. However, the idea that the sacraments are purely spiritual or some other aberration assumes a false dichotomy plagued by a fundamental misunderstanding of the sacraments—the fault lies beyond exegesis strictly speaking.

If there is a bourgeois habit that neglects the economic, which there certainly is, fault does not lie with a sacramental reading but with deficient sacramental doctrine and practice. This fact accords with my argument throughout this essay; it is precisely what we might expect. A broken body (persecuted church) reads suffering and scripture eucharistically. For such a body, the material dimension is inescapable. There exists an economic, material dimension in Mark, but it is clear only through a eucharistic reading.

First, we see an exchange of goods without money changing hands. No bread is bought; the proposed two hundred denarii are not used. Without need of money, the poor are invited to the table of the Lord, as Isaiah had proclaimed:

"Ho, everyone who thirsts,

    come to the waters

and you that have no money,

    come, buy and eat!

Come, buy wine and milk

    without money and without price." (Isa. 55:1)

If the wine and milk are *free*, why must these items be purchased? What would this mean? They are *had* and *given* (this is Jesus' pattern in the story: "How many loaves have you?"; he took . . . and gave). Mark is describing what contemporary theorists call a gift economy. Communities are brought together by the exchange of goods, but are kept apart by the exchange of money. For example, Pierre Bourdieu writes about how a French mason caused a scandal in 1955 "by going home when his work was finished without eating the meal traditionally given in the mason's honor when a house is built, and then demanding, in addition to the price of his day's work . . . an allowance of two hundred francs in lieu of the meal."[7] Related customs are easy to identify in experience. If you ask your teenage niece to babysit your children, you are not likely to pay her with money. If you decide to give her something in exchange for her babysitting services, you might give her something homemade—a knit hat or a loaf of home-baked bread. The small debts created by the exchange of gifts encourage the giving of more gifts in the future through reciprocity. If you were to pay your niece with money, however, you would be signaling that the transaction is complete. The debt created by the service (the babysitting) has been exactly remunerated so the relationship otherwise strengthened is now weakened. In short, non-monetary exchanges create and fortify communal bonds that will persist; monetary exchanges discourage these bonds and separate people from each other, leaving them in a "lonely place" (vv. 31, 32).

    The second point here is closely related. Money has no use for a

---

7. Pierre Bourdieu, *Outline of a Theory of Practice*, trans. Richard Nice (Cambridge: Cambridge University Press, 1977), 173.

generous person: "For thus says the Lord: You were sold for nothing, and you shall be redeemed without money" (Isa. 52:3). In Mark's narrative, this means that even when there is little, there is still enough. Belo sees this feeding story as a key instance of revolutionary messianic (but not sacramental) practice on the economic level. The *haves* pool what they have and redistribute it among the *have-nots*. This sharing is anti-capitalist and brings about a final blessing for all. The crowds are not only inwardly fed by Jesus' teaching; they are also physically fed with food that only some of them had brought.

What is the miracle? It is God's blessing on the process of sharing goods. God approves of it and so adds to it. But the sharing is not the part of the story that is miraculous—anyone can do this at any time. The miracle is that everyone "was satisfied" (cf. also Mark 8:8). Ched Myers agrees: "The only 'miracle' here is the triumph of the economics of sharing within a community of consumption over against the economics of autonomous consumption in the anonymous marketplace."[8] The disciples not only had more than they thought. They also handed out more than the crowd needed. This is a key lesson that Jesus highlights later in the boat.

While this is clearly a story about economics in the debt/gift mode rather than the capitalist/consumption mode, it is also sacramental. As I have said, Belo makes the mistake of assuming that we need to choose between an economic reading and a sacramental reading. Readers, he thinks, are likely to prefer one reading over another based on their class. The poor will want the economic for the same reason that the crowds in the desert were hungry: their want prompts Jesus to call on the rich—who wanted to buy more—to redistribute their wealth with the strong message that what they have with them is enough. The rich, on the other hand, prefer a sacramental reading

---

8. Ched Myers, *Binding the Strong Man: A Political Reading of Mark's Story of Jesus* (Maryknoll, NY: Orbis, 1988), 206.

that entirely spiritualizes the story, draining it of any economic meaning. The rich and poor alike receive sacramental grace from the breaking of the bread and everyone goes home *spiritually* satisfied.

Although Belo is wrong to force this choice along class lines, the reason is not that one's class doesn't influence one's reading but that his notion of sacrament is wanting. There are both historical and liturgical reasons that might lead one to believe that the sacrament has nothing to do with economics, or worse: that it positively reinforces capitalist forms of exchange. For example, how does the Eucharist function within the overall structure of the liturgy? Is the offering taken before or after the Eucharist? More self-conscious liturgical traditions will get the order right but may not know the reason for it. Others may get the order wrong without thinking. It is crucial that the church's practice of Eucharist resemble a potluck rather than a restaurant. In a potluck, everyone brings their contribution before the meal begins (offering, then Eucharist). In a restaurant, you pay after the meal (Eucharist, then offering). (This distinction alone isn't sufficient, though. Fast food restaurants have customers paying for their meal before they eat.[9]) A potluck isn't just about setting events in the right sequence; it is crucially also about sharing rather than buying, selling, and paying. The economic and the sacramental converge.

Losing

Jesus teaches an enigmatic lesson about the loaf and loaves in Mark 8. Mark's own narration of the setting is strange: "Now the disciples had forgotten to bring any bread; and they had only one loaf with them in the boat" (8:14). We once again notice what is eucharistic *and therefore economic* about the *loaf* and the *loaves*. The bread is broken

---

9. I owe these images to my colleague, Peter Slade.

and so made numerous for many, but the bodies that eat it are made one body through the bread. Paul uses the same image: "Because there is one bread, we who are many are one body, for we all partake of the one bread" (1 Cor. 10:17). The bread that Jesus gives—his loaf in the boat—is more than adequate.[10]

This economy of sharing accomplishes the opposite of the economies of consumption in which the more we consume the more we separate from each other. We can ask some hard questions about our own eucharistic observance: whether it is effective in uniting our own bodies with the bread that we eat, whether we associate within ourselves, through eucharistic identification, the broken body of Christ with our own brokenness as a community of disciples.

The disciples fret about only having one loaf with them in the boat because they are reflecting an anxiety that is aware of death and loss but not resurrection. Here, "breaking" means *breaking down*—having even less than we had to begin with: "[F]rom those who have nothing, even what they have will be taken away" (Mark 4:25). But Christians who believe in resurrection believe that Christ is present in the breaking of bread so that when the bread is broken, it is made more by the same promise and power that raised Jesus from the dead. The resurrection and the Eucharist are associated as conditions, as interpretive grills, for seeing the lesson of the bread.

I have been gesturing toward a eucharistic and economic reading of the one loaf and the many loaves. I believe this is what the text *means* and so have provided textual evidence for this interpretation. But we have also been relying on something prior to our search for meaning in this text; we have drawn on the fact that Christians are part of a tradition that approaches eating in particular ways. We look for how sharing a meal builds up the community of fellowship

---

10. See Norman A. Beck, "Reclaiming a Biblical Text: The Mark 8:14–21 Discussion about Bread in the Boat," *Catholic Biblical Quarterly* 43 (1981): 49–56.

because of how we understand taking part in it to be a sharing in the body of Christ.

Even more troubling, we became aware of the brokenness of bodies, those of Jesus and many of his followers throughout the centuries and throughout our world today. Their brokenness *reads* Mark for the whole church. Whether we are thinking about the reality or the memory or the association of Christian sufferers for the faith, the fact that by their suffering, Jesus' followers are included in the story of his own death casts the task of learning Mark's meaning onto the body that is characterized by that suffering. There are many sufferers, many broken bodies, but there is one Lord, one body, one loaf. This means that Christians of all kinds are united with the suffering of their fellows by sharing the one bread.

Mark combines the economic and the sacramental in still other ways. When the unnamed woman of Bethany anoints Jesus' head with ointment, Jesus says that she has anointed his body for burial (14:8). But this is not what she thinks she is doing. The woman anoints Jesus' head, not his feet, as in Luke's and John's similar stories. He is being anointed as Messiah, as king, but as Christopher Burdon says, "there is no way to the Kingdom apart from the breaking of his body."[11] Only in Mark is the jar *broken*. Some of Jesus' disciples object to the waste. The ointment might have been sold for three hundred denarii—more than the disciples had earlier proposed for feeding five thousand—and given to the poor.

Like the lesson of the loaves, there is not a zero sum game with Jesus' body and the poor. The problem with the world's economies is not finally that they neglect the poor; they sometimes make these sorts of provisions. The celebrations are curtailed, the parties end early, the pennies are carefully counted, the tips are meticulously

---

11. Christopher Burdon, *Stumbling on God: Faith and Vision through Mark's Gospel* (Grand Rapids: Eerdmans, 1990), 63.

calculated so that the poor can benefit from the moderation of the rich. Wealth is "wasted" when it only serves the rich; it is limited when it is shared with the poor. But Jesus' economy "wastes" everything, even the wealth of the poor!

This was the economic lesson of the widow's offering in chapter 12. She gave everything she had which, though little, was "more than all those who are contributing to the treasury" (12:43). Jesus has an economy of resurrection. Bread comes to starving people in the desert (8:4f); life comes out of death. After Jesus' body is entombed, the women bring spices "so that they might go and anoint him" (16:1). But he had already been anointed, the body already broken. What made these women's anointing unacceptable and unnecessary? For Mark, the answer is plain: they don't believe in resurrection. They are prepared to anoint him as Messiah only when the coast is clear (they were earlier described as those who "used to follow him" but "watched from a distance" Jesus being crucified; 15:40-41).

Later in the same chapter, a few of Mark's symbols combine:

"[H]e *took* a loaf of bread
And after *blessing* it
He *broke* it
Gave it to them
and said, '*Take*; this is my body'."
(14:22, emphasis added)

Here we have the reappearance of the loaf, a breaking, and a feeding. What has been hinted throughout is finally made explicit. Jesus' body is being broken; it is food for the hungry whose own bodies will be broken for others if they share in it.

The Last Supper has the same pattern from the feeding of the five thousand and the four thousand: taking bread, blessing it, giving it. As is typical, the blessing of the food (the bread and wine) is appropriated when it is eaten. But here the blessing is anything but typical: it is incorporation into and solidarity with the death and suffering of Jesus' body while it is also the destruction of that body by those who eat. There are no words of institution in Mark; Jesus doesn't tell his disciples to do this in remembrance of him.[12] This already happened in a combination of the feeding stories ("You give them something to eat") and the woman who anoints Jesus ("what she has done will be told *in remembrance of her*"). These eaters are destroying Jesus' body and are included with the betrayer in sharing the meal—everyone will desert him, like these whom the Psalms condemn for devouring God's people like bread (Pss. 14:4, 53:4).

Sharing in the impending cross is living the way of the cross, a way of life that increases the likelihood that you will be killed. So sharing that life means sharing that death; this meal signals the willingness of those who share it to go the distance with Jesus—Mark has us envisioning thirteen crosses. Moreover, the meal doesn't only signal the eaters' willingness to stick with the Jesus movement to the end; it also anticipates an even more blessed "new" meal that awaits them "in the kingdom of God" (14:25). Once God's economy finally sorts out the injustice and ignominy of the ensuing events, those faithful to the end will be rewarded and betrayers, deniers, and murderers will be forgiven; they will all be reconciled and eat together.

As readers, we *ironically* include the disciples in this present hint toward a future meal since the narrative does not proceed with thirteen crosses, but one. Simon of Cyrene is the only person other than Jesus who takes up his cross (15:21), yet it is not his own. So while the meal signals for disciples their deficient commitment to the Jesus movement—we remember that Judas shares in it—in the scope of Mark's book, it is also a promise based on Jesus' own willingness

---

12. John Fenton, "The Passion Narrative in St. Mark's Gospel" in *The Reality of God: Essays in Honor of Tom Baker, Dean of Worcester, 1975–1986*, ed. James Butterworth (London: Severn House, 1986), 19–32 (30).

to eat with sinners, as he had done throughout his ministry. These sinners—these eaters—include readers whose participation in the church's eucharistic sharing is seldom more than bittersweet. We commit ourselves to the politics of the cross and are both included in Christ's suffering and refuse to share it. Like the disciples, we might insist that we are not the betrayer (v. 19) even while denier and betrayer eat from the one loaf. This is a paradox of the kingdom: this bread is "broken" by the ones who eat it, destroying it; but it is also the means of incorporating the many into it. No wonder it becomes evident that the oneness of the community is so bound up with its suffering together as its members look forward to drinking new wine together.

Breaking

Mark has written such that the resurrection of Christ is necessary for understanding and interpreting the text, especially when it comes to what is broken and breaks in it. Resurrection is more than a fact of history or the content of Christian confession; it also literally enables the text's deep meaning. Jesus' exasperation at unbelief discloses how his meaning and significance are only legible in light of the faith the resurrection makes possible. Faith in resurrection, furthermore, locates and places readers who are themselves suffering for the gospel. How do they know they understand? They read their lives and deaths in the life and death of Jesus. This is what I have been arguing is a political reading.

Resurrection is death's other side and not a way around it. Readers of Mark are prepared for misunderstanding on this score when a disciple remarks of the temple, "Look, Teacher, what large stones and what large buildings!" (13:1)—seeing but not perceiving, as Jesus' reply makes plain ("Do you see these great buildings?"). The disciples see something (the temple) that will one day be gone, but they do not understand. What don't they understand? As is normal for Mark, this is a question for both the disciples and readers. What they misunderstand is that *Jesus is the temple*. Mark hints at this, but John is more obvious: "he was speaking of the temple of his body." Though even for John, what is obvious for the reader is only available to the eyes of faith provided by the resurrection: "after he was raised from the dead, his disciples remembered that he had said this; and they believed the scripture and the word that Jesus had spoken" (John 2:21-22).

In Mark, we get the aside: "let the reader understand" (13:14, cf. 8:21 regarding the loaves). Mark uses this literary device to include his readers in the same seeing/perceiving and hearing/understanding difficulties with which Jesus confronts the crowds and disciples. Scholars usually offer three main ideas about what the desolating sacrilege refers to. On one level, it is a reference to the book of Daniel (12:11) in which the "abomination that desolates" is spoken of as a future event. The books of Maccabees also use this same language to refer to the pagan desecration of the temple in Jerusalem (see 1 Macc 1:54)—when for a time under Antiochus Epiphanes the temple was made into a shrine to Zeus and unclean (pig) sacrifices were offered on the altar. A third idea is that this is an enigmatic reference to the destruction of the temple by the Romans in 70 C.E.

The true meaning of the desolating sacrilege, however, is not likely to be gained through the work of exegesis alone, however helpful exegesis may be. We know that, in context, Jesus has been condemning the temple in many different ways: the cursing of the fig tree, disrupting the economic exchanges in the temple, and his final parable told against the religious leadership. Deeper down, though, the reader's attention is shifted away from the temple's future and toward Jesus' own future. There will come a time when Jesus will be destroyed.

Later, while Jesus is being crucified, passers-by mock him, recalling that he had claimed he would destroy the temple and build it in three days (14:58, 15:30). Jesus' death is marked by three hours of darkness (15:33, cf. 13:24) and the temple's curtain tearing (15:38). The temple and Jesus' body are destroyed simultaneously. Something much more creative is happening than simply foretelling (in ch. 13) an event that will happen later, the Roman destruction of the temple in 70 c.e. Mark is enfolding Jesus' fate with the end of the cultic practice. The temple is no longer holy, nor are its priests doing God's will; Jesus' body replaces both temple and priesthood (Heb. 8–9). But like the disciples, we need to be reminded "the end is not yet" (13:7).

Mark seems to be saying, "Don't you see? Some of you will focus on the temple and think that the story is over. But this is just like disbanding once Jesus is arrested and crucified. You think the end has come. You flee; you run away. But you need to wait and watch and listen. The end is not yet for those who have the ears to hear and the eyes to see." I propose that the cross replaces what seems straightforwardly political, whether it is the desolating sacrilege described in Maccabees or the temple destruction foretold, in a way that deliberately permits readers to misunderstand, to come away with a layer of meaning nearer the surface if it suits their lack of faith.

Mark isn't going to force readers to see something they can't see. Let us again appreciate the way that Mark is involving his readers in the very dynamics about which he is writing. A reader may see Mark's story and even "get" a perfectly wonderful story about Jesus; but she may still not understand and believe. The *politics of the broken body* will either be at work as a grill for understanding or it won't. Christ appears to the one who reads with and through the eucharistic, broken body.

This is not simply to say that *knowledge* of the resurrection enables a political reading. In fact, close to the opposite is what is actually happening and we may conclude by noting it. The resurrection in Mark is, notoriously, not knowledge at all. The ending is contested, but in its likely original version, the risen Jesus is not seen, does not visit with disciples, nor grill fish over a fire. Instead, the manner in which Mark makes the risen Christ available to us, and to which the reader must respond by following, sets the stage for the church's present political struggle to be read as Christ's own struggle. This is not reading scripture politically, but *reading politics scripturally*.[13] The present experience of the church's struggle as a broken body is the politics necessary for reading scripture. The politics "lets the reader understand" what we read. But in addition, Mark is aware that this hermeneutic is necessary because of the kind of resurrection to which his book is bearing witness, that is, a resurrection whose completion cannot be witnessed within his book. The gospel completes only through invitation for the church to complete it in its legibility of its own situation in light of the Jesus story.

---

13. This is a praxological hermeneutic of the sort one reads in Ernesto Cardenal's *The Gospel in Solentiname*, trans. Donald D. Walsh (Maryknoll, NY: Orbis, 2010).

www.ingramcontent.com/pod-product-compliance
Lightning Source LLC
Chambersburg PA
CBHW071148070526
44584CB00019B/2712